Groovy for Domain-specific Languages

Second Edition

Extend and enhance your Java applications with domain-specific scripting in Groovy

Fergal Dearle

[PACKT] PUBLISHING

BIRMINGHAM - MUMBAI

Groovy for Domain-specific Languages

Second Edition

First published: June 2010

Second edition: September 2015

Production reference: 1230915

Published by Packt Publishing Ltd.
Livery Place
35 Livery Street
Birmingham B3 2PB, UK.

ISBN 978-1-84969-540-4

www.packtpub.com

Credits

Author
Fergal Dearle

Reviewers
David W Millar
Pietro Martinelli
Jason Winnebeck

Commissioning Editor
Erol Staveley

Acquisition Editors
Tushar Gupta
Antony Lowe

Content Development Editor
Adrian Raposo

Technical Editor
Siddhi Rane

Copy Editors
Janbal Dharmaraj
Kevin McGowan

Project Coordinator
Kinjal Bari

Proofreader
Safis Editing

Indexer
Hemangini Bari

Production Coordinator
Shantanu N. Zagade

Cover Work
Shantanu N. Zagade

About the Author

Fergal Dearle is a seasoned software development professional with almost 30 years' experience in software product development across a wide variety of technologies. He is currently the principal consultant with his own software development consulting company, Dearle Technologies Ltd., engaged in design, development, and architecture of new software products for client companies. Recent projects have included the integration of the Telegraph (`http://www.telegraph.co.uk`) into Apple's new Apple News application for iOS 9 and the reengineering of the G-Cloud Digital Marketplace for the United Kingdom Cabinet Office (`https://www.digitalmarketplace.service.gov.uk`).

He is a committed mentor in his local CoderDojo in Wexford Town where he teaches Groovy to the young coding ninjas. He has been recently nominated as a CoderDojo Hero for his work.

In the past, Fergal has worked in lead architect and developer roles for Candle Corporation on the OMEGAMON product, which is now part of IBM's Tivoli product suite, and as the development manager for Unix implementations of Lotus 1-2-3. In the early 1990s, Fergal led the team at Glockenspiel that developed CommonView, the first object-oriented UI framework for Microsoft Windows. The team was awarded one of the first ever Jolt Productivity Awards by Dr. Dobbs Journal.

Acknowledgments

Being part of the extended Groovy community has been one of the most fulfilling periods of my professional life. I have had the privilege to work with some of the best and most talented software developers and Groovy programmers around the world, and I have learned a lot from them all. There are so many to mention; first names will have to do: George, Elliot, Adam, Steve, Rob, Glenn, Zsolt, Chris, Tao, Adi, Grezg, Brendan, Alex, Sean, Atilla, Eugen, Alvaro, Jet, Dom, and Tim … to name but a few.

Special thanks must go to Peter Ledbrook for his tireless work running the London Groovy Grails User Group, and to the organizers of GGX and GR8 conferences. Some of the great blogs and conference talks that inspired me to write this book were presented by Guilliame Laforge, Cédric Champeau, Marco Vermeulen, Mr Haki, and Jeff Scott Brown.

Closer to home, I could not have finished this book were it not for the tireless support of my coworker and comentor at CoderDojo, Tony Davidson.

Last, but not least, I want to thank my girls, Caroline, Eabha, Nessa and Sadhbh, who put up with my long absences during the writing, and without whose love and tolerance I would never have completed this book.

About the Reviewers

David W Millar is a veteran software craftsman who holds a degree in computer science from Drexel University. He has had the pleasure of working in a wide variety of environments from small start-ups and research groups to industry giants such as IBM and Comcast. He is an active member of the Philadelphia tech scene and a contributor to the Groovy ecosystem. In his free time, he can be found hacking on open source projects; eagerly following tech trends such as the container revolution, IoT, DevOps, and infrastructure automation; or playing with his cats.

Pietro Martinelli is a software engineer, who has been working in enterprise application development since 2003. In 2002, he received his degree in computer engineering at the University of Brescia with highest honors. His main technical interests are languages development (primarily parsers and code generation tools development), enterprise application design, build and deployment automation, and quality-oriented development methodologies. He's an object orientation and testing bigot who loves teaching and mentoring students and colleagues on software design and testing methodologies. He writes about his technological experiences and his technical vision of the world in his blog, Java Peanuts, `http://javapeanuts.blogspot.com`.

> My wife Cristina and my daughters Irene and Laura beautifully fill every moment of my spare time.

Jason Winnebeck is a full-stack software developer with both frontend and backend development experience, including 15 years of experience with Java technologies and 4 years' experience with Groovy, specifically. He holds a master's degree in computer science from the Rochester Institute of Technology. He is married with two children, and enjoys volleyball and traveling.

www.PacktPub.com

Support files, eBooks, discount offers, and more

For support files and downloads related to your book, please visit www.PacktPub.com.

Did you know that Packt offers eBook versions of every book published, with PDF and ePub files available? You can upgrade to the eBook version at www.PacktPub.com and as a print book customer, you are entitled to a discount on the eBook copy. Get in touch with us at service@packtpub.com for more details.

At www.PacktPub.com, you can also read a collection of free technical articles, sign up for a range of free newsletters and receive exclusive discounts and offers on Packt books and eBooks.

https://www2.packtpub.com/books/subscription/packtlib

Do you need instant solutions to your IT questions? PacktLib is Packt's online digital book library. Here, you can search, access, and read Packt's entire library of books.

Why subscribe?

- Fully searchable across every book published by Packt
- Copy and paste, print, and bookmark content
- On demand and accessible via a web browser

Free access for Packt account holders

If you have an account with Packt at www.PacktPub.com, you can use this to access PacktLib today and view 9 entirely free books. Simply use your login credentials for immediate access.

Table of Contents

Preface

The Java virtual machine runs on everything from the largest mainframe to the smallest microchip and supports every conceivable application. But Java is a complex, and sometimes arcane, language to develop with. Groovy allows us to build targeted single-purpose mini languages, which can run directly on the JVM along with the regular Java code.

This book provides a comprehensive tutorial on designing and developing mini Groovy-based domain-specific languages (DSLs). It is a complete guide to the development of several mini DSLs with a lot of easy-to-understand examples. This book will help you gain all of the skills needed to develop your own Groovy-based DSLs.

Groovy for Domain-specific Languages, *Second Edition*, guides you from the basics through to the more complex metaprogramming features of Groovy. The focus is on how the Groovy language can be used to construct domain-specific mini languages.

Practical examples are used throughout to demystify these seemingly complex language features and to show how they can be used to create simple and elegant DSLs. The examples include a quick and simple Groovy DSL to interface with Twitter.

The book concludes with a chapter focusing on integrating a Groovy-based DSL in such a way as the scripts can be readily incorporated into your own Java applications. The overall goal of this book is to take developers through the skills and knowledge they need to start building effective Groovy-based DSLs to integrate into their own applications.

What this book covers

Chapter 1, Introduction to DSLs and Groovy, discusses how DSLs can be used in place of general-purpose languages to represent different parts of a system. You will see how adding DSLs to your applications can open up the development process to other stakeholders in the development process. You'll also see how, in extreme cases, the stakeholders themselves can even become co-developers of the system by using DSLs that let them represent their domain expertise in the code.

Chapter 2, Groovy Quick Start, covers the basics of installing Groovy and running simple Groovy scripts.

Chapter 3, Essential Groovy DSLs, covers two essential Groovy-based tools, Gradle and Spock. Gradle is a build, test, and deployment automation tool, which is powered by a Groovy DSL. Spock is a unit testing and specification framework built over JUnit. Both tools are used extensively throughout the book.

Chapter 4, The Groovy Language, covers a whistle-stop tour of the Groovy language. It also touches on most of the significant features of the language as a part of this tour.

Chapter 5, Groovy Closures, covers closures in some depth. It covers all of the important aspects of working with closures. You can explore the various ways to call a closure and the means of passing parameters. You will see how to pass closures as parameters to methods, and how this construct can allow the adding of mini DSL syntax to our code.

Chapter 6, Example DSL – GeeTwitter, focuses on how we can start with an existing Java-based API and evolve it into a simple user-friendly DSL that can be used by almost anybody. You'll learn the importance of removing boilerplate code and how you can structure our DSL in such a way that the boilerplate is invisible to our DSL users.

Chapter 7, Power Groovy DSL Features, covers all of the important features of the Groovy language, and looks in depth at how some of these features can be applied to developing DSLs.

Chapter 8, AST Transformations, covers how to use the Groovy abstract syntax tree (AST) transformations. AST transformations are a mechanism for us to hook into the Groovy compilation process. Here we look at compile time metaprogramming and see how we can use AST transformations to build code on the fly during the compilation process.

Chapter 9, Existing Groovy DSLs, discusses some existing Groovy DSLs that are in current use and are free to download.

Chapter 10, Building a Builder, explains how Groovy provides two useful support classes that make it much simpler to implement our own builders than if we used the MOP. You'll see how to use `BuilderSupport` and `FactoryBuilderSupport` to create our own builder classes.

Chapter 11, Implementing a Rules DSL, takes a look at Groovy bindings to see how they can be used in our DSL scripts. By placing closures strategically in the binding, you can emulate named blocks of code. You can also provide built-in methods and other shorthand by including closures and named Boolean values in the binding. These techniques can be used to great effect to write DSL scripts that can be read and understood by stakeholders outside of the programming audience.

Chapter 12, Integrating It All, takes all the knowledge from the previous chapters and builds a fully functioning web application based on a simple Game Engine DSL for Tic Tac Toe.

What you need for this book

It is highly recommended that you download the example code to use while you read the book. You will also need to download and install three key pieces of software, Groovy, Spock, and Gradle. Download and installation instructions for these are included in *Chapter 2, Groovy Quick Start,* and *Chapter 3, Essential Groovy DSLs.*

Who this book is for

This book is for any software developers who have an interest in building domain scripting into their applications. No knowledge of Groovy is required, although it will be helpful. This book will not teach Groovy, but will quickly introduce the basic ideas of Groovy. An experienced developer should have no problems with this and will move quickly onto the more involved aspects of creating DSLs with Groovy. No experience of creating a DSL is required.

The book should also be useful for experienced Groovy developers who have so far only used Groovy DSLs, such as Groovy builders, and would like to start building their own Groovy-based DSLs.

Conventions

In this book, you will find a number of text styles that distinguish between different kinds of information. Here are some examples of these styles and an explanation of their meaning.

Code words in text, database table names, folder names, filenames, file extensions, pathnames, dummy URLs, user input, and Twitter handles are shown as follows: "Before you go to the Groovy documentation for `MarkupBuilder` to look for the book, author, and surname methods in `MarkupBuilder`, let me save you the effort."

A block of code is set as follows:

```
<?xml version="1.0"?>
<book>
    <author>
                <first_name>Fergal</first_name>
                <surname> Dearle</surname>
    </author>
    <title>Groovy for DSL</title>
</book>
```

Any command-line input or output is written as follows:

```
Hello, World!
Goodbye, World!
```

New terms and **important words** are shown in bold. Words that you see on the screen, for example, in menus or dialog boxes, appear in the text like this: "Click on the button to **Create New App**, then complete the form to create you app."

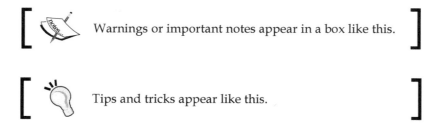

Warnings or important notes appear in a box like this.

Tips and tricks appear like this.

Reader feedback

Feedback from our readers is always welcome. Let us know what you think about this book—what you liked or disliked. Reader feedback is important for us as it helps us develop titles that you will really get the most out of.

To send us general feedback, simply e-mail feedback@packtpub.com, and mention the book's title in the subject of your message.

If there is a topic that you have expertise in and you are interested in either writing or contributing to a book, see our author guide at www.packtpub.com/authors.

Customer support

Now that you are the proud owner of a Packt book, we have a number of things to help you to get the most from your purchase.

Downloading the example code

You can download the example code files from your account at http://www.packtpub.com for all the Packt Publishing books you have purchased. If you purchased this book elsewhere, you can visit http://www.packtpub.com/support and register to have the files e-mailed directly to you.

Errata

Although we have taken every care to ensure the accuracy of our content, mistakes do happen. If you find a mistake in one of our books—maybe a mistake in the text or the code—we would be grateful if you could report this to us. By doing so, you can save other readers from frustration and help us improve subsequent versions of this book. If you find any errata, please report them by visiting http://www.packtpub.com/submit-errata, selecting your book, clicking on the **Errata Submission Form** link, and entering the details of your errata. Once your errata are verified, your submission will be accepted and the errata will be uploaded to our website or added to any list of existing errata under the Errata section of that title.

To view the previously submitted errata, go to https://www.packtpub.com/books/content/support and enter the name of the book in the search field. The required information will appear under the **Errata** section.

Piracy

Piracy of copyrighted material on the Internet is an ongoing problem across all media. At Packt, we take the protection of our copyright and licenses very seriously. If you come across any illegal copies of our works in any form on the Internet, please provide us with the location address or website name immediately so that we can pursue a remedy.

Please contact us at copyright@packtpub.com with a link to the suspected pirated material.

We appreciate your help in protecting our authors and our ability to bring you valuable content.

Questions

If you have a problem with any aspect of this book, you can contact us at questions@packtpub.com, and we will do our best to address the problem.

1
Introduction to DSLs and Groovy

It has been over 10 years since my first contact with the Groovy language. The occasion was an introductory talk about Groovy at JavaOne in the Moscone Centre, San Francisco, by James Strachan, the creator of the Groovy language. Java itself was just 10 years old at that time and Groovy was one of the very first languages other than Java to run on the **Java Virtual Machine (JVM)**.

Just this year, Java celebrated its twentieth birthday. In 2005, there were an estimated 3 million Java developers worldwide. Now, in 2015, Wikipedia estimates it as 11 million. The Groovy language has also taken off. There were an estimated 5 million downloads of Groovy in the last year alone. So what are the benefits of Groovy and why should you consider using it?

The Groovy project site at `http://www.groovy-lang.org` explains this better than I ever could with six major benefits:

- A flat learning curve
- Powerful features
- Smooth Java integration
- Domain-specific languages
- A vibrant and rich ecosystem
- The scripting and testing glue

In this book, we will cover all the key benefits of the Groovy language. The main focus, however, is on how Groovy supports the development of domain-specific languages through its metaprogramming features.

One of the big benefits of Groovy is how its dynamic features support the development of **domain-specific languages** (**DSLs**) or "mini languages", which we can run directly on the JVM alongside your existing Java code. Groovy DSLs integrate seamlessly into the Groovy language itself in such a way that it's not always apparent where the regular Groovy code stops and the DSL starts.

In fact, large parts of almost any Groovy application are written using Groovy-based DSLs. For instance, a new developer starting out with Groovy might assume that the builder code he uses to output some XML is a part of the core Groovy language. But it is, in fact, a mini internal DSL implemented using the Groovy metaprogramming features.

If you are an Android developer, the chances are you may have programmed in Groovy already. Since 2013, the build system in the Android SDK has been a tool called Gradle (`http://www.gradle.org`). Gradle is a Groovy-based DSL for dependency management and build automation.

Whether you are one of the 11 million existing Java developers, looking to add DSL features to you application, or you are an existing Groovy developer looking to improve your knowledge of DSL writing, metaobject programming or AST transformations, this book is intended for you.

By the end of this book, I hope that you will have the knowledge and the confidence to start building your own DSLs with Groovy, and be able to integrate them into your Java applications. To begin with, in this chapter, we will take some baby steps. This chapter will give you a brief background on DSLs and their usage. We will also dip a toe into the Groovy language, and briefly touch on the features of the language that distinguish it from Java and make it a great tool for developing DSLs on top of the Java platform.

DSL – a new name for an old idea

I've mentioned **domain-specific language** (**DSL**) several times now, so what does this really mean? The term "DSL" describes a programming language that is dedicated to a specific problem domain. The idea is not new. DSLs have been around for a long time. One of the most exciting features of Unix has always been its mini languages. These include a rich set of typesetting languages (troff, eqn, pic, and so on), shell tools (awk, sed, and so on), and software development tools (make, yacc, and lex).

The Java platform has a multitude of mini DSLs in the form of XML config files for configuration of everything from EJBs to web applications. In many JEE applications, **Enterprise Java Beans (EJB)** can be configured using an XML configuration file, `ejb-jar.xml`. While the `ejb-jar.xml` file is written in the general-purpose language XML, the contents of the file need to conform to a **document type definition (DTD)** or XML schema, which describes the valid structure of the file.

XML configuration files can be found across a wide range of libraries and frameworks. Spring is configured by using a `spring-config.xml` file, and Struts with `struts-config.xml`. In each case, the DTD or schema defines the elements and tags, which are valid for the specific domain, be it EJB, Spring, or Struts. So, `ejb-jar.xml` can be considered a mini DSL for configuring EJB, `spring-config.xml` is a mini DSL for configuring Spring beans, and so on.

In essence, DSL is a fancy name for something that we use every day of our professional programming lives. There are not many applications that can be fully written in a single general-purpose language. As such, we are the everyday consumers of many different DSLs, each of which is specific to a particular purpose.

A typical day's work could involve working with Java code for program logic, CSS for styling a web page, JavaScript for providing some dynamic web content, and Ant, Maven, or Gradle to build the scripts that tie it all together. We are well used to consuming DSLs, but seldom consider producing new DSLs to implement our applications — which we should.

The evolution of programming languages

My own background is probably typical of many of my generation of old-school programmers. Back in 1986, I was a young software engineer fresh out of college. During my school and college years, I studied many different programming languages. I was fortunate in high school to have had a visionary Math teacher who taught us to program in BASIC, so I cut my teeth programming as early as 1974. Through various college courses, I came to know about Pascal, C, Fortran, Lisp, Assembler, and COBOL.

My school, college, and early professional career all reinforced a belief that programming languages were for the exclusive use of us programmers. We liked nothing better than spending hours locked away in dark rooms writing reams of arcane and impenetrable code. The more arcane and impenetrable the better! The hacker spirit prevailed, and annual competitions such as the **International Obfuscated C Code Contest (IOCCC)** were born.

The IOCCC runs to this day. The point of the contest is to write valid but impenetrable C code that works. Check out http://www.ioccc.org to see how not to write code.

General-purpose languages

All of the teaching in college in those days revolved around the general-purpose languages. I recall sitting in class and being taught about the "two" types of programming language: machine language, and high-level languages. Both were types of general-purpose languages, in which you could build any type of application, but each language had its own strengths and weaknesses. The notion of a DSL was not yet considered as part of the teaching program. Nor was the idea that anyone other than a cadre of trained professional programmers (hackers) would ever write programs for computers. These days, the word "hacker" has bad connotations of being synonymous with virus writers and the likes. In those days, a good "hack" was an elegant programming solution to a hard problem and being called a hacker by one's peers was a badge of pride for most programmers.

The high-level programming language you used defined what type of an application programmer you were. COBOL was for business application programming, Fortran was for scientific programmers, and C was for hackers building Unix and PC software. Although COBOL and Fortran were designed to be used in a particular business domain, they were still considered general-purpose languages. You could still write a scientific application in COBOL or a business application in Fortran if you wanted to. However, you were unlikely to try any low-level device driver development in COBOL.

Although it was possible to build entire applications in assembly language (and many people did), high-level languages, such as C, BASIC, and COBOL, were much better suited to this task. The first version of the world-beating spreadsheet Lotus 1-2-3 was written entirely in 8086 assembly language, and ironically, it was the rewrite of this into the supposed high-level language C that nearly broke the company in the late 1980's.

Languages such as C and C++ provide the low-level functionality in a high-level language, which enabled them to be used across a much greater range of domains, including those where assembly was utilized before. These days, Java, C# and C++ compete with each other like the Swiss Army knives of general-purpose languages. There are almost no application domains to which these languages have not been applied, from space exploration, through to enterprise business systems, and mobile phones.

Spreadsheets and 4GLs

Programs such as Lotus 1-2-3 and its precursor VisiCalc revolutionized people's view of who would program computers. A whole generation of accountants, financial analysts, scientists, and engineers came to realize that they can develop sophisticated turnkey solutions for themselves, armed only with a spreadsheet and a little knowledge of macros. Spreadsheet macros are probably one of the first DSLs to find their way out of the cloisters of the IT community and into the hands of the general business user.

Around this time, there was also much media attention paid to the new **4GL** (**fourth-generation language**) systems. 4GLs were touted as being hugely more efficient for developing applications than traditional high-level languages, which then became known as **third-generation language** (**3GL**). From the hype in the media at the time, you would be forgiven for thinking that the age of the professional programmer was coming to an end and that an ordinary business user could use a 4GL to develop their own business applications. I viewed this claim with a degree of healthy skepticism—how could a non-programmer build software?

Like DSLs, 4GLs were, generally speaking, targeted at particular problem spaces, and tended to excel at providing solutions in those narrow target markets. The sophistication of most applications in those days was such that it was possible to build them with a few obvious constructs. 4GLs tended to be turnkey environments with integrated tools and runtime environments. You were restricted by the environment that the 4GL provided, but the applications that could be built with a 4GL could be built rapidly, and with a minimal amount of coding.

4GLs differ from our modern understanding of a DSL. We generally think of a DSL as being a mini language with a particular purpose, and they do not generally impose an entire runtime or tool set on their use. The best DSLs can be mixed and matched together, and used in conjunction with a general-purpose programming language, such as C++ or Java, to build our applications.

Language-oriented programming

Martin Fowler has spoken about the use of many mini DSLs in application development. He advocates building applications out of many mini DSLs, which are specific to the particular problem space, in a style of development called language-oriented programming. In a way, this style of programming is the norm for most developers these days, when we mix and match HTML, CSS, SQL, and Java together to build our applications.

The thrust of language-oriented programming is that we should all be going beyond exploiting these generally available languages and implementing our own DSLs that represent the particular problem space that we are working on. With a language-oriented programming approach, we should be building DSLs that are as narrowly focused as the single application that we are currently working on. A DSL does not need to be generally applicable to be useful to us.

Who are DSLs for?

It's worth considering for a moment who the different types of users of a DSL might be. Most DSLs require some programming skills in order to get to grips with them, and are used by software and IT professionals in their daily chores, building, and maintaining and managing systems. They are specific to a particular technical aspect of system development. So the domain of CSS as a DSL is web development in general, and specifically page styling and layout. Many web developers start from a graphic design background and become proficient as coders of HTML, CSS, and JavaScript simply because it gives them better fine-grained control of the design process.

Many graphic designers, for this reason, eventually find themselves eschewing graphical tools such as Dreamweaver in favor of code. Hopefully, our goal in life will not be to turn everybody into a coder. Whereas most DSLs will remain in the realm of the programmer, there are many cases where a well-designed DSL can be used by other stakeholders in the development process other than professional developers. In some cases, DSLs can enable stakeholders to originate parts of the system by enabling them to write the code themselves. In other cases, the DSL can become a shared representation of the system. If the purpose of a particular DSL is to implement business rules then, ideally, that DSL should express the business rule in such a way that it can be clearly understood upon reading by both the business stakeholder who specified it and the programmer who wrote it.

A DSL for process engineers

My own introduction to the concept of DSLs came about in 1986 when I joined **Computer Products Inc. (CPI)** as a software engineer. In this case, the DSL in question was sophisticated enough to enable the stakeholders to develop large parts of a running system.

CPI developed a process control system, which was primarily sold to chemical and pharmaceutical industries. It was a genuinely distributed system when most process control systems were based on centralized mini or mainframe computers. It had its own real-time kernel, graphics, and a multitude of device drivers for all types of control and measurement devices. But the most innovative part of the system, which excited customers, was a scripting language called **EXTended Operations Language** (**EXTOL**). EXTOL was a DSL in the purest sense because it drew the domain experts right into the development process, as originators of the running code.

With EXTOL, a chemical process engineer or chemist could write simple scripts to define the logic for controlling their plant. Each control block and measurement block in the system was addressable from EXTOL. Using EXTOL, a process engineer could write control logic in the same pseudo English that they used to describe the logic to their peers.

The following script could be deployed on a reactor vessel to control the act of half-filling the vessel with the reactant from VALVE001:

```
drive VALVE001 to OPEN
when LEVELSENSOR.level >= 50%
drive VALVE001 to CLOSED
```

This was an incredibly powerful concept. Up to this point, most process control systems were programmed in a combination of high-level languages on the main process system, and relay logic on PLCs in the plant. Both tasks required specific programming skills, and could not generally be completed by the chemists or chemical engineers, who designed the high-level chemical processing undertaken at the plant. I recall a room full of white-coated chemists at one plant happily writing EXTOL scripts, as we commissioned the plant.

The proof of the pudding is always in the eating, and I don't recall a CPI engineer ever being called upon to write a single line of EXTOL code on behalf of a customer. Given an appropriate DSL that fit their needs, our customers could write all of the code that they need themselves, without having to be programmers.

This shows the power of DSLs at their best. At this extreme end of the spectrum, a DSL becomes a programming tool that a domain expert can use independently, and without recourse to the professional programmer. It's important to remember, however, that the domain experts in this case were mostly process engineers. Process engineers are already well accustomed to devising stepwise instructions, and building process flows. They will often use the same visual representations as a programmer, such as a flow chart to express a process that they are working on.

When devising a DSL for a particular domain, we should always consider the stakeholders who need to be involved in using it. In the case of EXTOL, the DSL was targeted at a technical audience who could take the DSL and become part of the system development process. Not all of our stakeholders will be quite as technical as this. But, at the very least, the goal when designing a DSL should be to make the DSL understandable to nontechnical stakeholders.

Stakeholder participation

It's an unfortunate fact that with many DSLs, especially those based on XML, the code that represents a particular domain problem is often only legible to the programming staff. This leads to a disconnect between what the business analysts and domain experts define, and what eventually gets implemented in the system. For instance, a business rule is most likely to be described in plain English by a business analyst in a functional specification document. But these rules will most likely be translated by developers into an XML representation that is specific to the particular rules engine, which is then deployed as a part of the application. If the business analyst can't read the XML representation and understand it, then the original intent of the rule can easily be lost in translation.

With language-oriented programming, we should aim to build DSLs that can be read and understood by all stakeholders. As such, these DSLs should become the shared living specification of the system, even if in the end they must, by necessity, be written by a programmer with a technical understanding of the DSL.

DSL design and implementation

DSLs can take many different forms. Some DSLs, such as Unix mini languages, (sed, awk, and troff) have a syntactical structure, which is unique to that particular language. To implement such DSLs, we need to be able to parse this syntax out of the text files that contain the source code of that particular language. To implement our own DSL in this style involves implementing a mini compiler that uses lexing and parsing tools such as lex, yacc, or antlr.

Compiler writing is one particular skill that is outside the skill set of most application development teams. Writing your own parser or compiler grammar is a significant amount of effort to go to, unless the DSL is going to be used generally, and is beyond the scope of most application-specific DSLs.

EXTOL circumvented this problem by having its own syntax-sensitive editor. Users edited their EXTOL scripts from within the editor, and were prompted for the language constructs that they needed to use for each circumstance. This ensured that the scripts were always well-formed and syntactically correct. This also meant that the editor can save the scripts in an intermediate p-code form so that the scripts never existed as text-based program files, and therefore never needed to be compiled.

Many of the DSLs that we use are embedded within other languages. The multitude of XML configuration scripts in the Java platform are an example of this. These mini DSLs piggyback on the XML syntax, and can optionally use an XML DTD or schema definition to define their own particular syntax. These XML-based DSLs can be easily validated for "well-formedness" by using the DTD or schema.

External versus internal DSLs

We generally refer to DSLs that are implemented with their own unique syntax as external DSLs, and those that are implemented within the syntax of a host language as embedded or internal DSLs. Ideally, whenever building a new DSL, it would be best to give it its own unique and individual syntax. By designing our own unique syntax, we can provide language constructs, which are designed with both the problem domain and the target audience in mind.

If the intended user of the DSL is a non-programmer, then developing an XML-based syntax can be problematic. XML has its own particular rules about opening, closing, and properly terminating tags that appear arcane to anybody except a programmer. This is a natural constraint when working with DSLs that are embedded/internal to another language. An XML-based DSL cannot help being similar to XML.

Embedded/internal DSLs will never be as free-form as a custom external DSL due to the constraints of the host language. Fortunately, Groovy-based DSLs are capable of being structured in a more human-readable format. However, they always need to use well-formed Groovy syntax, and there are always going to be compromises when designing Groovy-based DSLs that are readable by your target audience.

Operator overloading

Some general-purpose languages, such as C++, Lisp, and now Groovy, have language features that assist in the development of mini language syntaxes. C++ was one of the earliest languages to implement the concept of operator overloading. By using operator overloading, we can make non-numeric objects behave like numeric values by implementing the appropriate operators. So, we can add a plus operator to a `String` object in order to support concatenation. When we implement a class that represents a numeric type, we can add the numeric operators again to make them behave like numeric primitives. We can implement a `ComplexNumber` class, which represents complex numbers, as follows:

```
class ComplexNumber {
public:
double real, imag;
        ComplexNumber() { real = imag = 0; }
        ComplexNumber(double r, double i) { real = r; imag = i; }
        ComplexNumber& operator+(const ComplexNumber& num);
};
```

To add one complex number to another, we need to correctly add each of the real and imaginary parts together to generate the result. We implement an equality operator for `ComplexNumber` as follows:

```
ComplexNumber& ComplexNumber::operator=(const ComplexNumber& num) {
        real = num.real;
        imag = num.imag;
        return *this;
}
```

This allows us then to add `ComplexNumber` objects together as if they were simple numeric values:

```
int main(int argc, const char* argv[]) {
        ComplexNumber a(1, 2), b(3, 4);
        ComplexNumber sum;
        sum = a + b;
        cout << "sum is " << sum.real << " ; "
            << sum.imaginary << "i" << endl;
}
```

One of the criticisms of the operator overload feature in C++ is that when using operator overloading, there is no way to control what functionality is being implemented in the overloaded function. It is perfectly possible—but not very sensible—to make the + operator subtract values and the – operator add values. Misused operator overloading has the effect of obfuscating the code rather than simplifying it. However, sometimes this very obfuscation can be used to good effect.

The preceding example illustrates what could be considered as a classic case of obfuscation in C++. If your use of C++ predated the introduction of the standard C++ libraries and the streams libraries in particular, you will probably do a double take when looking at this code.

The example uses what has become commonly known as the stream operator <<. This operator can be used to send a character stream to standard output, the logic being that it looks very much like how we stream output from one program to another in a Unix shell script. In fact, there really is no such thing as a stream operator in C++ and what has been overloaded here is the binary left shift operator <<. I have to admit that my first encounter with a code like this left me perplexed. Why would anybody want to left shift the address of a string into another object was beyond me? Common use over the intervening years means that this is now a perfectly natural coding style for all C++ programmers. In effect, the streaming operator implements a mini internal DSL for representing streaming. It subverts the original language a little by using an operator out of context, but the end effect is perfectly understandable and makes sense.

During a fireside chat event at JavaOne some years ago, James Gosling was asked if he would ever consider operator overloading for the Java language, and the answer was a resolute no! Fortunately, we don't have to wait and see if Oracle will ever add operator overloading to Java. With Groovy, we can have it now. Groovy has an extensive set of features, including operator overloading that allow us to implement feature-rich DSLs from within the language. We'll take a look at some of those features that distinguish it from Java, now.

Groovy

In the later chapters of this book, we will discuss the Groovy language in detail, but let's begin with a brief introduction to the language and some of the features that make it a useful addition to the Java platform.

The Java platform has expanded over the years to cover almost all conceivable application niches — from Enterprise applications, to mobile and embedded applications. The core strengths of Java are its rich set of APIs across all of these problem domains and its standardized **virtual machine** (**VM**) interface. The standard VM interface has meant that the promise of "write once, run anywhere" has become a reality. The JVM has been implemented on every hardware architecture and operating system from the mightiest mainframe down to the humble Lego Mindstorms robotic kits for kids.

On top of this standard VM, the list of APIs that have been built extends into every conceivable domain. In addition to the standard APIs that are a part of JME, JSE, and JEE, which are extensive in themselves, there are literally thousands of open source component libraries and tools to choose from. All of this makes for a compelling argument for using Java for almost any software project that you can think of.

For many years of its evolution, the JVM was considered to be just that—a virtual machine for running Java programs. The JVM spec was designed originally by James Gosling to be used exclusively for the Java language. In recent years, there have been a number of open source projects that have started to introduce new languages on top of the JVM, such as JRuby (an implementation of the Ruby language), Jython (an implementation of the Python language and Groovy), Clojure, and Scala.

A natural fit with the JVM

Groovy differs from the preceding languages, as the Groovy language was designed specifically to be a new language to run on the JVM. Groovy is designed to be source compatible with the Java language as well as being binary-compatible at the byte code level.

James Strachan and Bob McWhirter started the Groovy project in August 2003 with the goal of providing a new dynamic and object-oriented language, which can run on the JVM. It took several existing dynamic languages, such as Ruby, Python, Dylan, and Smalltalk, as its inspiration. James had looked at the Python scripting language and had been impressed with the power that it had over Java. James and Bob wanted to design a language that had the powerful scripting features of Python, but stayed as close to the Java language as possible in terms of its syntax.

Groovy is code compatible with Java, and for this reason, it is possible in most cases to take an existing `.java` file and rename it to `.groovy` and it will continue to work. Groovy has its own compiler, `groovyc`, which generates Java byte code from Groovy source files just as the `javac` compiler does. Groovyc generates class files, which run directly on the JVM. Methods defined in a Groovy class can be called directly from Java and vice versa.

Groovy classes and interfaces are 100 percent binary compatible with their Java counterparts. Uniquely, this means that we can create a new Groovy class that extends a Java class or implements a Java interface. You can also create Java classes that extend Groovy classes or implement Groovy interfaces.

Groovy language features

Groovy adds a number of unique features that distinguish it from Java and allow developers to code at a higher level, and use a more abstract idiom, than is possible with Java. Placing all of these powerful features on top of a language that is code and API compatible with the Java platform is a powerful proposition.

Static and optional typing

In Java, as in other statically-typed languages, variables must first be declared with a type before they can have a value assigned to them. In Groovy, type can be left to be determined at the time of assignment. Groovy supports both static and optional typing as follows:

```
String str1 = "I'm a String"
def str2 = "I'm also a String"
```

Both variables `str1` and `str2` are of the type `String`. The late binding of the type in the Groovy-style assignment allows for a much less verbose code.

Native support for lists and maps

One of the great bugbears of the Java language is the cumbersome interfaces required for list and map manipulation. Groovy adds native support for all of the Java collection types through a very intuitive and readable syntax. The following code:

```
def authors = [ 'Shakespeare', 'Beckett', 'Joyce', 'Poe' ]
println authors
println authors[2]
```

Produces this output:

```
[Shakespeare, Beckett, Joyce, Poe]

Joyce
```

Maps are also declared with ease:

```
def book = [ fileUnder: "Software Development",
        title: "Groovy for DSL" , author: "Fergal Dearle"]
println book
println book['title']
println book.title
```

This produces the following output:

```
[fileUnder: Software Development, title: Groovy for DSL, author: Fergal
Dearle]
Groovy for DSL
Groovy for DSL
```

Closures

Closures are one of the most powerful language features in Groovy. Closures are anonymous code fragments that can be assigned to a variable. Closures can be invoked by the `call` method as follows:

```
def biggest = { number1, number2 ->
  number1<number2?number2:number1
}
// We can invoke the call method of  the Closure class
def result = biggest.call(7, 1)
println result
// We can use the closure reference as if it were a method
result = biggest(3, 5)
println result
// And with optional parenthesis
result = biggest 13, 1
println result
```

Closures can contain multiple statements and can therefore be as complex as you like. In the following example, we iterate through a `list` looking for the `biggest` number, and return it when we are done:

```
def listBiggest = { list ->
    def biggest = list[0]
    for( i in list)
        if( i > biggest)
            biggest = i
    return biggest
}
def numberList = [ 8, 6, 7, 5, 3, 9]
println listBiggest( numberList)
```

Groovy operator overloading

Operator overloading is a powerful feature of the C++ language. Java inherited many of the features of the C++ language, but operator overloading was significantly left out. Groovy introduces operator overloading as a base language feature.

Any Groovy class can implement a full set of operators by implementing the appropriate corresponding method in the class. For example, the plus operator is implemented via the `plus()` method.

Regular expression support

Groovy builds regular expression handling right into the language via the `=~` operator and matcher objects. The following example creates a regular expression to match all multiple occurrences of the space character. This creates a matcher object from this expression and applies it to a string by using the `replaceAll` method:

```
def lorem =
"Lorem ipsum dolor sit amet, consectetur adipisicing elit"
println lorem
def matcher = lorem =~ " +"
def removed = matcher.replaceAll(" ")
println removed
```

Optional syntax

Optional typing means that variable type annotations are optional. This does not mean that variables have an unknown variable type. It means that the type will be determined at run time based on the value that gets assigned to the variable. All of the following are legal syntax in Groovy:

```
int a = 3
def b = 2
String t = "hello"
def s = 'there'
```

Trailing semicolons at the end of statements are optional. The only time that you explicitly need to use a semicolon in Groovy is to separate statements that occur on the same line of code, as shown in the first and third lines in the following code:

```
int a = 3; int b = 4;
def c = 2
def d = 5; def e = 6
```

Method call parentheses are also optional when the method being invoked has passed some parameters. We saw earlier, with closures, that we can invoke a closure through its reference as if it were a method call. When invoking a closure in this way, we can also drop the parentheses when passing parameters, as shown in the following code:

```
println( a );
c = 2
print c
printit = { println it }
printit c
```

These make for a much looser programming style, which is closer to the scripting syntax of Ruby or Python. This is a big benefit when we are using Groovy to build DSLs. When our target audience is nontechnical, being able to drop parentheses and semicolons will make our code much more legible. Consider the following example, where we have two methods, or closures, to get an account by ID and then credit the account with some funds:

```
Account account = getAccountById( 234 );
creditAccount( account, 100.00 );
```

With optional types, such as parentheses and semicolons, this can be used to write code that is far more legible to our target audience:

```
account = getAccountById 234
creditAccount account, 100.00
```

Groovy markup

There are a number of builder classes built in Groovy. There are markup builders for HTML, XML, Ant build scripts, and for Swing GUI building. Markup builders allow us to write code to build a tree-based structure directly within our Groovy code. Unlike API-based approaches for building structures, the tree-like structure of the resulting output is immediately obvious from the structure of our Groovy markup code. Consider the following XML structure:

```
<?xml version="1.0"?>
<book>
    <author>Fergal Dearle</author>
    <title>Groovy for DSL</title>
</book>
```

In Groovy markup, this XML can be generated simply with the following code fragment:

```
def builder = new groovy.xml.MarkupBuilder()
builder.book {
    author 'Fergal Dearle'
    title 'Groovy for DSL'
}
```

At first glance, this looks like strange special case syntax for markup. It's not! The structure of this code can be explained through the use of closures and the optional syntax that we've discussed in this chapter. We will go into this in great detail in *Chapter 5, Groovy Closures,* but it is interesting at this point to see how the clever use of some language features can yield a powerful DSL-like markup syntax.

Breaking down the preceding code a little, we can rewrite it as:

```
def builder = new groovy.xml.MarkupBuilder()
def closure = {
    author 'Fergal Dearle'
    title 'Groovy for DSL'
}
// pass a closure to book method
builder.book( closure)
// which can be written without parentheses
builder.book closure
// or just inline the closure as a parameter
builder.book {
    ...
}
```

In other words, the code between the curly braces is in fact a closure, which is passed to the book method of MarkupBuilder. Parentheses being optional, we can simply declare the closure inline after the method name, which gives the neat effect of seeming to mirror the markup structure that we expect in the output.

Similarly, author and title are just method invocations on MarkupBuilder with the optional parentheses missing. Extending this paradigm a little further, we can decide to have author take a closure parameter as well:

```
def builder = new groovy.xml.MarkupBuilder()
builder.book {
    author {
```

```
            first_name 'Fergal'
            surname 'Dearle'
        }
    title 'Groovy for DSL'
}
```

This will output the following nested XML structure:

```
<?xml version="1.0"?>
<book>
    <author>
            <first_name>Fergal</first_name>
            <surname> Dearle</surname>
    </author>
    <title>Groovy for DSL</title>
</book>
```

Downloading the example code

You can download the example code files from your account at
http://www.packtpub.com for all the Packt Publishing books
you have purchased. If you purchased this book elsewhere, you
can visit http://www.packtpub.com/support and register to
have the files e-mailed directly to you.

The method calls on `MarkupBuilder` start off by outputting an opening XML tag,
after which they invoke the closure if one has been passed. Finally, the XML tag
is properly terminated before the method exits. If we analyze what happens in
sequence, we can see that `book` invokes a closure that contains a call to `author`.
Additionally, the `author` tag contains a closure with calls to `first_name`, `surname`,
and so on.

Before you go to the Groovy documentation for `MarkupBuilder` to look for the `book`,
`author`, and `surname` methods in `MarkupBuilder`, let me save you the effort. They
don't exist. These are what we call pretend methods. We will see later in the book
how Groovy's metaprogramming features allow us to invoke methods on closure
that don't really exist, but have them do something useful anyway.

Already, we are seeing how some of the features of the Groovy language can
coalesce to allow the structuring of a very useful DSL. I use the term DSL here for
Groovy builders because that is essentially what they are. What initially looks like
special language syntax for markup is revealed as being regular closures with a
little bit of clever metaprogramming. The result is an embedded or internal DSL
for generating markup.

Summary

So, now we have a feel for DSLs and Groovy. We have seen how DSLs can be used in place of general-purpose languages to represent different parts of a system. We have also seen how adding DSLs to our applications can open up the development process to other stakeholders in the development process. We've also seen how, in extreme cases, the stakeholders themselves can even become co-developers of the system by using DSLs that let them represent their domain expertise in code.

We've seen how using a DSL that makes sense to a nontechnical audience means it can become a shared resource between programming staff and business stakeholders, representing parts of the system in a language that they all understand. So, we are beginning to understand the importance of usability when designing a DSL.

We have dipped a tentative toe in the water by looking at some Groovy code. We've gained an appreciation of how Groovy is a natural fit with the Java language due to its binary and class level compatibility. We have touched on the features of the Groovy language that make it unique from Java, and looked at how these unique features can be used as a basis for building on the base Groovy language with internal DSLs.

In the next chapter, we will go into more depth with the language itself and see how we can use these features to build programs. In subsequent chapters, we will dive deeper and see how the language can be exploited as an ideal platform for building DSLs on top of the Java platform.

2
Groovy Quick Start

In this chapter, we will jump straight into getting you up and running with the language on your computer. We will explore the various ways you can get Groovy installed and running on your environment, and look at how we make use of the various tools that come packaged in the Groovy installation:

- We will start out with a section on using GVM. This is definitely the preferred mechanism for installing Groovy and a host of other Groovy-related tools.

- We will follow this with a section on how to find the Groovy binaries and install them on your system.

- The next section will guide you through running Groovy scripts by using the various shell tools provided with the Groovy download.

- Most of you will be using one of the popular IDE environments, so we'll look at the various integration options for the popular IDEs and programmer's editors.

Installing Groovy with GVM

The Groovy ecosystem continues to evolve and is not too proud to take inspiration from other sources. While the language itself has moved forwards in leaps and bounds over the last few years, by far my favorite addition to the ecosystem is **GVM** (**Groovy enVironment Manager**). GVM was inspired by tools such as **RVM** (**Ruby Version Manager**).

GVM is the ideal tool for maintaining parallel versions of the various tools in the Groovy ecosystem. GVM has a simple and intuitive command-line interface for installing and using Groovy, and a whole collection of other useful Groovy-based tools. Switching between different versions of the Grails framework is achieved with a simple command:

```
$gvm use grails 3.0.5
$grails run-app
$gvm u grails 3.0.5
$grails upgrade
```

As well as Groovy itself, GVM can be used to install most of the popular Groovy tools such as Grails, Griffon, Gradle, and Vert.x. This list is being extended by the Groovy community all the time, so for the latest list of supported tools, see the GVM tool site at http://gvmtool.net.

Installing GVM

On Linux, Mac OS X, Solaris, and FreeBSD, installation of GVM can be achieved with one simple command:

```
$curl -s get.gvmtool.net | bash
```

I like the elegance and simplicity of this installation method. If you load http://get.gvmtool.net into a browser, you will see that it is the bash installation script for GVM. The curl command downloads the script and pipes it into bash to execute. You can immediately open a new terminal window and start using GVM. Use the following commands to check the available options:

```
$gvm help
```

Installing GVM on Windows

In my experience, Windows developers fall into two camps: those who love Cygwin because it gives them the power of a Linux style Command Prompt on Windows, and those who just hate it because it imposes too many constraints. If you are the former type of developer, then you already have Cygwin and the curl package installed, which means you have already run the previous curl command, so job done!

If you are the latter, then GVM has got to be your best reason yet for giving Cygwin a spin. You can install Cygwin by running the setup program from the following address: http://cygwin.com/install.html. Pick the setup program appropriate to your system, either 32-bit or 64-bit. Cygwin does not install all packages by default, so at the end of the installation process, you will need to pick curl from the **Net** package category and unzip from the **Archive** category.

From the directory where you installed Cygwin, you can now launch the Cygwin command prompt using the Cygwin.bat command file:

```
C:\cygwin\Cygwin.bat

Fergal@mypc ~
```

You can now issue the curl command we used earlier to install GVM in your Cygwin session.

> Cygwin will pick up all your Windows environment and path variables. GVM itself depends on there being a valid JDK available and will look first for JAVA_HOME and then for the javac command executable to determine where this is. Make sure you have a properly configured JDK in your path somewhere. You can download and install the latest JDK from http://www.oracle.com/technetwork/java/javase/downloads/index.html.

How to find and install Groovy from binaries

The Groovy project is hosted at http://www.groovy-lang.org/download.html and can be downloaded as a ZIP archive or a platform-specific installer for Windows and certain Linux distributions. At the time of writing this book, the latest version of the language available is Groovy 2.4.4.

In five simple steps, you can run Groovy and start experimenting with the language:

1. Download the latest build from http://www.groovy-lang.org/download.html.
2. Unzip the archive into a directory on your computer.
3. Set an environment variable in your command line or shell for GROOVY_HOME. This should point to the base directory to which you unzipped the archive.

4. Add the Groovy bin directory to your PATH. This will be %GROOVY_HOME%\bin (Windows) or $GROOVY_HOME/bin on Linux and Unix systems.

5. Open a new command shell and test your setup by issuing the Groovy version command groovy -v.

 Windows users can also make use of the Windows Installer, which can be found at http://www.groovy-lang.org/download.html.

If all goes well, you should see something like the following:

```
$ groovy -v
Groovy Version: 2.4.4 JVM: 1.8.0_51 Vendor: Oracle Corporation OS: Mac OS
X
```

Your Groovy installation relies on having a working Java version set up already on your computer. Groovy will work with any version of Java from 1.4.1 onwards, but if you want to use some of the language features, such as generics and annotations, you will need to have a minimum of Java 1.5 installed. You can check your Java version with the command java -version, if you are not sure. You can find an upgrade at http://www.oracle.com/technetwork/java/javase/downloads/index.html.

Running Groovy

Now that you have Groovy installed, let's introduce some of the tools that come with the Groovy package. Groovy can be compiled into a Java class file and deployed as part of an application, the same as for any other Java class file. In addition to this, Groovy has several tools that allow us to execute a Groovy program as a script without the need to package it into a Java application.

There are three commands that we can use to launch a script. In the following sections, we will demonstrate the different methods of running Groovy scripts. As we progress through the book, you can use these methods to execute the Groovy scripts that we will describe.

The Groovy script engine – groovy

Let's start by writing a Groovy version of the ubiquitous **Hello World** program. We can start by creating a file called `Hello.groovy`, which contains the following code:

```
public class HelloGroovy {
public static void main(String [] args) {
        System.out.println("Hello, World!");
}
}
```

To any Java developer, this looks strangely like Java code. That's because it is Java code. In the first instance, Groovy is Java source code compatible. Almost anything you write in Java is source-level compatible with Groovy. To prove this, let's try and run the following code as a script from the command line:

$groovy HelloWorld.groovy

Hello, World!

This is interesting, and it is a feature that we can make good use of in the future, but we are not gaining many of the benefits of Groovy by writing in Java. Let's rewrite this script to be more Groovy.

Groovy is also a scripting language, so we don't need to write our code within a class to execute it, and we don't need a static `main` method either. A lot of useful methods from the JDK, such as `println`, are provided as wrapper shortcuts by the Groovy class `DefaultGroovyMethods`. Thus, we can rewrite our **Hello World** program in one line of code as follows:

```
println "Hello, World!"
```

The Groovy script engine also defaults the filename suffix, so the following command works just as well:

$groovy HelloWorld

Hello, World!

We can also invoke the Groovy script engine and pass it a single statement to execute:

$groovy -e "println 'Hello, World'"

Hello, World!

We already know that Groovy is a language built on top of the JVM and that it runs as Java bytecode. So, how is it possible for a Groovy script to run without being compiled to a Java class? The answer is that the Groovy scripting engine compiles scripts on the fly and loads the bytecode onto the JVM. We will find out how to compile our Groovy script later in the chapter.

The important thing to note for now is that even though our scripts seem to be running on the command line, they are in fact running on a JVM, and as a result, we have access to all of the power of the JVM and Java APIs. To demonstrate, let's look at a more complicated script.

The Java management extension JMX is an extremely useful component of the Java platform. JMX is a framework for managing and monitoring applications, system objects, and devices. In JMX, resources are represented as MBeans and we can use the JMX APIs to access the resources to monitor the state of our application.

Typical JMX clients such as jManage tend to be heavy-weight GUI applications that allow application resources to be inspected. Sometimes, I just want to monitor one or two values that are relevant to the performance of my application, such as its current heap usage, and log it to a file at intervals.

Consider the following Groovy script, `monitor.groovy`, which connects to the platform MBean of a remote JVM and monitors its heap usage before and after a garbage collection operation:

```
import java.lang.management.*
import java.lang.management.ManagementFactory as Factory
import javax.management.remote.JMXConnectorFactory as JMX
import javax.management.remote.JMXServiceURL as ServiceURL

def serverUrl = 'service:jmx:rmi:///jndi/rmi://localhost:3333/jmxrmi'
def server = JMX.connect(
                new ServiceURL(serverUrl)).MBeanServerConnection

println "HEAP USAGE"
def mem = Factory.newPlatformMXBeanProxy(server,
                Factory.MEMORY_MXBEAN_NAME, MemoryMXBean.class)
def heapUsage = mem.heapMemoryUsage
println """Memory usage : $heapUsage.used"""
mem.gc()
heapUsage = mem.heapMemoryUsage
println """Memory usage after GC: $heapUsage.used"""
```

You can try this script against any running Java application. Just add the following switches to the Java startup command of the application. This instructs your JVM to start up with an open JMX connection on the port `3333`. For simplicity, we have abstained from using a secure connection or password authentication:

```
-Dcom.sun.management.jmxremote.port=3333-Dcom.sun.management.jmxremote.
authenticate=false-Dcom.sun.management.jmxremote.ssl=false
```

After running the script and connecting to an application, we get instant feedback about the state of our heap usage:

```
$groovy monitor.groovy
HEAP USAGE
Memory usage : 1118880
Memory usage after GC: 607128
```

If you are not familiar with JMX, don't worry. The point to be grasped here is that Groovy unleashes the power of the JVM and APIs, and puts them at your disposal through the command-line shell. My starting point for the previous script was an existing Java program that implemented the JMX API calls I needed. This is a slightly cleaned up version of the script, which exploits some Groovy syntax that we will learn about later. In practically no time, it is possible to drop Java API code into a Groovy script and you have a command-line version to play with. The possibilities for tool development are endless.

Shebang scripts

If you are running Groovy on UNIX, Linux, Mac OS X, or in the Cygwin shell for Windows, you can go one step further with this approach. The Groovy script engine is designed to work as a proper shell scripting language and supports the "shebang" `#!` characters. By placing `#!/usr/bin/env groovy` as the first line of a script, the shell will pass the remainder of the script for processing by Groovy. These are commonly referred to as **shebang scripts**. We can modify our `Hello.groovy` as follows:

```
#!/usr/bin/env groovy
println "Hello, World!"
```

Now, if we change the permissions of the file to executable, we can call it directly from the shell:

```
$mv Hello.groovy Hello
$chmod a+x Hello
$./Hello
Hello, World!
```

The Groovy shell – groovysh

The Groovy shell is a useful command-line tool for trying out snippets of Groovy code interactively. The shell allows you to enter Groovy code line by line and execute it. We can run the `groovysh` command and immediately start entering Groovy statements:

```
$ groovysh
Groovy Shell (2.4.4, JVM: 1.8.0_51)
Type ':help' or ':h' for help.
-------------------------------------------------------------groo
vy:000> "Hello, World!"
===> Hello, World!
groovy:000>
```

The Groovy shell evaluates each line and outputs the return value of the statement. The preceding statement contains just one instance of a string, so the string `Hello, World!` is returned. By contrast, our single line Hello script outputs **Hello, World!**, but returns `null`, as follows:

```
groovy:000> println "Hello, World!"
Hello, World!
===> null
groovy:000>
```

This is an important point to remember if you make use of the Groovy shell, as it sometimes can be the cause of unexpected error messages in otherwise correct scripts. The Groovy shell will try to interpret and print the return value of your statement irrespective of whether it makes sense to do so or not.

With the Groovy shell, statements can span more than one line. Partially complete Groovy statements are stored in a buffer until completion. You can use the `:display` command to output a partially complete statement, as follows:

```
groovy:000> class Hello {
groovy:001> :display
 001> class Hello {
groovy:001> String message
groovy:002> :display
 001> class Hello {
 002> String message
groovy:002> }
===> true
groovy:000>
```

The `load` command allows scripts to be loaded into `groovysh` from a file. However, some limitations of the Groovy shell make this problematic. The Groovy shell works by using an instance of the `GroovyShell` class to evaluate each line of script in turn. When we run any Groovy script, the variables local to the script are stored in the binding object. Variables in the binding object behave exactly like variables that are in a global scope. Since `groovysh` evaluates the script piecemeal as it encounters each line, only variables that find their way into the binding are preserved. So, the following code works because the `message` variable is stored in the binding, which is shared between evaluations:

```
groovy:000> message = "Hello, World!"
===> Hello, World!
groovy:000> println message
Hello, World!
===> null
groovy:000>
```

However, this version causes an error as `message` is now treated as a local variable and not stored in the binding:

```
groovy:000> String message = "Hello, World!"
===> Hello, World!
groovy:000> println hello
Unknown property: message
groovy:000>
```

The Groovy console – groovyConsole

The limited set of commands and crude command-line operations make `groovysh` problematic for anything other than trying out single expressions or statements. A much more useful tool is the Groovy console. The Groovy console is a GUI editor and runtime environment. You only need to type your Groovy statements in the top pane and the output gets listed in the bottom pane.

You can launch the Groovy console from the command line with the following command:

```
$groovyConsole
```

This launches the following Groovy console:

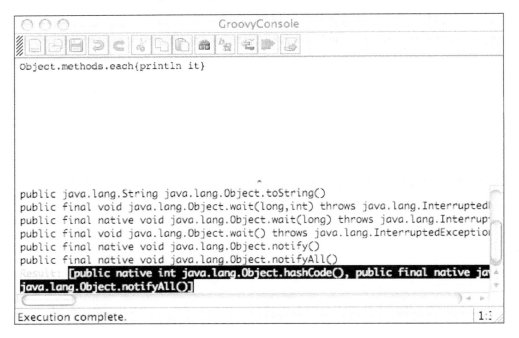

In the preceding **GroovyConsole**, we are trying out a handy feature of Groovy, which is the ability to find class methods on the fly. This simple line of code exploits a few of the Groovy language features. `Object.methods` is analogous to calling `getMethods()` for the `Object` class. Instead of a method array, a Groovy list is returned containing the method objects. We use the built-in iteration method to pass each element in the list to the closure that prints the method details. We will go over all of these language features in depth later.

On the other hand, `GroovyShell`, the class on which `groovysh` is built, is an extremely useful class. Later in this book, we will use `GroovyShell` to evaluate DSL scripts on the fly, but other uses can be made of it including building an on-the-fly Groovy interpreter into your application, if necessary.

The Groovy console has several other features, such as the ability to select a part of the buffer and run it, and also has a useful object browser. This allows you to inspect the last result object from the console. Combined with the ability to select part of the display buffer and run it independently, the console is the ideal sandbox for playing with code snippets—whether debugging existing code or learning the Groovy language.

The Groovy compiler – groovyc

Using the Groovy script engine, we can execute Groovy scripts from the command line. For experimenting and debugging our scripts, we can run them interactively in the Groovy shell or the Groovy console. To build our Groovy programs into larger apps that require more than one class, or to integrate our Groovy programs into existing Java applications, we need to be able to compile Groovy.

The groovyc command works exactly the same way as javac does. It takes a Groovy source file and compiles it into a corresponding class file that can be run on the JVM. Our script examples up to now have not defined a class. The Groovy compiler will wrap our Groovy scripts into an executable class file, which can be invoked with the java command as if they had a public static void main() method.

Let's take the JMX monitor.groovy script that we wrote earlier, and compile and run it:

```
$ groovyc monitor.groovy
$ java -cp $GROOVY_HOME/embeddable/groovy-all-2.4.4.jar:. monitor
HEAP USAGE
Memory usage : 1118880
Memory usage after GC: 607128
```

The Groovy IDE and editor integration

If you are going to do any amount of serious Groovy coding, you will want to work with Groovy in your favorite IDE.

NetBeans

Of the popular IDE environments, NetBeans was the first to provide built-in Groovy support. From NetBeans 6.5 onwards, Groovy support is available from within any of the Java bundles without any additional plugins being required. By default, you have excellent Groovy source editing with syntax highlighting, source folding, and code completion. You can mix and match Groovy with Java in your projects, or build a full Groovy on Grails-based project from scratch. You can download the latest NetBeans installation from https://netbeans.org/downloads/.

Eclipse

Eclipse was the first Java IDE to have Groovy support integrated through the Groovy-Eclipse plugin. You can install the Groovy-Eclipse plugin from the update site at `http://dist.springsource.org/snapshot/GRECLIPSE/e4.5/`.

The Groovy-Eclipse plugin has full support for source-level Groovy editing with syntax highlighting, auto completion, and refactoring.

Spring STS

If you don't want the hassle of managing individual plugins in your Eclipse installation, then it's worth downloading and installing the Groovy/Grails Tool Suite from `http://spring.io/tools`.

IntelliJ IDEA

All the latest versions of IntelliJ IDEA have excellent built-in support for Groovy, including excellent support for Grails, Gradle, and Spock. For the purpose of most of the examples in this book, the free Community Edition of IntelliJ IDEA is sufficient for your needs.

Other IDEs and editors

Other IDEs with Groovy support are JDeveloper and JEdit. In addition, many of the popular program editors, such as TextMate and UltraEdit, also now have Groovy support. There is even a plugin available to download for Emacs. Check out `http://www.groovy-lang.org/ides.html` for a full list of available plugins, and extensive instructions on setting up and running Groovy in your preferred environment.

Summary

In this chapter, I gave you all the tools to get started with the Groovy language, but we have barely touched the language itself. Whatever your own personal preference for an operating system or IDE, you should now be ready to start coding.

In the next chapter, we will start to look at some of the essential Groovy DSLs that are available. Gradle is a Groovy-based build and dependency management tool. Spock is a Groovy-based unit testing framework that used DSL syntax to implement **behavior-driven development (BDD)** syntax into your tests.

3
Essential Groovy DSLs

It's tempting at this point in the book to dive into the Groovy language. Instead in this chapter we will take a slightly different tack. Here we will take a look at two essential Groovy tools and, more importantly, the DSLs that they provide. Gradle is a build, test and deployment automation tool, which is powered by a Groovy DSL. Spock is a unit testing and specification framework built over JUnit. The stand out feature of Spock is its highly expressive Groovy based DSL, which allows the tests to be written in **behavior-driver development** (**BDD**) style semantics.

In this chapter we will cover some of the basic features of both DSLs. Both Gradle and Spock are used extensively in the code examples that accompany this book. Where possible throughout the rest of the book we will use Spock's BDD syntax to illustrate Groovy features. I urge you to read this chapter first before continuing with the rest of the book. Familiarity with Spock and Gradle will be assumed in the text from this chapter forward.

Installing Gradle

Let's start by installing Gradle using the GVM tool we used in the last chapter. Installing Gradle is simplicity itself if you have followed the instructions from *Chapter 2*, *Groovy Quick Start*, to install the GVM tool. Just issue the following GVM command:

```
$gvm install gradle
```

This will install the latest available version of Gradle into your environment. The Gradle developers, Gradleware, have a policy of first deprecating old features and then removing them entirely. So, to avoid any future compatibility issues, you can use the GVM tool to install the version of Gradle used when this book was written as follows:

```
$gvm install gradle 2.4
```

If you already have Gradle installed with a different version you can switch versions as follows:

```
$gvm use gradle 2.4
```

GVM takes care of all the detail of installing Gradle and setting up the path and GRADLE_HOME environment for you. If you are not using the GVM tool, you can find the Gradle installation packages at http://www.gradle.org/downloads. Then configure the Gradle environment by following the instructions at http://www.gradle.org/docs/current/userguide/installation.html.

Gradle basics

To understand Gradle builds, you need to only consider three basic concepts initially:

- **The build script**: Gradle automatically looks for a file called build.gradle in the current directory. This file is the build script, which defines the projects and tasks that make up the build.

- **Projects**: Gradle can work with a single or multiple projects per build. For the purpose of this chapter, we will only be looking at single project builds.

- **Tasks**: Gradle tasks are the building blocks of the build, for example, compile, test, and clean.

Gradle build scripts

Gradle automatically looks for a file called build.gradle in the current directory and uses this as the build script. For most simple projects, all you ever need to write is a build.gradle file. The source package that accompanies this book has a build.gradle file in the root directory. This is a very simple build script file from which we only care about one main task.

You can test all the code in the book with one Gradle command:

```
$gradle test
```

We will look at this build.gradle script in more detail later in the chapter to see how this is achieved. But first, let's look at some basic Gradle tasks. In the following examples, we will use build scripts with different names to build.gradle. This is purely so that we can have more than one build script in the same directory. To run a build script other than build.gradle from the command line, we will use the following code:

```
$gradle -b hello.gradle
```

Gradle tasks

As we saw previously, Gradle tasks are the building blocks of a Gradle build. We can define as many tasks as we like within our build script. Here is an example of a very simple task:

```
task hello {
    doLast {
        println "Hello, World!"
    }
}
```

What the preceding Gradle script snippet is doing is declaring a single task called `hello`. Tasks can be comprised of multiple actions. In this case, there is one action defined for the task, that is, the code block:

```
{
println "Hello, World!"
}
```

This is actually a Groovy closure. We will dedicate a full chapter later to learning about closures. It is sufficient for now to know that by declaring this as the `doLast` action we are asking for this block of code to be executed last as part of the `hello` task. You can run this script from the command line as follows:

$gradle -q -b hello.gradle hello

> For the rest of the Gradle examples in this chapter, we will always use the `-q` "quite execution" option. This will ensure that only the output from the tasks is printed and not the other Gradle status messages on startup.

Adding actions to tasks

There is also a `doFirst` method we can use to add an action to the start of a task. The `doFirst` and `doLast` methods are useful notational conveniences if you have a very simple task to define like the one that follows:

```
task helloWithActions {
    doFirst {
        print "Hello, "
    }
    doLast {
        println "World Actions!"
    }
}
```

If we add multiple doFirst and doLast actions in a task, Gradle gives us what seem to be illogical results. So, the first doFirst action is last and the last doLast action is last to be executed. Confused? Look at this task and then check out the output, and it will be clearer:

```
task confused {
    doFirst {
        println "The First doFirst will be last"
    }
    doFirst {
        println "The last doFirst will be first"
    }
    doLast {
        println "The first doLast will be first"
    }
    doLast {
        println "The last doLast will be last"
    }
}
```

You can execute the preceding task from the root directory of the sample code package with the following command:

```
$gradle -q -b scripts/ChapterThree/hello.gradle confused
The last doFirst will be first
The First doFirst will be last
The first doLast will be first
The last doLast will be last
```

From the preceding output, we can see that the order of our actions is not quite what we might have expected. The reason is that each of the doFirst and doLast methods are executed in turn as they occur in the task definition. When Gradle encounters a doFirst method in the definition, it is established as the first action to execute, but subsequent doFirst actions are inserted before it. The same happens with doLast, except that doLast at least adds actions to the action list in the order they are encountered.

For the preceding reasons and to avoid hours spent scratching your head wondering why actions are not performing in the order you expect, I suggest not using doFirst and doLast in anything except a trivial Gradle task. The better notation to use is the << operator as follows:

```
task  helloSimple << {
    println "Hello, Simple World!"
}
```

The << operator is synonymous with doLast, so we can use it over again in the build script to add actions to the end of the task. In this example, we create a task called actionsInOrder. Once this task is created, we can continue to use << to action actions to the task.

```
task actionsInOrder << {
    println "The first will be first"
}
actionsInOrder << {
    println "The last will be last"
}
```

When we run this script, the actions are executed in the order they are encountered in the script as follows:

```
$gradle -q -b scripts/ChapterThree/hello.gradle actionsInOrder
The first will be first
The last will be last
```

Default tasks

Sometimes, in a build system, we need to define a default task or tasks to execute whenever the build is run. We define default tasks in a Gradle build script with the defaultTasks method. For instance, here we have two tasks; clean and runTests, which we want to run by default whenever the build is executed without a task specified.

```
defaultTasks 'clean', 'runTests'

task clean << {
    println 'Cleaning'
}
task runTests << {
    println 'Running Tests'
}
```

The preceding Gradle script when run produces the following output:

```
$gradle -q -b scripts/ChapterThree/default.gradle
Cleaning
Running tests
```

Creating task dependencies

Any build tool is incomplete without the ability to create dependencies between build tasks. With Gradle, we create dependencies using the dependsOn attribute. We can create a dependency between two tasks as follows:

```
task  helloSimple << {
    println "Hello, Simple World!"
}
task helloWithDepends (dependsOn: 'helloSimple') << {
    println "Hello, Dependent World!"
}
```

Invoking the helloWithDepends task will first cause the helloSimple task to be executed.

```
$gradle -q -b scripts/ChapterThree/hello.gradle helloWithDepends

Hello, Simple World!

Hello, Dependent World!
```

Dependent tasks can be chained together by declaring one task to depend on another task. This task in turn can already depend on a third task. We can also make a single task dependent on multiple other tasks:

```
task clean << {
    println 'Cleaning'
}
task runTests << {
    println 'Running Tests'
}
task buildApplication (dependsOn: 'clean') << {
    println 'Building Application'
}
task deploy (dependsOn: ['runTests','buildApplication']) << {
    println 'Deploying'
}
```

When we run the preceding script, it produces the following output:

```
$gradle -q -b scripts/ChapterThree/default.gradle deploy

Cleaning

Building Application

Running Tests

Deploying
```

Built-in tasks and plugins

So far, we've looked at tasks we provide ourselves in the build script. While Gradle is a powerful tool, it would be tedious to use if we had to script every build task ourselves by hand. Luckily, Gradle provides a plugin mechanism to overcome this. There are many different plugins, which provide focused functionality for various use cases building.

Java and Groovy are supported via Gradle plugins. In addition to these core plugins that are supported by Gradleware themselves, there are numerous other plugins supported by the community for everything from the Cobertura plugin for code coverage support to the Tomcat plugin, which supports deployment of your web app to an embedded Tomcat container.

Let's take a look at the `build.gradle` script supplied with the example code package for this book:

```
apply plugin: "groovy"
apply plugin: "idea"
apply plugin: "eclipse"

repositories {
  mavenCentral()
}
dependencies {
    compile "org.codehaus.groovy:groovy-all:2.4.4"
    testCompile "org.spockframework:spock-core:0.7-groovy-2.0"
}
```

What is unusual about this in light of what we've read already about Gradle is the fact that this script does not define any tasks. However, as was stated already in this build script is all we need to build and run all the example code for the book. The reason we don't need to add any tasks is that the plugins defined are providing all the tasks we need in this case.

Even an empty build script has some default tasks provided by Gradle itself. One of these is `tasks`, which we can use to list the available tasks in a build script. Try the `tasks` task against some of the build scripts in the code package. If we run it on a completely empty script, it reports the basic built-in tasks that Gradle provides out of the box.

```
$gradle -b scripts/ChapterThree/empty.gradle tasks --all
```

This includes some useful tasks as follows:

- `tasks`: This lists available tasks as we've seen earlier
- `wrapper`: This is a useful way of packaging your Gradle build with a self-installing `gradle` jar
- `projects`: This lists the available projects in your build
- `dependencies`: This lists the dependencies in your build

The same command run against our `hello.gradle` example script will also report the tasks listed in the build script itself: `hello`, `helloSimple`, `helloWithActions`, and so on. When we run it against the `build.gradle` script from our previous examples, it will report they additional tasks provided by the plugins.

Plugins

You will also notice that the script declares three plugins to use, Groovy, IDEA, and Eclipse. Plugins bundle additional tasks into Gradle that focus on a specific functionality. By applying these plugins, we are in effect adding additional built-in tasks to our build that we can call upon.

The Gradle Groovy plugin

The first plugin we have included is the Gradle Groovy plugin. We can see what additional tasks are applied to our build by running `gradle tasks --all` in the sample root directory. The Groovy plugin bundles some useful tasks into our build to facilitate the compilation, testing, and packaging of the Groovy code. Here are some of the tasks provided:

- `classes`: This task builds the classes from source
- `testClasses`: This task builds test classes from source
- `test`: This builds all classes and runs the tests
- `clean`: This cleans up all target classes and other output files from the build
- `groovydoc`: This generates documentation from the JavaDoc style comments in Groovy classes

The IDEA plugin

As the name suggests, the IDEA plugin is used to support IntelliJ IDEA. This plugin provides two main tasks: `cleanIdea` and `idea`. These tasks will clear and create the support files that allow you to view a project in IntelliJ IDEA. Running the following command from the example source's root will enable you build the project files that will allow you to view all the sample sources in IDEA:

```
$gradle cleanIdea idea
```

The Eclipse plugin

The Eclipse plugin does exactly the same for Eclipse users. To generate a project setup to allow the samples to be viewed in Eclipse, all we need to do is run:

```
$gradle cleanEclipse eclipse
```

Repositories

The next section in our preceding build script is the `repositories` section. The `repositories` section tells Gradle where to look to resolve dependencies in the build.

```
repositories {
  mavenCentral()
}
```

In this build script, all of our dependencies can be resolved in the Maven central, so we get all that we need to declare. We can also declare our own company Maven, Ivy, or local repository if we have one.

```
repositories {
  maven {
    url "https:repos.company.com/nexus"
  }
  ivy {
    url "https:repos.company.com/ivy"
  }
  ivy {
    url "../local-ivy"
  }
}
```

Gradle will search the defined repositories in the order they are specified in the `repositories` section and stop at the first repository that has the required dependency.

Dependencies

The final section in our preceding build script declares the dependencies we need
to resolve. Gradle is a Groovy-based tool, so it already ships with Groovy library.
However, in order to declare what version of Groovy we want used by our own
builds, we need to declare that as a dependency. The previous `dependencies`
section declares a compile time dependency on the latest Groovy version available
at time of publication:

```
dependencies {
  compile "org.codehaus.groovy:groovy-all:2.4.4
  testCompile "org.spockframework:spock-core:0.7-groovy-2.0"
}
```

Dependencies can be declared for compile and runtime phases of the build. We can
declare a dependency that is just to be used at the test compilation phase with a
`testCompile` configuration. In the previous example, we configured a dependency
for the Spock test framework, which is the second of our essential Groovy DSLs.

Spock tests

The Spock Framework is a **behavior-driven development** (BDD) tool built on top
of JUnit. Spock uses the features of the Groovy language to add BDD style syntax
to JUnit tests. Spock allows us to write our test specifications as "given, when, then"
style expressions, but under the covers, they still run as JUnit tests and can still be
run by the JUnit runner. This means that Spock tests are compatible with most build
tools, IDEs, and continuous integration servers.

Given, when, then

The main characteristic of BDD is the concept of expressing tests in plain English
sentences. User stories should be accompanied with clear descriptive acceptance
criteria, which describe expected behavior in the system under test.

In support of this concept, an accepted dialect has evolved to describe acceptance
tests. The general form follows the pattern: **given** (some initial context), **when**
(some event or stimulus occurs), **then** (a certain outcome is expected).

A simpler version when no stimulus is involved is **given** (some initial context) and
expect (certain condition to be true). The Spock DSL allows us to specify tests using
these familiar terms.

Spock specification structure

Spock specifications are written as a Groovy class that extends one of the core Spock specification classes. We will use `spock.lang.Specification` for our tests. The anatomy of the specification itself breaks down as follows:

- **Feature methods**: These are the core of the Spock specification. They describe the feature of the system under test and how it is expected to work.

- **Blocks**: Within a feature method, Spock specification comprise of blocks. These are the conceptual elements of the test and describe initial state and expected outcomes of a test specification.

- **Fields**: Class instance fields are where we store objects belonging to a specifications fixture.

- **Fixture methods**: These are the methods Spock uses for setup and cleanup operations.

- **Helper methods**: Spock aims through its rich syntax to make specification as expressive as possible. Often, however, our specifications get large or contain duplication. Helper methods are not run as features by the Spock, but are used within the feature methods themselves.

Feature methods

The fundamental building block of a Spock test specification is the feature method. Feature methods in a Spock specification are any method in the specification class that contains Spock blocks, which we will describe in the next section. We can declare a feature method using classic Java style method naming, or we can do so using a special Groovy naming style, which allows method names as string.

The latter style is the convention in Spock, which supports the BDD goal of defining tests in plain English. We can in fact chose whatever we like as a feature method name, but the more descriptive we make these names, the more readable our test specifications become. Once you make regular use of BDD, it starts to become natural to define your tests in the same plain English used in the acceptance tests written in your user stories.

Here is a simple Spock test specification. The specification itself is a Groovy class extended from the `spock.lang.Specification` class. It contains one feature method called "the truth could not be truer" and it has two blocks. The specification itself is written in the Groovy language, and so far in the book, we have barely touched on the syntax of the language at all. However, it still should be possible to read this test specification and understand what it is aiming to achieve.

```groovy
import spock.lang.Specification

class ChapterThreeSimpleSpec extends Specification {
    def "the truth could not be truer" () {
        given:
            def truth = true

        expect:
            truth
    }
}
```

Blocks

Spock feature methods comprise of combinations of blocks. In the following example, we will see how we can specify a BDD style `given`, `when`, `then` sentence. We have a block for each of the BDD keywords. The string description after each keyword is entirely optional, but it is best practice to provide it because it adds readability to your specifications:

```groovy
void "two wrongs don't make a right" () {
    given: "two false statements"
        def theWorldIsFlat = false
        def theEarthOrbitsTheSun = false

    when: "we combine the two falsehoods"
        def copernicusWasWrong =
        theWorldIsFlat && theEarthOrbitsTheSun

    then: "Copernicus was telling the truth"
        ! copernicusWasWrong
}
```

For the most part, we can write whatever we like within the block itself. However, Spock applies some rules, which make sense. The `then:` and `expect:` blocks should only contain expressions that can be evaluated as Boolean expressions. In the next chapter, we will cover how Groovy's interpretation of truth is wider than Java. In effect any expression which, evaluates to Boolean true, is a positive or non null value or a collection with elements in it will all evaluate to true.

As you would expect the code can have multiple lines in any block. However, it may make sense to logically separate this to aid the readability of a test. For instance, the previous `given:` block can be been broken up as follows:

```
given: "a flat world"
    def theWorldIsFlat = false
and: "two celestial bodies"
    def theEarthOrbitsTheSun = false
```

We can extend any block of our test specification with an additional `and:` block. Here, we will add a second `expect:` to the specification:

```
void "we can extend Spock specs with and blocks" () {
    given: "Two Integer numbers"
        Number a = 10
        Number b = 5

    expect: "Integer multiplication and addition are commutative"
        a * b == b * a

    and:
        a + b == b + a
}
```

Spock does its best to preserve the logical structure of our BDD style specification, so it will disallow sequences of blocks that don't make sense. Odd block sequences such as `given/then` or `given/expect/when` will either result in a polite suggestion from Spock to use an alternative or a syntax error.

Fields

Spock test specifications can contain class instance fields, which is a good place to store fixture objects. It's important to note however that while fields are declared as class instance fields their values are not shared between feature methods. In the following example, `truth` will be reinitialized to `false` for each feature method:

```
class ChapterThreeSimpleSpec extends Specification {
    def truth = false

    void "the truth could not be truer" () {
        given: "the unvarnished truth"
            truth = true

        expect: "its true"
            truth
    }
}
```

Sometime, it might be desirable to subvert this feature of Spock and have a field whose state is preserved between feature methods. The `@Shared` annotation will overcome the default Spock behavior for fields and share the value between feature method executions.

```
@Shared def truth = false
```

Fixture methods

Spock provides four special fixture methods that allow setup and cleanup of objects in the specification. These can be used in combination with fields in our specification to handle any setup and cleanup required by the specification or the individual feature methods:

- `setupSpec()`: This is called once per test specification, before the first feature method is run. This can be used for any specific test initialization required by the system under test, but it cannot access any instance fields.

- `cleanupSpec()`: This is called once per test specification, after the last feature method has been called. Here, we can do any final teardown of services required by the test, but we cannot access any instance fields.

- `setup()`: This is called before every feature method. It's good practice to initialize fixture data in here.

- `cleanup()`: This is called after each feature method. We can release any resources consumed in `setup()` here.

Here is a slightly complex but very useful example of a use for fixture methods. We will go into more detail in later chapters about how to use the `GroovyShell` class. In this example, we will set up a Groovy shell in our test specification and a `PrintStream` object to capture the output from the shell. The `GroovyShell` class will allow us to execute Groovy source code from a file in our path without the need to compile it and include it in the class path:

```
GroovyShell shell
Binding binding
PrintStream orig
ByteArrayOutputStream out

def setup() {
    orig = System.out
    out = new ByteArrayOutputStream()
    System.setOut(new PrintStream(out))
    binding = new Binding()
    shell = new GroovyShell(binding)
}
def cleanup() {
    System.setOut(orig)
}
```

Helper methods

A feature method is any method that has a Spock block in it. Any method that does not have a Spock block defined, and is not one of the four fixture methods, will be treated by Spock as a helper method and will be compiled into the test as a regular instance method.

We can call a helper method from anywhere in one of our feature methods. For instance, the following helper method works alongside our `GroovyShell` fixture methods to return the output after executing a Groovy script in the Groovy shell:

```
protected String output() {
    out.toString().trim()
}
```

Together these fixtures and helper methods give us a neat way to test the expected outcome of running an external Groovy script. Remember this one because we will make use of it in the following chapters of the book:

```
def "HelloWorld says Hello World"() {
    given: "we have a Hello World script"
        def script = new File("scripts/ChapterTwo/Hello.groovy")
    when: "we run the script"
        shell.evaluate script
    then: "the script outputs the correct details"
        "Hello, World!" == output()
}
```

Where blocks

The BDD style syntax provided in Spock allows us to write very expressive tests, but because of its nature can become very repetitive when we have multiple expectations we want to test, which have the same or different outcomes and which are data-driven. Spock fortunately has a very useful `where:` block to cover this scenario.

The `where` blocks always come at the end of a feature method. In the following example, the `where` block defines two feature method variables, `filename` and `expectedOutput`. The feature method will iterate the values for each of these variables applying each in turn and asserting the outcomes in turn.

```
def "HelloWorld says Hello World in Java and Groovy styles"() {
    given: "we have a Hello World script"
        def script = new File(fileName)
    when: "we run the script"
        shell.evaluate script
    then: "the script outputs the correct details"
        expectedOutput == output()
    where: "we have different versions of HelloWorld"
        fileName                              | expectedOutput
        "scripts/ChapterTwo/Hello.groovy"     | "Hello, World!"
        "scripts/ChapterTwo/HelloWorld.groovy" | "Hello, World!"
}
```

Fixture blocks

Sometimes, we will have fixture data which is specific to a feature method and is not something we want to be shared across multiple feature methods. Spock provides `setup:` and `cleanup:` for this purpose.

```
def "Fixtures can be in blocks too"() {
    setup:
        orig = System.out
        out = new ByteArrayOutputStream()
        System.setOut(new PrintStream(out))
        binding = new Binding()
        shell = new GroovyShell(binding)
    and: "we have a Hello World script"
        def script = new
        File("scripts/ChapterTwo/Hello.groovy")
    when: "we run the script"
        shell.evaluate script
    then: "the script outputs the correct details"
        "Hello, World!" == output()
    cleanup:
        System.setOut(orig)
}
```

Note that the `setup:` block is synonymous with `given:` and can often be used interchangeably.

Testing Gradle using Spock

We started out the chapter by describing some of the features of Gradle. If we take **test-driven development** (TDD) seriously, it should be possible to assert any expected outcome using a test tool. As it happens, it is not difficult to use Spock to verify the assertions we made earlier about how Gradle itself works. Consider the following feature method:

```
def "hello task says Hello, World!"() {
    given: "we have a gradle build command"
        def command = "gradle -q -b hello.gradle hello"
    when: "we run the build command"
        def proc = command.execute()
        proc.waitFor()
    then: "the script outputs the correct details"
        "Hello, World!" == proc.in.text.trim()
}
```

Further reading

I encourage you to read the detailed documentation for both these tools at their respective sites. The Gradle DSL has full and comprehensive documentation hosted at `http://www.gradle.org/docs/current/dsl/index.html`. A detailed documentation on Spock can be found at `http://spockframework.github.io/spock/docs/1.0/index.html`.

As further reading take a look at the `ChapterThreeGradleSpec.groovy` example in the code sources. Most of the Gradle examples from the start of the chapter are asserted via Spock feature methods in this specification. Now, take the time to explore the sample code associated with the book. Spock is used extensively to illustrate and assert the code examples in the book. Gradle is used as the primary build tool for building all the examples in the book.

Summary

The purpose of this chapter was to give you sufficient background in both Gradle and Spock so that you are comfortable with them when we make reference to these tools later in the book. We covered enough material to serve this purpose, but for both Gradle and Spock, there is a lot more to learn. Gradle alone is the subject of several books, including one excellent title by this publisher, Packt Publishing.

In the next chapter, we will take a tour of the Groovy language. While this will not be a comprehensive guide of all aspects of the language, I will cover enough of the language so that you will be able to start coding in Groovy yourself, and start to follow the examples in the rest of the book.

4
The Groovy Language

In this chapter, we will conduct a whistle-stop tour of the Groovy language. We don't have the scope in this book to cover the whole language in a tutorial fashion, but by the end of the book, we will have covered most of the aspects of the language that you need to be able to write your own Groovy-based DSLs. For now, in this chapter, we will just touch on some of the main points that differentiate Groovy from its parent language—Java.

This chapter makes extensive use of Spock style test assertions throughout. If you have not already read *Chapter 3, Essential Groovy DSLs*, I would strongly suggest you at least read the *Spock tests* section of that chapter and familiarize yourself with the unique Spock syntax.

Introducing the Groovy language

In the following sections, we will cover some of the fundamental concepts and features of the Groovy language. A working knowledge of Java is assumed, so we will focus on what is different between the Groovy and Java languages.

The module structure

Groovy programs and scripts are generally stored in Groovy source files with the `.groovy` extension. The exception to this are the Unix "shebang" scripts described in *Chapter 2, Groovy Quick Start*. Unlike Java source files, which must always contain a class definition, Groovy source files can contain both class definitions and inline scripting. When we compile or run a Groovy script, Groovy generates a class object for each Groovy class that it encounters in the source. If the source file contains some scripting elements, it also generates a class object for these.

To see how this works, let's take an example script and compile it with the Groovy compiler. We can use the GVM tool we encountered in *Chapter 2, Groovy Quick Start*, to make Groovy available on the command line:

```
$gvm use groovy 2.4.4

$groovyc AccountTest.groovy
```

The following example contains two class definitions and some script that uses these classes:

```groovy
// AcountTest.groovy
class Customer {
  int id
  String name
}

class Account {
  int id
  double balance
  Customer owner
  void credit (double deposit) {
    balance += deposit
  }
  String toString() {
    "Account id ${id} owner ${owner.name} balance is ${balance}"
  }
}
customer = new Customer(id:1,name:"Aaron Anderson")
savings = new Account(id:2, balance:0.00, owner:customer)

savings.credit 20.00
println savings
```

Compiling the preceding code with `groovyc` will result in the generation of three class files: `Customer.class`, `Account.class`, and `AccountTest.class`. If we were to name our script `Customer.groovy` or `Account.groovy`, the Groovy compiler will see this example as having duplicate class definitions because it is also trying to generate a class file for us.

This extra, generated, class is the key to what makes a script runnable. The generated class will have a regular Java main method generated along with a run method. When we run a Groovy script in a shell script or via the `groovy` command, we are invoking the `main()` method of the generated class, which in turn calls the run method. The code within the script itself is actually within this run method.

In Java, we are used to the idiom of writing a single class per Java file. The previous style of coding is common in Groovy when writing standalone scripts and DSLs. For regular coding circumstances, we make use of Groovy classes in the same idiom as Java with a single class per Groovy source file, so the coding style will not be unfamiliar to you.

Another important difference to remember when writing Groovy classes versus Groovy scripts is that Groovy scripts have a special binding for variable references. In scripts, we can immediately start using a variable from the point that we initialize it without having to declare it first. Script variables are stored in this binding scope. So, we can initialize the previous savings variable with the following line of code:

```
savings = new Account(id:2, balance:0.00, owner:customer)
```

This will result in the savings variable being automatically added to the binding scope. At this point, we make use of savings:

```
println savings
```

At this point, savings must be in the binding scope or we will get an error.

If we rewrite the script portion of our preceding example to include a class definition and a static main method, then savings and customer must be explicitly defined by using the def keyword, as follows:

```
class AccountSample {
    public static void main (args) {
        def customer = new Customer(id:1,name:"Aaron Anderson")
        def savings = new Account(id:2, balance:0.00,
        owner:customer)

        savings.credit 20.00
        println savings
    }
}
```

Groovy shorthand

We have seen already that Groovy is source compatible with Java. To be more script-like, Groovy has some syntax elements that are optional and other syntax shortcuts that make code easier to read and write. By examining the AccountTest example, we can see some of these shorthand features in action.

Implicit imports

Java automatically imports the `java.lang` package for you. Groovy goes a step further and automatically imports some of the more commonly-used Java packages, as follows:

- `java.lang.*`
- `java.util.*`
- `java.net.*`
- `java.io.*`
- `java.math.BigInteger`
- `java.math.BigDecimal`

Two additional packages from the **Groovy JDK (GDK)** are also imported:

- `groovy.lang.*`
- `groovy.util.*`

Default visibility, optional semicolon

The majority of classes that I have written in Java have been declared public. Java requires us to always explicitly express the public visibility of a class. This is because the default visibility of classes is "package private", which, to be honest, is a visibility that is seldom used and is often misunderstood. "Package private" visibility means classes are accessible by other classes in the same package, but not by classes in other packages. Groovy makes the more sensible decision that public visibility is the default visibility, so it does not need to be stated in the class definition.

Java uses the semicolon to separate statements even when they end on the same line. In Groovy, semicolons are optional as long as we limit ourselves to a single statement per line. This small change makes for much cleaner looking code:

```
def customer = new Customer(id:1,name:"Aaron Anderson")
def savings = new Account(id:2, balance:0.00, owner:customer)
```

The previous snippet from our `Account` example would have been more syntactically verbose in Java, without adding to the clarity of the code:

```
Customer customer = new Customer(id:1,name:"Aaron Anderson");
Account savings = new Account(id:2, balance:0.00, owner:customer);
```

If we have multiple statements on a line, a semicolon is required. The semicolon can still be left off the last statement in the line:

```
class Account {
    def id; double balance;  Customer owner
...
}
```

Optional parentheses

The parentheses around method call parameters are optional for top-level statements. We have been looking at this language feature since the start of the chapter. Our Hello World program is:

```
println "Hello, World!"
```

This is, in fact, a call to the built-in Groovy println method and can be expressed with parentheses if we want, as follows:

```
println ("Hello, World!")
```

Similarly, the call to the Account.credit method in our Account example could have been written with parentheses:

```
savings.credit( 20.00 )
```

When a method call or closure call takes no arguments, then we need to supply the parentheses. The compiler will interpret any reference to a method without parameters as a property lookup for the same name. A reference to a closure will return the closure itself:

```
getHello = { return "Hello, World" }

// Prints the closure reference
hello = getHello
println hello

// Parens required because
// println
// on its own is a reference to a property called println
println ()

// calls the closure
hello = getHello()
println hello
```

When method calls are nested, the parentheses are also needed to let the compiler distinguish between the calls:

```
greeting = { name -> return "Hello, " + name }

// Parens are optional for println but required for nested
// greeting call
println greeting ( "Fergal" )
```

The optional dot in method chains

Version 1.8 of the Groovy language added another nice feature. When we chain methods, the dot notation as well as the parentheses becomes optional. We will see in a later chapter how we can use this feature to enhance our DSLs. Here is a simple example that illustrates how it works:

```
class Message {
    String message

    def to( String person) {
        println "$message, $person!"
    }
}

def say (String message) {
    new Message(message:message)
}
```

Here we have a simple Groovy class that has a `to` method. The `say` method returns a `Message` object, so we can chain calls together. Using regular Java style syntax, we can call:

```
say("Hello").to("Fred");
```

However, with Groovy's optional parentheses plus the option dot notation, we can shorten this to:

```
say "Hello" to "Fred"
```

We can also invoke closures without the dot notation. We can modify the preceding example so that the `say` method returns a map with closure entries as follows:

```
def say (String message) {
    [ to: { person ->
        println "$message, $person!"
    }]
}
```

Now, when we invoke, say as before we are retrieving the entry in the returned map for `to` which is a closure. We can invoke this closure without needing the dot notation as follows:

```
say "Hello" to "Fred"
// which is similar to calling
say("Goodbye")['to'].call('Barney')
```

Dynamic types

Groovy also has the concept of dynamic types. We can define variables and member fields with explicit types if we wish. In our `Customer` and `Account` class, we declare our `id` fields with the `def` keyword. This allows us to decide at runtime what actual type we want our IDs to be.

> Note that the `def` keyword is required when declaring properties within the context of a class, but is optional when we write Groovy scripts. Another way to look at the `def` keyword is that it declares a variable of the type `Object`; so the two lines are analogous: `def number = 1` and `Object number = 1`.

The optional return keyword

Every statement in Groovy has a resulting object value. We can see this clearly by running the Groovy shell `groovysh` and typing in statements. The shell outputs the resulting value of each statement as it is executed. Sometimes, this value is `null`, as in the case of our `Hello World` script:

```
groovy:000> println message
Hello, World!
===> null
```

In Groovy, the `return` keyword is optional because the value of the last statement is always returned from a method call, with the exception of methods declared with a return type of void. The type of the returned object will depend on the return type defined. If no return type is defined, then the type will be determined at runtime. If the method is a `void` method, then the value returned will be `null`. We can try using Spock test notation to illustrate some of the possibilities. Imagine we have the following method:

```
String returnString(param) {
    param
}
```

The preceding method returns `String` object, while the type of the object passed in is dynamic, so Groovy will attempt to coerce the return object to a `String` and return that value:

```
when: "calling a method with a typed return"
    def result = returnString("Fred")
then: "type of returned value is String"
 result instanceof String


when: "we pass the same function an Integer"
 result = returnString(123)
then: "the type returned is still String"
 result instanceof String
 result == "123"
```

No matter what type of object we try to return, the return type defined in the method will determine the type that is actually returned:

```
String returnIntegerCoercedToString(Integer param) {
    param
}

when: "we pass a typed Integer"
    result = returnIntegerCoercedToString(123)
then: "the type returned is still String"
    result instanceof String
    result == "123"
```

However, if the method uses the `def` keyword as its return type, then the return type is considered to be dynamic, so the type we get back is determined by the type of the returned object:

```
def returnDef(param) {
    param
}
when: "calling a method with dynamic return type"
    def result = returnDef("Fred")
then: "type of returned value is String"
    result instanceof String

when: "we pass the same function an Integer"
    result = returnDef(123)
then: "the type returned is Integer"
    result instanceof Integer
    result == 123
```

No matter what value is contained in the last statement in a method, if the return type is void, the value returned will always be null:

```
void returnVoid(param) {
    param
}
```

```
when: "calling a method with void return, passing String"
    def result = returnVoid("Fred")
then: "type of returned value is null"
    !result
    result == null
```

```
when: "calling a method with void return, passing Integer"
    result = returnVoid(123)
then: "type of returned value is null"
    !result
    result == null
```

Properties and GroovyBeans

We know from Java that a JavaBean is a class that implements getters and setters for some or all of its instance fields. Groovy automatically generates getters and setters for instance fields in a class that have the default visibility of public. It also generates a default constructor. This means that a Groovy class is automatically accessible as a JavaBean without any additional coding. Instance fields that have automatically generated getters and setters are known in Groovy as properties, and we refer to these classes as **GroovyBeans**, or by the colloquial **POGO (Plain Old Groovy Object)**:

```
given: "a Groovy class"
    Customer customer = new Customer()
when: "we set a value via the Setter"
    customer.setName "Brian Beausang"
then: "we can use either the getter or property notation"
    "Brian Beausang" == customer.getName()
    customer.getName() == customer.name
when: "we set a value via property notation"
    customer.name = "Carol Coolidge"
then: "we can use either the getter or property notation
    "Carol Coolidge" == customer.name
```

This code snippet shows how we can optionally use getter/setter methods to manipulate the name field of our Customer class, or we can use field access syntax. It's important to note that when we use the field access syntax customer.name, we are not accessing the field directly. The appropriate getter or setter method is called instead.

 If you want to directly access the field without going through a getter or setter, you can use the field dereference operator @. To access customer.name directly, you would use customer@.name.

A JavaBean version of our Customer class would require getters, setters, and a default constructor, as follows:

```
public class Customer implements java.io.Serializable {
    private int id;
    private String name;

    public Customer () {
    }
        public int getId() {
        return this.id;
    }
        public void setId(final int id) {
        this.id = id;
    }
        public String getName() {
        return this.name;
    }
        public void setName(final String name) {
        this.name = name;
    }
}
```

GroovyBeans have a very useful initialization feature. We can pass Map to the constructor of a bean that contains the names of the properties, along with an associated initialization value:

```
given: "we initialize some beans with a Map of values"
    def map = [id: 1, name: "Barney Rubble"]
    def customer1 = new Customer( map )
    def customer2 = new Customer( id: 2, name: "Fred Flintstone" )
expect: "the bean properties have been set"
    customer1.id == 1
    customer2.id == 2
    customer1.name == "Barney Rubble"
    customer2.name == "Fred Flintstone"
```

When passing the `map` directly to the `Customer` constructor, we can omit the map literal square brackets, as seen here when initializing `customer2`. However, this is another case where the method's parentheses cannot be omitted.

Every GroovyBean has this default built-in `Map` constructor. This constructor works by iterating the `map` object and calling the corresponding property setter for each entry in the `map` object. Any entry in `map` that doesn't correspond to an actual property of the bean will cause an exception to be thrown. The beauty and simplicity of this approach is that it allows us to have absolute flexibility when initializing beans.

We can name properties in any order that we want, and omit properties if we see fit.

 This feature is often referred to as **named parameters** as it gives the impression that we are providing a flexible parameter list where we name those parameters, even though we are just passing a `Map` object.

Assertions

Groovy has a built-in assertion keyword `assert`. The `assert` keyword can be used in conjunction with any Boolean conditional statement. Groovy assertions work similarly to Java assertions, however, since Groovy 1.7, they provide much more information about assertion failures, including a visual representation of each subexpression in the assertion, and its corresponding value. If the asserted statement is not true, the `assert` keyword can cause a `java.lang.AssertionExceptionAssertionExceptionError` exception to be thrown. Assertions have two forms:

```
assert 1 == 1
assert 1 == 2 : "One is not two"
```

This gives the following output:

java.lang.AssertionError: One is not two. Expression: (1 == 2)

The first assertion passes silently, whereas the second throws the `AssertionError` exception and the test inserted after the colon is injected into the exception log for more clarity. Groovy 1.7 introduced the "power assert". If we use the first form of preceding assertion without the failure message, Groovy will automatically introspect the full expression within the assertion and give a detailed breakdown of what was wrong.

```
def map = [a:'a',b:'b',c:[d:'d',e:['f','g']]]
assert map.c.e[1] == 'h'
```

Here, we are asserting a value within a complex structure of arrays and maps. Groovy will happily breakdown each element of the structure in the assertion output, as follows:

```
Assertion failed:

assert map.c.e[1] == 'h'
        |   | ||   |
        |   | |g   false
        |   | [f, g]
        |   [d:d, e:[f, g]]
        [a:a, b:b, c:[d:d, e:[f, g]]]
```

From time to time in the text, we will use assertions as a shorthand means of validating and illustrating the code. For instance, in the Account examples, we could have illustrated setting and getting property values using assertions as follows:

```
Customer customer = new Customer()
customer.setName("Carol Coolidge")
assert customer.name == customer.getName()
```

Autoboxing

Java has two ways of handling numeric values. We can either use the numeric primitive types, such as int, float, double, and so on, or their equivalent classes, such as Integer, Float, Double, and so on. Unfortunately, you can't put an int or any other primitive type into a collection; so you must box the int object into an Integer object to put it into the collection, and unbox it if you need to use the primitive int type again.

From Java 1.5 onwards, Java introduced the concept of **autoboxing**, whereby primitive types are automatically promoted to their object-based equivalent when the need arises. Groovy goes a step further with the autoboxing concept. In essence, Groovy behaves as if primitives don't exist. Numeric fields of classes are stored as the declared primitive type; however, as soon as we make use of that variable and assign it to a local variable, it is automatically converted to the equivalent wrapper type object. Even numeric literals behave like objects:

```
expect: "numeric literal is implemented with Numeric class"
    2.0 instanceof BigDecimal
    2 instanceof Integer
    2.00000f instanceof Float
    21 instanceof Long
```

For all intents and purposes, you can treat any numeric value as if it is both an object-based numeric value and a primitive. You can pass a Groovy numeric object to a Java method that requires a primitive, and Groovy automatically unboxes it to the equivalent primitive.

If we need to explicitly coerce a numeric type to its equivalent primitive, for example, to call a Java method that takes a primitive parameter, we can do this unboxing with the (as) operator:

```
javaMethodCall(3.0 as double))
```

In most cases, this is redundant as Groovy will automatically unbox to the correct type. However, it can be useful as a hint about which method call we need to select when multiple methods signatures exist.

Strings

Regular Groovy strings can be defined with either the single quote (') or double quotes ("") characters. This makes it easy to include either type of quotes in a string literal:

```
String singleQuote = "A 'single' quoted String"
String doubleQuote = 'A "double" quoted String'
```

Strings declared with double quotes can also include arbitrary expressions by using the ${expression} syntax. Any valid Groovy expression can be included in the ${..}. Normal strings in Groovy are instances of the java.lang.String class. Strings that contain the ${...} syntax are instantiated as Groovy GString objects:

```
given: "a Groovy object"
    Customer customer = new Customer(name:"Daniel Dewdney")
    def string1 = "Customer name is Daniel Dewdney"
    def string2 = "Customer name is ${customer.name}"
expect: "We can compare both strings as if the are equivalent"
    string1 == string2
and: "they are implemented by two different classes"
    string1 instanceof String
    string2 instanceof GString
```

Multiline strings can be defined by surrounding them in a triple quote, which can use single quote (''') or double quote (""") characters as follows:

```
given: "some multiline strings with single and double quotes"
    String multiLine = '''Line one
        Line two
```

```
        "We don't need to escape quotes in a multi-line string"
    '''
    def name = "Daniel Dewdney"
    def customerSelectSQL = """
        select * from customer where name = ('${name}');
    """
expect:
    multiLine instanceof String
    customerSelectSQL instanceof GString
```

Multiline strings are useful for embedding XML, HTML, and SQL. Combined with GStrings, they are ideal for building templates in our code.

Regular expressions

Groovy supports regular expressions natively within the language. There are three built-in convenience operators specifically for this purpose:

* The `regex` match operator, `==~`
* The `regex` find operator, `=~`
* The `regex` pattern operator, `~String`

The match operator is a simple Boolean operator that takes the operands `String ==~ regex string`. The match returns true if the string operand is a match to the `regex` string. Regex strings are a sequence of characters that define a pattern to apply when searching for a match within a string. They can consist of specific characters or character classes, such as \d (any digit), and \w (any word character). Later, we'll look at a table with some of the more commonly-used character classes.

In the simplest case, a regular expression can just consist of a sequence of regular characters. So, a `regex` string `Match Me` will match only strings containing exactly the characters `Match Me`. In other words, it can be used to just test equality. We can use this feature to show how the different ways of expressing strings in Groovy result in the same string:

```
given: "A String we want to match"
    def matchMe = "Match Me"
expect: "We can do an exact match using single quoted Strings"
    matchMe ==~ 'Match Me'
and: "using multiline style String"
    matchMe ==~ """Match Me"""
and: "using slashy String"
    matchMe ==~ /Match Me/
```

The final assertion shown in the preceding code introduces yet another Groovy string syntax, which goes under the name slashy strings. Slashy strings are most commonly used when defining `regex` strings, but they can be used anywhere you wish to define a string object.

The biggest advantage of the slashy string is the fact that the backslash character \ does not need to be escaped. In a literal string, \\ is a single backslash. So, to place the character class \d in a string literal, we need to write \\d. To match the backslash character itself, we need to write \\\\. In slashy string format, these become /\d/ and /\\/ respectively.

A further refinement was added to slashy strings in Groovy 1.8. Dollar slashy strings are denoted by a starting $/ and ending /$ and have different escaping rules to the regular GStrings. Slash and backslash do not need to be escaped. However, $ can be used as an escape if needed. The differences are best illustrated with an example:

```
given: "a dollar slashy"
    def dollarSlashy = $/
$ dollar
$$ dollar
\ backslash
/ slash
$/ slash
/$
and: "an old style multiline string"
    def multi = """
\$ dollar
\$ dollar
\\ backslash
/ slash
/ slash
"""
expect:
    multi == dollarSlashy
```

Groovy adds some neat usability features to Java regular expression handling, but under the covers, it still uses the `java.util.regex` classes. Groovy `regex` pattern strings are identical to their Java equivalents. The most comprehensive documentation for all of the pattern options available can be found in your Java SE.

You can find JavaDoc under the class documentation for `java.util.regex.Pattern`. The following is a truncated list of some of the more commonly-used patterns:

Construct	Matches
.	Any character
^	The start of a line
$	The end of a line
X	The character x
\d	A digit character
\D	Any character except a digit
\s	A whitespace character
\S	Any character except whitespace
\w	A word character
\W	Any character except word characters
\b	A word boundary
(x|y|z)	x or y or z, that is, (apple|orange|pear)
[a-f]	The character class containing any character between a and f
[abc]	a, b, or c

The Groovy find operator (=~) is similar to match but returns a `java.util.regex.Matcher` object. In the following code, we use `find` to return a matcher for all three-letter words with a middle letter of o. The pattern we use is /\b.o.\b/. Groovy allows us to use the collection convenience method "each" to iterate over the resulting matches and invoke a closure on each match to output the result. There will be more on collections and closures shortly:

```
given: "A String with words we want to match"
    def quickBrownFox =
            "The quick brown fox jumps over the lazy dog."
and: "a matcher built via the find operator"
    def matcher = quickBrownFox =~ /\b.o.\b/
expect: "to match all three letter words with middle letter o"
    matcher.findAll() == ['fox','dog']
```

Every time we use the `match` and `find` operators, behind the scenes, Groovy transforms the `regex` string into a `java.util.regex.Pattern` object and compiles it. The pattern operator does the same thing, and transforms the string it operates on into a compiled `Pattern` object. For most applications, using `find` and `match` directly on a pattern string is fine because the overhead of transformation and compilation to a `Pattern` object is not significant. The rationale behind the pattern operator is that complex patterns are often expensive to compile on demand, so the precompiled pattern object will be faster to use.

A simple change to the previous code is all that is required to use a precompiled pattern instead:

```
given: "A String with words we want to match"
    def quickBrownFox =
            "The quick brown fox jumps over the lazy dog."
and: "a matcher built via a pattern object"
    def pattern = ~/\b.o.\b/
    def matcher = pattern.matcher( quickBrownFox )
expect: "to match all three letter words with middle letter o"
    matcher.findAll() == ['fox','dog']
```

Methods and closures

Closures will be dealt with in detail in the next chapter, so we won't go into them in depth here. In order to do justice to the Groovy control structures and the special built-in support Groovy has for collections, we need to take just a brief excursion into closures for now.

Closures are snippets of Groovy program code enclosed in curly braces. They can be assigned to an instance property, or a local variable, or even passed as parameters to a method. In Java, program logic can only be found in class methods. The inclusion of static member functions in classes gives some flexibility to Java in allowing methods to be invoked outside of the context of an object instance.

In Groovy, methods can exist both inside classes and outside of classes. We already know that Groovy scripts get compiled to classes that have the same name as the script. Groovy methods within scripts just get compiled into member methods of the script class. Groovy has a slightly different syntax from Java to support the concept of a dynamic return type.

Groovy methods look very similar to Java methods except that public visibility is the default, so the `public` keyword can be left out. In addition, Groovy methods support optional arguments, as do closures. As with dynamic variables, we need to use the `def` keyword when defining a method that has a dynamic return type:

```
// Java method declaration
public String myMethod() {
...
}
// Groovy method declaration
String myMethod() {
...
}
// And with dynamic return type
def myMethod() {
}
```

Groovy script methods, which are declared in the same script, can be called directly by name:

```
def greet(greeting) {
    println greeting + ", World!"
}

greet ("Hello")
greet ("Goodbye")
```

The previous code gives the output:

Hello, World!

Goodbye, World!

Class methods are called by object reference, similar to Java:

```
class Greeting {
    def greet(greeting) {
        println greeting + ", World!"
    }
}
greeting = new Greeting()
greeting.greet ("Hello")
greeting.greet ("Goodbye")
```

Closures can look deceptively similar to method calls in their usage. In the next code snippet, we will create a variable called `greet` and assign a closure to it. This closure is just a snippet of code enclosed in braces, which prints a greeting. Regular methods have their own local scope and can only access variables defined within that scope or member fields in the containing class. Closures, on the other hand, can reference variables from outside their own scope, as illustrated in the following code. Closures can be invoked by applying the method call syntax to the variable containing the closure:

```
given: "a variable in scope"
    def greeting = "Hello"
and: "a closure that can access the variable"
    def greet = { println "$greeting, World!"}
when: "we invoke the closure with variable different"
    greet()
    greeting = "Goodbye"
    greet()
then: "the output is as expected"
    """Hello, World!
Goodbye, World!""" == output()
```

Closures can also accept parameters, but they have their own particular syntax for doing so. The next closure accepts a parameter, `greeting`. Multiple parameters can be defined by separating them with commas. Parameters can also have an optional type annotation:

```
given: "a closure which takes a single parameter"
    def greet = { greeting -> println "$greeting, World!"}
when: "we call closure with a single parameter"
    greet("Hello")
then: "that parameter was what was passed"
    "Hello, World!" == output()

given: "a closure which takes a several parameters"
    def greet = { String greeting, name ->
        println "$greeting, $name!"
    }
when: "we call closure with two parameters"
    greet("Goodbye", "Fred")
then: "that parameter was what was passed"
    "Goodbye, Fred!" == output()
```

We can pass a closure as a method parameter. Many useful collection methods take a closure as a parameter. The list `each()` method takes a closure as its parameters. The `each()` method iterates over a list and applies the closure to each element in the list:

```
given: "a list of fruits"
    def fruits = ["apple","orange","pear"]
and: "a closure that can operate on a single String"
    def likeIt = {String fruit -> println "I like ${fruit}s"}
when: "we invoke the each method of list passing the closure"
    fruits.each likeIt
then: "each element of the list is passed to the closure in turn"
    """I like apples
I like oranges
I like pears""" == output()
```

Now, if we look back at our matcher example, at the first glance, it seems to be using some specialized collection iteration syntax:

```
matcher.each { match -> println match }
```

However, if we remember that matcher is a collection of matches, and that parentheses in Groovy are optional, we can see that all that is happening here is that a closure is passed to the `each` method of the matcher collection. We could have written the same statement as:

```
matcher.each ({ match -> println match })
```

Groovy also has a neat shorthand for closures, which have just one parameter. We don't need to explicitly name this parameter and can just refer to it as `it`. So, our matcher statement can be even more succinct:

```
matcher.each { println it }
```

Control structures

Groovy supports the same logical branching structures as Java. The Groovy versions of the common branching are identical in structure to those of Java:

```
// Simple if syntax
if (condition) {
}
// If else syntax
if (condition) {
} else {
}
// Nested if then else syntax
```

```
if (condition) {
} else if (condition) {
} else {
}
```

Groovy Truth

The only difference is in how Groovy interprets the `if` conditions. Groovy can promote a number of non-Boolean conditions to `true` or `false`. So, for instance, a non-zero number is always `true`. This wider, more all-encompassing notion of what can be true is often referred to as "Groovy Truth":

```
// Java non zero test
int n = 1;
if ( n != 0) {
}
// Groovy equivalent does not need to form a boolean expression
def n = 1;
if (n) {
}
```

Other "Groovy Truths" are as shown in the following code. In other words, when taken in the context of a predicate, these values will all equate to a Boolean `true` value:

```
given: "An initialized value"
    String initialized = "Some Value"
    Customer customer = new Customer(name: "Joey")
    def array = [1,2,3]
    def map = [a:1,b:2]
expect: "it will evaluate to true"
    initialized
    customer
    array
    map
```

Now, let's look at some "Groovy Falsehoods". Things which when used as a predicate will equate to a Boolean `false` value are:

```
given: "A null uninitialized or empty value"
    String nullString = null
    String uninitializedString
    Customer customer = null
    def array = []
    def map = [:]
    def emptyString = ''
```

```
expect: "it will evaluate to false"
    !nullString
    !uninitializedString
    !customer
    !array
    !map
    !emptyString
```

As with many Groovy language features, Groovy's loose interpretation of what can be `true` allows for much more succinct and understandable branching conditions. From Groovy 1.7, Groovy Truth got even more useful. Now, any class can implement the `asBoolean` method to define what it means for it to be true:

```
enum Status {
    ACTIVE,
    INACTIVE,
    DELETED
    def asBoolean () {
        this == Status.ACTIVE
    }
}
```

In this example, we will implement a `Status` enum where only `ACTIVE` is considered to be true:

```
expect: "Only Status.ACTIVE will return true from asBoolean"
    Status.ACTIVE
    !Status.INACTIVE
    !Status.DELETED
```

Ternary and Elvis operators

The standard Java ternary operator (a ? b : c) is supported. Groovy also has another similar operator, the bizarrely named Elvis operator (a ? : b). We can express the ternary operation as a traditional `if-else` branch as follows:

```
// Ternary operator
x > 0 ? y = 1 : y = 2

// Is same as
if (x > 0)
    y = 1
else
    y = 2
```

We can set up a Spock test to assert that this is true for various values of a:

```
given:
    def b = 'value1'
    def c = 'value2'
and: "a ternary expression"
    def result1 = (a ? b : c)
and: "the logical equivalent using if and condition"
    def result2
    if (a) {
        result2 = b
    } else {
        result2 = c
    }
expect: "these expressions are equivalent for various values of a"
    result1 == result2
where:
    a << [1,0,2,true,false]
```

The Elvis operator's behavior is best illustrated as a version of the ternary operator. So, (a ? : b) is equivalent to (a ? a : b). The use of the Elvis operator makes more sense in the light of our previous discussion on Groovy Truth where the Boolean condition used can be something other than a regular expression:

```
given:
    def b = 'value1'
and: "a ternary expression"
    def result1 = (a ?: b)
and: "the logical equivalent using if and condition"
    def result2
    if (a) {
        result2 = a
    } else {
        result2 = b
    }
expect: "these expressions are equivalent for various values of a"
    result1 == result2
where:
    a << [1,0,2,true,false]
```

The Elvis operator has the added benefit of avoiding a second evaluation of the initial predicate. This may be important if x is either expensive to evaluate, has unwanted side effects, or results in an operation that we don't necessarily want to repeat (such as a database retrieval). The Elvis operator works by maintaining a hidden local variable, which stores the initial result. If that result is true according to the rules of Groovy Truth, then that value is returned, otherwise, the alternative value is used.

Suppose that we want to retrieve shopping cart items in a Map so that we can display a list of selected items. If the check database and the cart contain entries, then that is the Map that we want to display. If there are no items in the cart, then we want to return a Map, which contains a dummy entry to display that just says that the cart is empty. If we use regular conditional logic, we can't use a ternary operator because we don't really want to check the cart twice. We would have to write something like the following to manage a temporary map while we decide what to do with it:

```
cartItemsMap = Cart.getItems()

if ( cartItemsMap ) // Groovy true if map has entries in it
    return cartItemsMap
else
    return ["-1": "empty"]
```

Cart.getItems returns a Map, which in Groovy Truth is true if it has elements and false if it is empty. Knowing this, we can rewrite the same code as a succinct one-liner:

```
return Cart.getItems() ?: ["-1": "empty"]
```

Spaceship and Elvis operators

We can't look at the Elvis operator without also looking at the other oddly name "spaceship" operator. The spaceship operator is comprised of two angle brackets and an equals sign <=> and is so named because it resembles a UFO or spaceship in flight. Spaceship is a shorthand operator that works the same as Java's compareTo method. In other words, it compares two operands and returns 0 if they are equal, -1 if the first is less than the second, and 1 if the first is greater than the second. We can express how the spaceship operator works with a simple block of Spock code. Try this out yourself and play with different values for b and c:

```
expect:
    a == (b <=> c)
and:
    (b <=> c) == b.compareTo(c)
```

```
where:
    a  |  b  |  c
   -1  |  1  |  2
    0  |  1  |  1
    1  |  2  |  1
```

One of my favorite Groovy shortcuts is what we can do if we combine the spaceship operator with the Elvis operator. Suppose we have an object, which has three fields that define an account balance, first name and last name, we might want to sort these balances highest first, but then order them by the last name and then first name:

```
class Balance {
    String first
    String last
    BigDecimal balance
    String toString() { "$last, $first : $balance"}
}
```

We can express the sort very succinctly using a combination of spaceship comparators and Elvis operators:

```
a.balance<=>b.balance ?: a.last<=>b.last ?: a.first<=>b.first
```

Let's take a look at this in practice with a Spock test:

```
given: "we have a few customer account objects"
    def accounts = [
        new Balance(balance: 200.00,
                first:"Fred", last:"Flintstone"),
        new Balance(balance: 100.00,
                first:"Wilma", last:"Flintstone"),
        new Balance(balance: 100.00,
                first:"Barney", last:"Rubble"),
        new Balance(balance: 100.00,
                first:"Betty", last:"Rubble"),
    ]
when: "we sort these with spaceship Elvis operators"
    accounts.sort { a, b ->
        a.balance <=> b.balance ?:
            a.last <=> b.last ?: a.first <=> b.first
    }.each { println it }
then: "the accounts are sorted by balance - last - first"
    """Rubble, Barney : 100.00
Rubble, Betty : 100.00
Flintstone, Wilma : 100.00
Flintstone, Fred :200.00"""
```

The switch statement

Groovy adds some neat features to the `switch` statement by adding some extra options that can be tested in the `case` expression:

```
switch (x) {
case 1:
// if x is number 1 we end up here
break;

case "mymatch":
// if x equals string "mymatch" we end up here
break;
case /.o./:
// if x is a string and matches regex /.o./ we end up here
break;

case ["apple", "orange","pear", 1, 2, 3]:
// if x is found in the list we end up here
break;
case [a: 1, b: 2]:
// If x is a key of the map we end up here
break;

case 1..5:
// if x is one of the values 1, 2, 3, 4 or 5 we end up here
break;
}
```

Loops

Groovy does not support the traditional Java `do { } while (condition)` style of looping. This does support traditional `while` loops, as follows:

```
int n = 0;
while ( n++ < 10) {
    println n
}
```

Groovy makes up for this lack of looping options with its own style of looping. Groovy loops are simpler and in many ways more powerful than the Java equivalent. In Groovy, we can iterate over any range of values, as follows:

```
for ( n in 0..10)
    println n
```

We can iterate all the values of a list without any funky `Iterator` objects:

```
for ( x in ["apple", "orange", "pear"])
    println x
```

In fact, as we will see in the following section on collections, we can use the `in` expression to iterate over any collection type. We can even iterate over the characters in a string, as follows:

```
def hello = "Hello, World!"
for ( c in hello)
    println c
```

Collections

Groovy has enhanced the Java collection classes by adding to, and improving on, the declaration syntax and additional convenience methods. It also adds the new collection type range, which provides a special-purpose syntax for managing ranges of values.

Ranges

Groovy supports the concept of a **range of values**. We define a range of values with the range operator (. .). So, a range of integers from 1 to 10 is defined with `1..10`. A range value can be any object that belongs to a class that defines the `previous()` and `next()` methods and implements the `Comparable` interface. We saw previously how we can use the `for (variable in range)` style loop to iterate through a range. We can define ranges that are inclusive or exclusive, as follows:

```
given: "an inclusive and exclusive range"
    def inclusive = 1..10
    def exclusive = 'a'..<'e'
when: "we collect all the possible values of that range"

    def inclusiveValues = inclusive.collect { it }
    def exclusiveValues = exclusive.collect { it }
then: "result is an inclusive/exclusive list of those values"
    inclusiveValues == [1,2,3,4,5,6,7,8,9,10]
    exclusiveValues == ['a','b','c','d']
```

Range objects have two properties, `to` and `from`, that define their limits, as shown in the following code:

```
given: "some ranges"
    def numbers = 1..100
    def letters = 'a'..'z'
expect: "range has to and from properties"
    numbers.from == 1
    numbers.to == 100
    letters.from == 'a'
    letters.to == 'z'
```

Ranges are implemented under the covers by the `java.util.List` class. This means that all of the Java APIs that are available on a `List` object can also be applied to a range:

```
and: "range is a java.util.List so we can use contains"
    numbers.contains 2
    numbers.contains 5
```

We can also use the `in` keyword as part of a predicate to test if a particular value is contained within the range:

```
and: "we can use the in keyword with ranges"
    5 in numbers
```

Lists

Groovy supports the notion of list literals. List declarations look like array declarations in Java. Lists declared in this way are in fact `java.util.List` objects. Let's prove the last statement that ranges are equivalent to lists:

```
given: "a range and the list equivalent"
    def numberList = [1,2,3,4,5,6,7,8,9,10]
    def numberRange = 1..10
expect: "they are equal"
    numberList == numberRange
```

There are some useful list operators that we can use as shortcuts with lists, including plus, minus, and left shift:

```
given: "a list within a list"
    def multidimensional = [1,3,5,["apple","orange","pear"]]

expect: "we can add to lists together using the plus operator"
```

```
    [1,3,5] + [["apple","orange","pear"]] == multidimensional
and: "also with the left shift operator"
    [1,3,5] << ["apple","orange","pear"] == multidimensional
and: "we can Subtract elements with the minus operator"
    multidimensional - [["apple","orange","pear"]] == [1,3,5]
and: "we can flatten that multi dimensional list"
    multidimensional.flatten() == [1,3,5,"apple","orange","pear"]
```

There are also some convenience functions that make list management easier. In the preceding code, we use the flatten method to flatten a multidimensional List. Next, we can see the use of the reverse, collect, and grep `find` and `sort` methods and their effect on a List:

```
given: "some Lists"
    def odds = [1,3,5]
    def evens = [2,4,6]
    def animals = ["cat", "dog", "fox", "cow"]
expect: "we can reverse the order of a list"
    odds.reverse() == [5,3,1]
and: "can apply a closure to a list to transform it using collect"
    odds.collect { it + 1 } == evens
and: "we can find in the list using regex"
    animals.grep( ~/.o./ ) == ["dog", "fox", "cow"]
and: "we can sort a list"
    [5,1,3].sort() == odds
and: "we can find elements matching an expression"
    animals.find { it == "dog" } == "dog"
```

We can iterate over a list in both directions by applying a closure to each item:

```
given:
    def list = [1,3,5]
    def number = ''
when: "we iterate forwards"
    list.each { number += it }
then: "the numbers are added to the string in order"
    number == '135'
when: "we iterate backwards"
    number = ''
    list.reverseEach { number += it }
then: "the numbers are added in reverse order"
    number == '531'
```

Groovy adds two additional new methods to lists: `any` and `every`. These return a Boolean value if any or every member of the list, respectively, satisfies the given closure:

```
given:
    def list = [1,2,3,5,7,9]
expect: "any member is even because 2 is even"
    list.any { it % 2 == 0 }
and: "every member is not even"
    ! list.every { it % 2 == 0 }
```

Maps

Groovy provides a map literal syntax as well. The declaration syntax for maps is very similar to that of lists. We declare a map as a list of key-value pairs delimited by colons. Groovy is flexible in what type of objects can be used as keys or values. In principal, any object that has a `hashCode` function that returns consistent values can be used as either a key or value in a map. By consistent, I mean that any specific value that we define for the object will always return the same `hashCode` value. Let's start by looking at maps by using strings as keys.

The first thing we can try is accessing a property. We can access an element of a `Map` using both array style and property access:

```
given: "we declare a simple map"
    def fruitPrices = ["apple":20,"orange":25,"pear":30]
expect: "we can subscript a map with any key value"
    fruitPrices["apple"] == 20
and: "use the key like it was a property"
    fruitPrices.apple == 20
```

We can also access elements of the `Map` using the get method directly:

```
expect: "we can retrieve a value using the get method"
    fruitPrices.get("apple") == 20
and: "we can supply a default value for items that are not found"
    fruitPrices.get("grape", 5) == 5
```

Empty maps can be declared as `[:]` this creates an empty `Map` that can be added to later:

```
given: "we can declare a variable that is empty but is a map"
    def empty = [:]
expect: "it is an empty map"
    empty instanceof Map
    empty.size() == 0
```

When assigning values to `Map` elements, we can use either the array superscript syntax or property access syntax:

```
when: "assigning a value, it can be done via superscript"
    fruitPrices['apple'] = 21
then: "the expected value was set"
    fruitPrices['apple'] == 21
when: "we try the same with property access"
    fruitPrices.apple = 22
then: "that also works"
    fruitPrices['apple'] == 22
when: "assign a value to a key that does not exist"
    fruitPrices.grape = 6
then: "a new item is added to the Map"
    fruitPrices == [apple:22,orange:25,pear:30, grape:6]
```

Maps support the plus operator for adding maps together:

```
given:
    def fruit = [apple:20, orange:25 ]
    def veg = [pea:1, carrot:15]
expect: "we can add these Maps using plus"
    fruit + veg == [apple:20, orange:25, pea:1, carrot:15]

and: "map  equality is agnostic to order"
    fruit + veg == [ pea:1, carrot:15, apple:20, orange:25]
```

The most common use of maps in Groovy is with `String` keys. When we use a `String` as key, we can interchangeably use the key with or without quotes. We can also look up the value by using the subscript operator, or by using the property reference semantics. Because any object can be a key, this allows us to define some unusual looking maps:

```
given:
    def squares = [ 1:1, 2:4, 3.0:9]
expect:
    squares[1] == 1
    squares[2] == 4
    squares[3.0] == 9
```

Here we see how we can use what seem to be primitive numeric values as keys. Because Groovy autoboxes these primitives into their equivalent wrapper object and these wrappers implement consistent `hashCode` methods, we can use them as keys. Not only this, but we can mix the type of object that we use as a key.

We also can use object values as keys, but in order to do so, we need to add parentheses around them to assist the compiler in determining our intention. In the following code, we add two keys to the map. The first key is a string, `apple`, but the second is the value contained in the `apple` local variable, which is 1:

```
given:
    def apple = 1
    def map = [ apple:"Red", (apple):"Green"]
then:
    map[1] == "Green"
    map["apple"] == "Red"
```

Operators

Groovy implements all of the usual operators that we expect from Java, and adds a number of unique operators of its own. We have already encountered some of these in the preceding sections, such as the spaceship operator (`<=>`), the Elvis operator (`? :`), the manual type coercion operator (`as`) and the `regex` match (`==~`), find (`=~`), and pattern operators (`~`).

Spread and spread-dot

Collections also support some useful operators such as the spread-dot operator (`*.`). Spread-dot is used when we need to apply a method call or make a field or property accessible across all members of a collection. This is best illustrated with some examples, as shown in the following code:

```
given: "a map and two arrays with the same keys and values"
    def map = [a:"apple", o:"orange", p:"pear"]
    def keys = ["a", "o", "p"]
    def values = ["apple", "orange", "pear"]
expect: "we can use spread dot to access all keys/values"
    map*.key == keys
    map*.value == values
and: "which is equivalent to using the collect method"
    map.collect { it.key } == keys
    map.collect { it.value } == values
```

We can use spread-dot to invoke a method across all members of a list:

```
class Name {
    def name
    def greet(greeting) {
        println greeting + " " + name
    }
}
```

```
given: "An array of Name objects"
    def names = [ new Name(name:"Aaron"),
                  new Name(name:"Bruce"),
                  new Name(name:"Carol")]
when: "we invoke a method via spread dot"
    names*.greet("Hello")
then: "the method is called in sequence across all the members"
    """Hello, Aaron
Hello, Bruce
Hello, Carol""" == output()
```

A close relative of spread-dot is the spread operator. Spread has the effect of tearing a list apart into its constituent elements, as shown here:

```
and: "a closure that expects three parameters"
    def greetAll = { a, b, c ->
        println "Hello $a, $b and $c"
    }
when: "we use spread against the names array"
    greetAll(*names.name)
then: "It explodes the names array into three separate objects"
    "Hello Arron, Bruce and Carol"
```

Null safe dereference

One of my favorite operators in Groovy is the null safe dereference operator. How many times in your programming career with Java have you needed to write the following?

```
Customer customer = getCustomerFromSomewhere();
if (customer != null) {
   String name = customer.getName();
}
```

Groovy provides a neat (`?.`) operator that automatically does the null check for you before dereferencing, so the preceding code can be written, as follows:

```
Customer customer = getCustomerFromSomewhere()
String name = customer?.name;
```

All told, these syntactical shortcuts make for much more concise and readable code. Freed from the syntactical sugar of Java, we can write cleaner code more quickly. Once you've gotten used to this shorthand, going back to Java is like wearing a pair of lead boots.

Operator overloading

Java inherited many features from the C++ language, with one notable exception—operator overloading. Groovy implements operator overloading as a language feature, which means that any class can implement its own set of operators. In the simplest case, we can overload the arithmetic operators and make any object of the class behave as if it is a numeric value. Operators are overloaded by implementing the corresponding operator method in the class, for example, the `plus()` method to implement addition.

The Groovy version of the `Date` class implements some operators, including the `plus()` and `minus()` operators. Operator overloading is a fundamental feature in implementing DSLs, so we will go into this feature in significant detail later in the book:

```
given:
    def today = new Date()
    def tomorrow = today + 1
    def yesterday = today - 1
expect:
    today.plus(1) == tomorrow
    tomorrow.minus(1) == today
    today.minus(1) == yesterday
```

Summary

In this chapter, we conducted a whistle-stop tour of the Groovy language. We touched on most of the significant features of the language as a part of this tour.

In the subsequent chapters, we will delve deeper into some of these features, such as operator overloading. We will also cover some of the more advanced features that have not been touched on here, such as builders and metaprogramming. However, this book is not intended to be a complete tutorial on the Groovy language, and I recommend you delve further into the language by reading the Groovy user guide, which is available at `http://www.groovy-lang.org/documentation.html`.

5
Groovy Closures

In this chapter, we will focus exclusively on closures. We touched upon closures already in the previous chapter. Now, we will take a close look at them from every angle. Why devote a whole chapter of the book to one aspect of the language? The reason is that closures are the single most important feature of the Groovy language. Closures are the special seasoning that helps Groovy stand out from Java. They are also the single most powerful feature that we will use when implementing DSLs. In this chapter, we will discuss the following topics:

- We will start by explaining just what a closure is and how we can define some simple closures in our Groovy code

- We will look at how many of the built-in collection methods make use of closures for applying iteration logic, and see how this is implemented by passing a closure as a method parameter

- We will look at the various mechanisms for calling closures, and we will take a look under the covers at how Groovy implements its various `doCall()` methods for different parameter types

- We will go into some depth on how parameters are passed to closures, including a discussion on optional type annotations and default parameter values

- We will take a look at how return values are handled in closures, and finally, we will look into how scope affects closures, particularly the field variables that are visible in surrounding scopes

- Finally, we will look at some of the more advanced closure features such as parameter currying, closure composition, trampolines, and memorization

A handy reference that you might want to consider having to hand while you read this chapter is GDK JavaDocs, which will give you full class descriptions of all of the Groovy built-in classes, but of particular interest here is `groovy.lang.Closure`.

What is a closure?

Closures are such an unfamiliar concept to begin with that it can be hard to grasp initially. Closures have characteristics that make them look like a method in so far as we can pass parameters to them and they can return a value. However, unlike methods, closures are anonymous. A closure is just a snippet of code that can be assigned to a variable and executed later:

```
def flintstones = ["Fred","Barney"]
def greeter = { println "Hello, ${it}" }
flintstones.each( greeter )
greeter "Wilma"
greeter = { }
flintstones.each( greeter )
greeter "Wilma"
```

Because closures are anonymous, they can easily be lost or overwritten. In the preceding example, we defined a variable `greeter` to contain a closure that prints a greeting. After `greeter` is overwritten with an empty closure, any reference to the original closure is lost.

It's important to remember that `greeter` is not the closure. It is a variable that contains a closure, so it can be supplanted at any time.

Given that `greeter` is a variable with dynamic type, we could have assigned any other object to it. All closures are a subclass of the type `groovy.lang.Closure`. As `groovy.lang` is automatically imported, we can refer to `Closure` as a type within our code. By declaring our closures explicitly as `Closure`, we cannot accidentally assign a non-closure to them:

```
Closure greeter = { println it }
```

For each closure that is declared in our code, Groovy generates a `Closure` class for us, which is a subclass of `groovy.lang.Closure`. Our closure object is an instance of this class. Although we cannot predict which exact type of closure is generated, we can rely on it being a subtype of `groovy.lang.Closure`.

Closures and collection methods

In the last chapter, we encountered Groovy lists and saw some of the iteration functions, such as the each method:

```
def flintstones = ["Fred","Barney"]

flintstones.each {
    println "Hello, ${it}"
}
```

This looks like it could be a specialized control loop similar to a while loop. In fact, it is a call to the each method of Object. The each method takes a closure as one of its parameters, and everything between the curly braces {} defines another anonymous closure.

Closures defined in this way can look quite similar to code blocks, but they are not the same. Code defined in a regular Java or Groovy style code block is executed as soon as it is encountered. With closures, the block of code defined in the curly braces is not executed until the call() method of the closure is made:

```
println "one"
def two =
{
println "two"
}
println "three"
two.call()
println "four"
```

This will print the following:

one

three

two

four

Let's dig a bit deeper into the structure of each of the calls shown in the preceding code. We refer to each as a call because that's what it is—a method call. Groovy augments the standard JDK with numerous helper methods. This new and improved JDK is referred to as the Groovy JDK, or GDK for short. In the GDK, Groovy adds the each method to the java.lang.Object class. We will discover later in this book how to inject methods into existing classes ourselves. The signature of the each method is as follows:

```
Object each(Closure closure)
```

The java.lang.Object class has a number of similar methods such as each, find, every, any, and so on. Because these methods are defined as part of Object, you can call them on any Groovy or Java object. They make little sense on most objects, but they do something sensible if not very useful:

```
given: "an Integer"
    def number = 1
when: "we call the each method on it"
    number.each { println it }
then: "just the object itself gets passed into the Closure"
    "1" == output()

given: "a String"
    def string = "String"
when: "we call the each method on the String"
    string.each { println it }
then: "each knows to iterate the chars in the String"
    """S
t
r
i
n
g""" == output()
```

These methods all have specific implementations for all of the collection types, including arrays, lists, ranges, and maps. So, what is actually happening when we see the call to flintstones.each is that we are calling the list's implementation of the each method. Because each takes a Closure object as its last and only parameter, the following code block is interpreted by Groovy as an anonymous Closure object to be passed to the method.

The actual call to the closure passed to each is deferred until the body of the each method itself is called. The closure may be called multiple times—once for every element in the collection.

Closures as method parameters

We already know that parentheses around method parameters are optional, so the previous call to each can also be considered equivalent to:

```
flintstones.each ({ println "Hello, ${it}")
```

Groovy has special handling for methods whose last parameter is a closure. When invoking these methods, the closure can be defined anonymously after the method call parentheses. So, yet another legitimate way to call the preceding line is:

```
flintstones.each() { println "hello, ${it}" }
```

The general convention is not to use parentheses unless there are parameters in addition to the closure:

```
given:
    def flintstones = ["Fred", "Barney", "Wilma"]
when: "we call findIndexOf passing int and a Closure"
    def result = flintstones.findIndexOf(0) { it == 'Wilma'}
then:
    result == 2
```

The signature of the GDK `findIndexOf` method is:

```
int findIndexOf(int, Closure)
```

We can define our own methods that accept closures as parameters. The simplest case is a method that accepts only a single closure as a parameter:

```
def closureMethod(Closure c) {
    c.call()
}

when: "we invoke a method that accepts a closure"
    closureMethod {
        println "Closure called"
    }
then: "the Closure passed in was executed"
    "Closure called" == output()
```

Method parameters as DSL

Method parameters as DSL is an extremely useful construct when we want to wrap a closure in some other code. Suppose we have some locking and unlocking that needs to occur around the execution of a closure. Rather than the writer of the code locking via a locking API call, we can implement the locking within a locker method that accepts the closure:

```
def locked(Closure c) {
    callToLockingMethod()
    c.call()
    callToUnLockingMethod()
}
```

The effect of this is that whenever we need to execute a locked segment of code, we simply wrap the segment in a locked closure block, as follows:

```
locked {
    println "Closure called"
}
```

In a small way, we are already writing a mini DSL when we use these types on constructs. This call to the locked method looks, to all intents and purposes, like a new language construct; that is, a block of code defining the scope of a locking operation. We will be using this again and again in our DSL examples later in this book.

When writing methods that take other parameters in addition to a closure, we generally leave the `Closure` argument till last. As already mentioned in the previous section, Groovy has a special syntax handling for these methods, and allows the closure to be defined as a block after the parameter list when calling the method:

```
def closureMethodInteger(Integer i, Closure c) {
    println "Line $i"
    c.call()
}
```

```
when: "we invoke a method that accepts an Integer and a Closure"
    closureMethodInteger(1) {
        println "Line 2"
    }
then: "the Closure passed in was executed with the parameter"
    """Line 1
Line 2""" == output()
```

Forwarding parameters

Parameters passed to the method may have no impact on the closure itself, or they may be passed to the closure as a parameter. Methods can accept multiple parameters in addition to the closure. Some may be passed to the closure, while others may not:

```
def closureMethodString(String s, Closure c) {
    println "Greet someone"
    c.call(s)
}
```

```
when: "we invoke a method that accepts a String and a Closure"
    closureMethodString("Dolly") { name ->
        println "Hello, $name"
    }
then: "the Closure passed in was executed with the parameter"
    """Greet someone
Hello, Dolly""" == output()
```

This construct can be used in circumstances where we have a look-up code that needs to be executed before we can have access to an object. Say we have customer records that need to be retrieved from a database before we can use them:

```
def withCustomer (id, Closure c) {
    def cust = getCustomerRecord(id)
    c.call(cust)
}

withCustomer(12345) { customer ->
    println "Found customer ${customer.name}"
}
```

We can write an updateCustomer method that saves the customer record after the closure is invoked, and amend our locked method to implement transaction isolation on the database, as follows:

```
class Customer {
    String name
}
def locked (Closure c) {
    println "Transaction lock"
    c.call()
    println "Transaction release"
}

def update (customer, Closure c) {
    println "Customer name was ${customer.name}"
    c.call(customer)
    println "Customer name is now ${customer.name}"
}

def customer = new Customer(name: "Fred")
```

At this point, we can write code that nests the two method calls by calling `update` as follows:

```
locked {
    update(customer) { cust ->
        cust.name = "Barney"
    }
}
```

This outputs the following result, showing how the update code is wrapped by `updateCustomer`, which retrieves the `customer` object and subsequently saves it. The whole operation is wrapped by `locked`, which includes everything within a transaction:

Transaction lock

Customer name was Fred

Customer name is now Barney

Transaction release

Calling closures

In our previous examples, we were passing closures to the built-in collection methods. In the examples to date, we have deferred to the collection method to do the closure invocations for us. Let's now look at how we can make a call to the closure ourselves. For the sake of this example, we will ignore the fact that the GDK provides versions of the `Thread.start` method that achieves the same thing:

```
class CThread extends Thread {
    Closure closure

    CThread( Closure c ) {
        this.closure = c
        this.start()
    }
    public void run() {
    if (closure)
        closure() // invoke the closure
    }

}

CThread up = new CThread(
    {
        [1..9]* each {
            sleep(10 * it)
            println it
```

```
        }
    } )

CThread down = new CThread(
    {
    ["three","two", "one", "liftoff"]  each {
            sleep(100)
            println it
        }
    } )
```

Here we define a subclass of the Java `Thread` class, which can be constructed with a closure. The `run` method of the `Thread` invokes the closure using an `unnamed ()` invocation on the closure field. The `CThread` constructor automatically starts the thread. We can invoke a closure in two different ways, as follows:

- Using the `unnamed ()` invocation syntax, as described here:

```
public void run(Closure closure) {
    closure()
}
```

- By calling the `call()` method of `groovy.lang.Closure`, as follows:

```
public void run(Closure closure) {
    closure.call()
}
```

This example was useful as an illustration of how to call a closure that you have saved in a member field or variable. However, I think you will agree that the built-in `Thread.start` method taking a closure is far more elegant:

```
Thread.start
    {
        [1..9]*.each {
            sleep(10 * i)
            println i
        }
    }

Thread.start
    {
        ["three","two", "one", "liftoff"] .each {
            sleep(100)
            println i
        }
    }
```

The implicit doCall method

There is a third mechanism that you can use to invoke a Closure calling the doCall() method of the closure itself:

```
public void run(Closure closure) {
    closure.doCall()
}
```

The call and doCall methods might seem redundant, but there is an important distinction. The call method is part of the groovy.lang.Closure class and can accept any number of dynamic arguments. When we declare a closure in Groovy, the doCall method is generated dynamically for each closure that we define in our code, and has a signature that is specific to the individual closure.

The doCall method for the following closure will only accept a single string as its parameter list:

```
def closure = { String s -> println s }
```

The general convention is to use either the unnamed () syntax or groovy.lang. Closure.call() when invoking closures. The doCall method is used by the Groovy runtime, and we should never directly invoke it ourselves. It is good to understand its role however, if we ever want to write a closure in Java.

All closures we declare in our Groovy code will have a doCall method. However, it's worth remembering that the groovy.lang.Closure class, which is a Java class, is perfectly feasible for us to build a closure in Java:

```
public class MyClosure extends Closure{
    public MyClosure(Object owner) {
        super(owner);
    }
    public MyClosure(Object owner, Object thisObject) {
        super(owner, thisObject);
    }
    Object doCall(String message) {
        System.out.println(message);
        return null;
    }
}
```

We can then make use of this closure class in our Groovy code as normal. Groovy will match closure invocations with a `String` parameter and will throw a `MethodMissingException` for all others. Our closure will behave in the same way as if it was declared in Groovy:

```
given: "an instance of a Java Closure"
    def stringParams = new MyClosure(this)
when: "Invoking this with the parameters defined by the doCall"
    stringParams "String"
then: "we expect them to work"
    notThrown Exception
when: "we pass an incorrect type for the doCall parameter"
    stringParams 1
then: "we expect that Groovy won't find a matching Closure"
    thrown MissingMethodException
```

Closures declared using the regular Groovy method only have a single method signature. However, when declaring a closure in Java, we can add as many overloaded `doCall` methods as we like. It's also feasible to declare a closure in Java that did not implement `doCall` at all and overloaded the call methods of closure instead. However, according to the documentation for `groovy.lang.Closure`, this will have the unwanted side effect of disallowing the use of the unnamed `()` calling syntax, so it should be avoided.

Finding a named closure field

All of the previous techniques for calling a closure rely on us having prior knowledge of a field or variable that contains a closure. This is fine for most straightforward applications of closures, but this book is about developing DSLs, so let's dig a little deeper.

Take the Grails application framework as an example. You can download Grails from `http://grails.org/Download`. Grails uses closures as a neat way of defining actions for its user interface controllers. No further configuration is required for the Grails runtime to be able to dispatch requests to an action:

```
class UserController {
....
    def login = {
        .... Login closure code
    }
}
```

We can implement a login action for our user controller in Grails—simply by declaring a closure in the `controller` class and assigning it to a field called `login`. In the UI, Grails provides tags to automatically create a link that will dispatch to our login action:

```
<g:link controller="user" action="login">Login</g:link>
```

The Grails runtime can find the appropriate action, given the closure field name as a string, and call that closure when the user clicks on the link. We can achieve the same effect by simply using Java reflection:

```
class MyController {
  def public myAction = {
    println "I'm an action"
  }
}

void callPublicClosureField(Class clazz, String closure ) {
  def controller = clazz.newInstance()
  controller.getClass()
            .getDeclaredField(closure).get(controller).call()
}

callPublicClosureField(MyController.class, "myAction")
```

 Grails 2.0 has added the ability to define `Controller` actions as methods, and this is now the preferred method of defining actions. It is still worth looking at how this technique works.

Here we are using Java reflection to access a `public` field in our `controller` class. We then invoke this closure field with the `call` method. Java reflection honors class visibility, so we need to make the field `public` in order to be able to access it. Later in this book, we will explore other methods that allow us to access static and private fields in both classes and scripts.

This gives the ability to write code like:

```
def something = {
  snippet of code
}
```

Having a separate runtime that makes sense will be the key to writing some of our DSLs later in the book.

Closure parameters

In our previous examples, we have made use of the it keyword. When a closure accepts only a single parameter, we are able to refer to this parameter as it and are free from having to explicitly define the parameter. The possible syntax definitions for a closure are:

- The default case allows any parameters to be passed to the closure:

```
{
// statements
}
```

- The closure does not accept any parameters:

```
{ ->
// statements
}
```

- The closure can accept one to many parameters with optional type annotations:

```
{ [type] param (,[type] param)* ->
// statements
}
```

The parameter list is a comma-separated list of parameter names with optional type definitions. Closures behave slightly different depending on whether we supply the optional type:

```
given: "Closures with various parameter definition"
    def defaultParams = { println it; }
    def dynamicParams = { something -> println something; }
    def intParams = { int something -> println something; }
    def stringParams = { String something -> println something; }
    def noParams = { -> }
when: "Invoking these with valid parameters"
    defaultParams 1
    defaultParams "String"
    dynamicParams 1
    dynamicParams "String"
    intParams 1
    stringParams "String"
    noParams ()
then: "we expect them to work"
    notThrown MissingMethodException
when: "we pass an incorrect type for a typed parameter"
    stringParams 1
```

```
then: "we expect that Groovy won't find a matching Closure"
    thrown MissingMethodException
when: "we pass too many parameters"
    dynamicParams "String1", 1
then: "that should fail also"
    thrown MissingMethodException
when: "passing a parameter to a Closure that does not expect one"
    noParams "String"
then: "we expect that to fail"
    thrown MissingMethodException
```

The preceding examples illustrate the use of dynamic versus static typing for closure parameters. When we declare a closure with default parameters, then we can pass pretty much whatever parameters we like to the closure, and Groovy will not mind. When we declare a parameter but not its type, then Groovy will police the number of parameters we try to pass but not their type. If we declare the type of a parameter, then Groovy will check the parameters passed against that type. Finally, if we want to enforce that a Closure does not accept a parameter, we can use the -> operator with no parameter list.

Enforcing zero parameters

When we declare a closure with the default unnamed syntax, we will use the it keyword in place of the assumed parameter. If we then invoke this closure with no parameters, the closure gets called but a null is passed for the default parameter value:

```
given: "a closure which declares no params"
    def greet = { println "Hello, ${it}" }
when: "we invoke the closure"
    greet()
then:
    "Hello, null" == output()
```

Sometimes, we want to explicitly define a closure as having no parameters. Passing a parameter to a closure like this will result in an exception being thrown:

```
given: "a closure which should take zero parameters"
def greet = { -> println "Hello,World!" }
when: "we try and call this with a parameter"
greet "Hello"
then: "we should get an exception"
thrown MissingMethodException
```

Parameters and the doCall method

You will note from the preceding example that we check for whether `MethodMissingException` has been thrown to determine whether the method call was successful. Groovy calls to closure methods are always via a dynamic method lookup. `MethodMissingException` is the exception that the Groovy runtime throws whenever it can't find a match to the method/closure based on the parameters being passed.

`MethodMissingException` that is thrown relates to the generated `doCall()` method for the closure. We know that Groovy generates `Closure` classes for each closure that we define in our code. Therefore, we can imagine that Groovy is generating the following closure classes on our behalf for the previous examples:

- For a closure with no explicit parameter defined, we can expect a `doCall` method that accepts `varargs` to be generated. So, `doCall` for this closure will accept any parameter that we pass to it:

```
def defaultParams = { println it; }

class Closure1 extends groovy.lang.Closure{
    def doCall(Object [] params ) {
    }
}
closure1 = new Closure1()

closure1.doCall("hello")
closure1.doCall("hello",1,0.1)
```

- For a closure accepting only one dynamically typed parameter, we would expect our `doCall` method to also accept a single parameter. We can pass any value to this `doCall` method, but should expect an exception if we pass more than one parameter:

```
def dynamicParams = { something -> println something; }
class Closure2 extends groovy.lang.Closure{
    def doCall(something) {
    }
}

closure2 = new Closure2()

closure2.doCall("hello")
closure2.doCall(1)
closure2.doCall("hello",1,0.1) // exception
```

- A closure that accepts typed parameters will have a doCall method that accepts only the same specific types as the closure parameters to be generated:

```
def stringParams = { String something -> println something; }

class Closure3 extends groovy.lang.CLosure{
    def doCall(String s) {
    }
}

closure3 = new Closure3()

closure3.doCall("hello")
closure3.doCall(1) // exception

class Closure4 extends groovy.lang.Closure{
    def doCall(int s) {
    }
}

closure3 = new Closure3()

closure3.doCall("hello") // exception
closure3.doCall(1)
```

For this reason, closures are often best used with dynamically typed parameters, as it is difficult to guard against the side effects. Consider the following code. We would probably prefer it if the closure was applied to the whole of the list and not to only a part of it. In this case, the each method will process all of the elements in the list up until it encounters the string nine element, which causes an exception to be thrown:

```
given: "a hetrogeneous list"
    def list = [1,3,5,7, "nine"]
and: "a typed closure"
    def intParams = { int something -> println something; }
when: "we use the each method of the collection"
    list.each intParams
then: "Fails when we hit list[4]"
    thrown MissingMethodException
```

Passing multiple parameters

So far, our examples have all been using single parameters. To accept multiple parameters, we will list the parameters in order before the -> symbol:

```
given: "a closure which declares no params"
    def greet = { greeting, name -> println "$greeting, $name" }
when: "we invoke the closure"
    greet "Hello", "Dolly"
then:
    "Hello, Dolly" == output()
```

Default parameter values

We can define default parameters by supplying a value in the parameter list, as follows:

```
given: "a closure with default parameters"
    def greetString = {greeting, name = "World" ->
        return "${greeting}, ${name}!"
    }
expect:
    greetString("Hello") == "Hello, World!"
    greetString("Hello", "Dolly") == "Hello, Dolly!"
```

Implementing closures in Java

Earlier we looked at the Closure code generated for us by the Groovy compiler. We know that under the covers a closure is just a Java class extending the groovy.lang.Closure interface. So, let's try implementing a closure in pure Java:

```
public class StringClosure extends Closure{
    public StringClosure(Object owner) {
        super(owner);
    }
    public StringClosure(Object owner, Object thisObject) {
        super(owner, thisObject);
    }
    Object doCall(String message) {
        System.out.println(message);
        return null;
    }
}
```

In the preceding code, we implemented a simple closure, which accepts a single string parameter. We can now make use of this closure within our Groovy code, as follows:

```
given: "an instance of a Java Closure"
    def stringParams = new StringClosure(this)
when: "Invoking this with the parameters defined by the doCall"
    stringParams "String"
then: "we expect them to work"
    notThrown Exception
when: "we pass an incorrect type for the doCall parameter"
    stringParams 1
then: "we expect that Groovy won't find a matching Closure"
    thrown MissingMethodException
```

Now, we can try a more complex closure that accepts multiple different parameter types by implementing multiple doCall methods in the closure:

```
public class MultiClosure extends Closure{
    public MultiClosure(Object owner) {
        super(owner);
    }
    public MultiClosure(Object owner, Object thisObject) {
        super(owner, thisObject);
    }
    Object doCall(String message) {
        System.out.println(message);
        return null;
    }
    Object doCall(Integer number) {
        System.out.println(number);
        return null;
    }
}
```

We can then pass the different parameter types to this closure, and it will work fine:

```
given: "an instance of a Java Closure"
    def multiParams = new MultiClosure(this)
when: "Invoking these with the parameters defined by the doCall"
    multiParams "String"
then: "we expect them to work"
    notThrown Exception
when: "Invoking these with the parameters defined by the doCall"
    multiParams 1
then: "we expect them to work"
    notThrown Exception
```

Curried parameters

Curried parameters does not mean that we are including our parameters as ingredients in an Indian dish. **Currying** is a term borrowed from functional programming that is named after its inventor, the logician Haskell Curry. Currying involves transforming a function or method that takes multiple arguments in such a way that it can be called as a chain of functions or methods taking a single argument.

In practice, with Groovy closures, this means we can "curry" a closure by prepacking one or more of its parameters. This is best illustrated with an example:

```
given: "a closure taking three parameters"
def indian = { style, meat, rice ->
    return "${meat} ${style} with ${rice} rice."
}
when: "we curry the closure with different first parameters"
def vindaloo = indian.curry "Vindaloo"
def korma = indian.curry "Korma"
then: "it is as if we passed these parameters together"
vindaloo "Chicken","Fried" == "Chicken Vindaloo with Fried rice."
korma "Lamb","Boiled" == "Lamb Korma with Boiled rice."
```

The preceding indian closure accepts three parameters. We can prepack its first parameter by calling the curry method of the closure. The curry method returns a new instance of the closure with one or more of its parameters set. The variables vindaloo and korma contain instances of the indian closure with the first parameter style set. We refer to these as **curried closures**.

We can curry multiple parameters in one go. Parameters will always be curried in their order of declaration, so in this case, chickitikka will cause the style and meat parameters to be set:

```
when: "we curry the closure with multiple parameters"
def chickitikka = indian.curry "Tikka", "Chicken"
then: "it is the same as if we passed these parameters together"
chickitikka "Boiled" == "Chicken Tikka with Boiled rice."
```

If we take a curried closure such as korma and curry it again, we now curry the subsequent parameters from the original indian closure. The style and meat parameters are now curried into the variable lambKorma:

```
when: "we curry a curried closure"
def lambKorma = korma.curry "Lamb"
then:
lambKorma "Fried" == "Lamb Korma with Fried rice."
```

We can continue currying parameters until we run out of parameters (or curry powder). At this point, we have a curried closure `lambKormaBoiled` that can be invoked without passing any parameters:

```
when: "we exhaust all the parameters"
def lambKormaBoiled = lambKorma.curry "Boiled"
then:
lambKormaBoiled() == "Lamb Korma with Boiled rice."
lambKormaBoiled() == lambKorma("Boiled")
lambKormaBoiled() == korma("Lamb","Boiled")
lambKormaBoiled() == indian("Korma","Lamb","Boiled")
```

Curried closures can be used very effectively in circumstances where contextual data needs to be gathered on the fly and then acted upon. We can write an appropriate closure that acts on all parameters as if they were available. We curry the parameters of the closure as we discover them, and eventually invoke the closure to act on the data. The only limitation that we have is that our closure parameters need to be defined in the correct order.

Since the release of Groovy 1.8, we are no longer limited to currying parameters from left to right. Two new closure methods are available to curry right to left and to curry any arbitrary *n*th parameter:

```
when: "we curry the closure with right parameters"
def fried = indian.rcurry "Fried"
then:
fried "Vindaloo","Chicken" == "Chicken Vindaloo with Fried rice."

when: "we curry the closure with 2nd parameters"
def chicken = indian.ncurry 1, "Fried"
then:
chicken "Vindaloo","Fried" == "Chicken Vindaloo with Fried rice."
```

Closure return values

Closure declarations syntax provides no means of defining a return value. Every closure does, however, return a value with each invocation. A closure can have explicit `return` statements. If a `return` statement is encountered, then the value defined in the `return` statement is returned; otherwise, execution continues until the last statement in the closure block:

```
given: "a closure that returns values"
def closure = { param ->
    if (param == 1)
        return 1
```

```
    2
}
expect:
closure(1) == 1  // return statement reached
closure(-1) == 2 // ending statement evaluates to 2
```

If no `return` statement is encountered, then the value returned by the closure is the result of evaluating the last statement encountered in the closure block. If the last statement has no value, the closure will return `null`:

```
void voidMethod() {
}
given: "a closure returning void method"
def nullReturn = { voidMethod() }
expect:
nullReturn() == null
```

The closure scope

Closures have access to variables in their surrounding scope. These can be local variables or parameters passed to a method inside which the closure is defined. Here, we can access the `name` parameter and the local variable `salutation` in our closure:

```
def greeting ( name ) {
    def salutation = "Hello"
    def greeter = { println "$salutation , $name" }
    greeter()
}

when: "we call the greeting method"
    greeting("Dolly")
then:
    "Hello , Dolly" == output()
```

If the closure is defined within a `class` method, then the object instance fields are also available to the closure. The field member `separator`, shown in the following code, is also accessible within the closure:

```
class ClosureInClassMethodScope {
    def separator = ", "
    def greeting ( name ) {
        def salutation = "Hello"
        def greeter = { println "$salutation$separator$name" }
        greeter()
```

```
        }
    }

given: "A class with a closure in a method"
ClosureInClassMethodScope greeter = new
ClosureInClassMethodScope()
when: "we call the class method"
    greeter.greeting "Dolly"
then:
    "Hello, Dolly" == output()
```

In addition to directly accessing variables, we can also use GStrings to paste variables from the local scope into a string.

In essence, the closure simply inherits all of the visible variables and fields from the surrounding scope in which it is defined. The closure can update any of these fields or variables, and the class or local method scope will see these changes. Likewise, any changes that occur in the class or method scope will also be seen by the closure.

Unlike the regular method or class scope, we are able to pass a closure back from a method. At the time that a closure is defined, Groovy binds all of the variables that it accesses to the closure object. When this happens, Groovy converts any stack-based variables such as method parameters and local variables into heap-based duplicates of these objects. The values of these objects are now bound to the individual closure because the original values were lost once the method was returned. Take the following example, which illustrates this:

```
class MethodReturningClosure {
    def member = "first"
    def method (String param ) {
        def local = member
        return {
            "Member: $member Local: $local Parameter: $param"
        }
    }
}
```

```
given: "we have a class with a method returning a closure"
    MethodReturningClosure myClazz = new MethodReturningClosure()
when: "we invoke the method"
    def clos1 = myClazz.method("first")
then: "member and stack variables are bound to the closure"
    clos1() == "Member: first Local: first Parameter: first"
when: "we invoke again we get a new closure"
```

```
        myClazz.member = "second"
        def clos2 = myClazz.method("second")
    then: "new member, local and parameter values are bound"
        clos2() == "Member: second Local: second Parameter: second"
    and: "but the first still has the old parameter and locals bound"
        clos1() == "Member: second Local: first Parameter: first"
```

Here we are examining the effect on scoped variables when we make multiple calls to a method that returns a closure. To keep things simple in this example, we are not modifying any variables within the closure. The first time that we call `method`, we return a closure which, when invoked, outputs the following:

```
Member: first  Local: first Parameter: first
```

Both the field `member` and `local` variable reflect the `first` state of the `member` field because the `local` variable is just a copy of the field variable. The parameter variable reflects the parameter value that we just passed to `method`.

Before calling the method for a second time, we can change the `member` variable to `second`. When we invoke the closure that is returned from this call, we see:

```
Member: second Local: second Parameter: second
```

The field `member` and `local` variable reflect the `second` state of the `member` field, and the parameter value is what we just passed to the `method`. We then call the first closure for a second time, and we see:

```
Member: second Local: first Parameter: first
```

The `member` field shows the latest state of the field `member`, but the `local` variable and parameter are preserved in the same state as when the first call to `method` was made. If we had modified one or more local variables, then eventually all bets will be off in terms of the state of these variables in relation to any particular closure instance. I recommend caution whenever returning closures from methods. Ensure that you fully understand the impact of the variables that you are acting upon and the state they will have when called is truly the state that you expect.

This note of caution also extends to accessing field members from a returned closure. While we can at least be sure that the state of a field member is the same whether it is accessed from the class or the closure, there is also the impact on the encapsulation of the class to be considered. When we pass a closure back from a class method, we are potentially giving insecure access to the inner workings of the class.

The this, owner, and delegate variables

Groovy has three implicit variables in scope inside each closure. They are: `this`, `owner`, and `delegate`. The `this` variable refers to the enclosing class, providing that one exists. If the closure is defined within the scope of a script, the enclosing class is the script class. This will be autogenerated if we are running in the GroovyConsole or the Groovy shell.

The `owner` variable is the enclosing object of the closure. This is generally analogous to `this`, except in the case of nested closures where the enclosing object is another closure. The `delegate` variable is also usually the same as the `owner` variable, except that `delegate` can be changed.

In most closures, we only need to care about `this` as a means of accessing field variables in an outer scope. The `owner` and `delegate` variables will only become relevant later in the book when we deal with implementing our own builders.

Closure composition

In mathematics, we can compose a new function from other functions. Suppose we have a function *f: R -> R* given by *f(x) = 2x + 4* and another function *g: R -> R* given by *g(x) = x³*. We can compose a new function *fg: R -> R* given by *fg(x) = 2x³ + 4* or the reverse composition *gf: R -> R* given by *gf(x) = (2x + 4)³*:

Therefore:

- $fg(x) = f(g(x)) = f(x^3) = 2x^3 + 4$
- $gf(x) = g(f(x)) = g(2x + 4) = (2x + 4)^3$

In Groovy, we can compose a new closure from two existing closures using `<<` for composition and `>>` for reverse composition. So we can mimic the preceding functions in two closures, and compose them using Groovy closure composition.

This can be expressed with Groovy closures as follows:

```
given: "two closures for f(x) = 2x + 4 and g(x) = x cubed"
    def f = { it*2 + 4}
    def g = {it * it * it}
and: "a closure composed from these"
    def fg = f << g
and: "a reverse composition of the same"
    def gf = f >> g
expect:
    fg(10) == f(g(10))
```

```
    fg(7)  ==  f(7*7*7)
    fg(13) == (2*(13*13*13)+4)
and:
    gf(5)  == g(f(5))
    gf(7)  == g(7*2+4)
    gf(13) == (13*2+4)*(13*2+4)*(13*2+4)
```

Closure trampoline

Recursive method calls are notorious for causing stack overflow errors. Closures are no different. If we implement a recursive algorithm in a closure, then in all likelihood there is a limit to how deep it can be called before we get a stack overflow. For example, an algorithm to calculate factorials might be written as follows:

```
def factorial
factorial = { BigDecimal n ->
    println "Called"
    if (n < 2)
        1
    else
        n * factorial(n - 1)
}
factorial(1)
factorial(1000)
factorial(100000000)
```

Eventually, this will cause a `StackOverflowError` no matter how big our stack is. To overcome this problem, Groovy 1.8 introduced the concept of a closure trampoline. We create a trampoline by calling the `trampoline` method of the closure. Calls to the trampolined closure are invoked sequentially until the closure returns something other than another trampoline:

```
given: "a factorial algorithm using trampoline()"
    def factorial
    factorial = { int n, BigDecimal accumulator = 1 ->
        if (n < 2)
            accumulator
        else
            factorial.trampoline(n - 1, n * accumulator)
    }
and: "we use trampoline() to wrap the closure"
    factorial = factorial.trampoline()
expect: "it correctly calculates factorials"
    factorial(1) == 1
    factorial(3) == 1*2*3
```

```
    factorial(6) == 1*2*3*4*5*6
when: "we use value that overflows the stack for recursion"
    factorial(10000)
then: "it works"
    notThrown StackOverflowError
```

Closure memoization

The final closure feature we will look at is another useful addition from Groovy 1.8. Memoization allows the return values for closure invocations to be cached. This is useful for potentially expensive or long running closure calls, as long as the outcome of the closure call is predictable and does not have other side effects that impact the system state:

```
given: "a simple closure"
    def callCount = 0
    def memoized = { name ->
        callCount++
        "Hello, $name $callCount"
    }
and: "we memoize the closure"
    memoized = memoized.memoize()
when: "we make subsequent calls with the same parameter"
    def firstResult = memoized "Dolly"
    def secondResult = memoized "Dolly"
    def thirdResult = memoized "World"
then:
    firstResult == secondResult
    firstResult == "Hello, Dolly 1"
    secondResult != "Hello, Dolly 2"
    thirdResult == "Hello, World 2"
```

In the preceding code, we see that the first call to memoized is cached and the closure is not actually invoked again until we pass a different parameter value. Memoization can be combined usefully with a trampolined closure and will cut down the potential for repeated expensive processing:

```
given: "a factorial algorithm using trampoline()"
    def trampolined
    trampolined = { int n, BigDecimal accumulator = 1 ->
        if (n < 2)
            accumulator
        else
```

```
            trampolined.trampoline(n - 1, n * accumulator)
    }.trampoline()
and: "we memoize() the trampolined closure"
    def factorial = trampolined.memoize()
expect: "it still correctly calculates factorials"
    factorial(1) == 1
    factorial(3) == 1*2*3
    factorial(6) == 1*2*3*4*5*6
```

Summary

In this chapter, we covered closures in some depth. We covered all of the important aspects of working with closures. We explored the various ways to call a closure and the means of passing parameters. We saw how we can pass closures as parameters to methods, and how this construct can allow us to appear to add mini DSL syntax to our code.

Closures are the real "power" feature of Groovy, and they form the basis of most of the DSLs that we will develop later in this book. In the next chapter, we will build on this knowledge of closures and take a look at some more of the power features of the Groovy language, including builders and metaprogramming with the ExpandoMetaClass classes.

6

Example DSL – GeeTwitter

Before we dive any deeper into Groovy's more advanced features, let's take some time out to build a simple Groovy DSL, using some of the knowledge that we acquired in the previous chapters. In this chapter, we will use closures to build a simple and useful DSL that allows us to automate simple scripts that interact with Twitter.

We will take a stepwise approach to building our DSL. Starting with some vanilla Java APIs that require Groovy or Java programming skills, we will progressively apply some cool Groovy features to evolve a simple DSL that anybody can use.

Twitter

Since the first version of this book was released in 2010, Twitter has become an ubiquitous part of the social media landscape. So ubiquitous in fact, that the Oxford English Dictionary now recognizes words such as Tweet, Twitter, and Twitterati, with their own descriptions. Broadsheets, tabloids, and TV news channels now report what is trending on Twitter as news items in themselves.

Twitter has been variously described as a micro-blogging or social networking service. Twitter is a synergy between instant messaging, SMS, e-mail, and the Web, and allows users to make comments — "tweets" — and have them instantly sent to multiple recipients — "followers".

Using Twitter is the essence of simplicity. Once you have set up an account, you can log onto the service and set a status message. Status messages are text messages of up to 140 characters in length. Twitter keeps a log of your status messages so that you or any other Twitter user can view them. If you follow another user or they follow you, then you will see their status messages in your updates page, and they will see yours.

With Twitter, you can tweet from the Web or from your mobile phone. If you register your mobile phone with your account, you can send your tweets via SMS, and in certain countries, you can get the tweets of the folks that you follow sent directly to your mobile phone as SMS messages.

To begin with, like most people, I was very skeptical about Twitter. My initial Twitter experiences mostly involved reading friends' tweets about what they were having for breakfast. The experience was not unlike reading early bloggers blogging about the mundane aspects of their day. Since then Twitter has evolved, and many eminently sensible people are out there tweeting about stuff that really does have value.

Try searching Twitter for keywords such as "Groovy DSL" and you'll find tweets from folks such as Guillaume LaForge, who is a senior figure in the Groovy community. It's probably worth following the user @glaforge on Twitter for that reason. In fact, it's safe to say that it is worth following anybody who is tweeting about "Groovy DSL".

Like most major modern websites, Twitter has a self-contained API that allows us to interface with it. By providing an open API to developers, Twitter has fostered a community of developers who have developed numerous different client applications. As a result, there are numerous third-party and open source client applications for Twitter, for both mobile and desktop platforms.

Suppose we were able to use Twitter APIs to develop a Groovy-based scripting interface, what would it look like? Imagine a script that allows us to follow every Twitter user who has recently tweeted about "Groovy DSL". Based on our knowledge of Groovy, something like the following would probably make sense:

```
// Follow all that have tweeted recently about Groovy and DSL
search ("Groovy DSL") { from, tweet ->
    follow(from)
    println "Following ${from}"
}
```

For the rest of this chapter, we will walk through the steps it takes to turn this script into a working reality.

Working with the Twitter APIs

Twitter provides APIs that cover the whole gamut of operations that we might like to invoke for interacting with the service. Through the APIs, we can update our status, send direct messages to other users, list our friends and followers, and search for tweets by keyword, among many other useful features.

Twitter APIs are all pure HTTP-based requests. Any method that just retrieves data such as a search operation is implemented by using an HTTP GET request, whereas any method that updates, deletes, or creates, an object is implemented by using an HTTP POST request. Most of the APIs conform to REST design principals and support XML and JSON data formats, RSS, and Atom Syndication Formats.

We can interact with the Twitter APIs by using any tool or programming language that allows us to interact with a web server using HTTP requests.

In order to use the APIs, you first need to create an application with your own Twitter user account. To do this, you will need to log in to Twitter at `http://apps.twitter.com`. Click on the button to **Create New App**, then complete the form to create your app. Next, click on the **Permissions** tab and change the Access type to **Read, Write and direct messages**. Finally, navigate to the **Keys and Access Tokens** page, and click on the **Create my access token** button.

You now have four unique codes generated for this account. To run the examples, you will need to copy the generated keys and secrets into the `twitter4j.properties` file in the examples directories.

Before we go on, you can test out the raw APIs using the Twitter online OAuth tool. Just click on the **Test OAuth** button on the App page. Try a simple search via the APIs by typing the following into the request URI:

`https://api.twitter.com/1.1/search/tweets.json?q=Groovy`

This will generate the OAuth signature headers for you so that you can try the API out.

Try out the generated cURL command at the command line for example (your version will have keys and secrets that are generated for your account):

```
curl --get 'https://api.twitter.com/1.1/search/tweets.json'
--data 'q=Groovy' --header 'Authorization: OAuth oauth_consumer_
key="xxxxxxxxxxxxxxxxxxxxxxxxx", oauth_nonce="xxxxxxxxxxxxxxxxxxxxxxxx
xxxxxxxxxx", oauth_signature="xxxxxxxxxxxxxxxxxxxxxx", oauth_signature_
method="HMAC-SHA1", oauth_timestamp="1416572721", oauth_token="xxxxxxx-
xxxxxxxxxxxxxxxxxxxxxxxxx ", oauth_version="1.0"' --verbose
```

This will invoke the search API, searching for tweets containing the keyword `Groovy`. The resulting list of tweets is formatted as JSON. cURL is a command-line tool for fetching files using URL syntax. It's available by default on Mac OS X and most Linux distributions, or can be downloaded from `http://curl.haxx.se/download.html`. There is extensive documentation of the Twitter APIs that can be found at `https://dev.twitter.com/rest/public`.

Running the `curl` command will display the resulting HTTP response from Twitter. This will include the HTTP response headers along with the response body in JSON. The JSON returned is not formatted in a user-readable manner, so it can be hard to read. A favorite site of mine is `http://www.jsbeautifier.org`. Cutting and pasting the JSON file into the **Beautify JavaScript or HTML** input box will let you produce properly formatted JSON. The following code is a much simplified version of one response:

```
{
  "statuses": [
    {
      "entities": {
        "hashtags": [
          {
            "text": "Groovy",
            "indices": [
              13,
              19
            ]
          }
        ]
      },
      "text": "Let's talk #Groovy at GGX 2014",
      "metadata": {
        "iso_language_code": "en",
        "result_type": "recent"
      },
      "user": {
        "name": "Fergal Dearle",
        "created_at": "Mon Apr 26 06:01:55 +0000 2010",
        },
        "followers_count": 70,
        "statuses_count": 579,
        "friends_count": 110,
      }
    ]
}
```

The response JSON contains details about the tweet, including details about the user who tweeted.

Reading raw JSON tweets is obviously not user friendly. Fortunately, thanks to the vibrant developer community that has sprung up around Twitter APIs, there are high-level client libraries for most languages, including Java, C++, PHP, and Ruby. There are three Java-based client libraries to be found — Twitter4J, JTwitter, and java-twitter. So far, there is no Groovy library listed, but because Groovy is fully Java compatible, we can work with any of the Java libraries.

Using Twitter4J Java APIs

In the following examples, we will use Twitter4J by Yusuke Yamamoto. Twitter4J is an excellent open source Java library for Twitter APIs, released under the BSD license. Using Twitter4J greatly simplifies the code that we need to write in order to build a simple DSL scripting interface for Twitter. Twitter4J can be downloaded from `http://yusuke.homeip.net/twitter4j/en/index.html`. However, we will simply add the `twitter4j` dependency to `build.gradle` in the code in the example pack:

```
dependencies {
  compile "org.twitter4j:twitter4j-core:4.0.2"
}
```

To begin with, let's try out the Twitter4J APIs and see what we can do with them. Although Twitter4J is a Java API, all of the examples here will run as Groovy scripts. If we were to write the same code as Java, we would need to build the examples into full-blown classes with the main methods before we could see any results. With Groovy, we can be up and running almost immediately.

In the following examples, we will use Groovy scripts. These scripts can be run from the command line as follows:

`$ groovy Script.groovy`

We will use the `@Grab` annotation to resolve the Twitter 4J dependency in these scripts. Each script therefore needs to begin with `@Grab`, but we will omit this in the text for terseness sake:

```
@Grab(group='org.twitter4j', module='twitter4j-core',
version='[4.0,)')
import twitter4j.*
```

Our examples dip into Groovy features at times, but we could simply cut and paste the sample code from the Twitter4J site and run it unchanged. Used in this way, Groovy can be a sandbox for exploring the Twitter4J APIs even without writing any Groovy code.

You will find full documentation for using Grape and the @Grab annotation at http://docs.groovy-lang.org/latest/html/ documentation/grape.html.

If you are running the preceding example from behind an http proxy, you may need to refer to the *Proxy settings* section in this documentation.

Tweeting

We'll start by trying out the APIs to get and set our current Twitter status. We will use the Twitter class from Twitter4J to log in to our Twitter account and access the APIs to update and get our status, so you will need to have added your OAuth credentials into twitter4j.properties before you try this yourself:

```
// Get a twitter connection
def twitter = TwitterFactory.singleton
// Update twitter status
twitter.updateStatus("Updating my status via the Twitter4J APIS")
println twitter.showUser("groovydsl").status.text
```

The sample code pack has several examples that make use of the Twitter4J libraries. You will need to locate each of these twitter4j.properties files and edit them. Each file contains the following properties that will need to be filled in:

```
debug=true
oauth.consumerKey=
oauth.consumerSecret=
oauth.accessToken=
oauth.accessTokenSecret=
```

Once we've got a connection to the service with the Twitter object, we can start to play with the APIs. The Twitter.updateStatus method sets a new status message (tweet) for us on our Twitter account. Try out this script yourself. Check your Twitter status through your favorite Twitter client or on the Web, and you will see it has been updated.

Retrieving our status is just as simple. We can use the Twitter.showUser method to get a User object for any user, including ourselves. Calling getStatus on this object retrieves the current status message for any user.

Direct messages

Twitter has a direct message feature that allows you to send messages directly to another Twitter user. Direct messages don't show up in your general Twitter profile and are private to the sender and the recipient. We can use the APIs to send direct messages to a user and to check our own current messages from other users:

```
def twitter = TwitterFactory.singleton

// Send a direct messsage to twitter user GroovyDSL
twitter.sendDirectMessage(
    "GroovyDSL",
    "Hi Fergal read Groovy for DSL and loved it")

// Retrieve our latest direct messages
// same as visiting http://twitter.com/#inbox
messages = twitter.directMessages

messages.each { message ->
    println "Message from : $message.senderScreenName"
    println "      ${message.text}"
}
```

 You can only direct message to users in Twitter who follow you. This also applies to the preceding example. If you try it out yourself, you will need to use a user ID that is one of your Twitter followers.

In the code snippet that we've just seen, we used the `Twitter.sendDirectMessage` method to send a message to the Twitter user `GroovyDSL`. We then use the `Twitter.directMessages` method to retrieve our latest direct messages from our inbox. This, in fact, is a shortcut to the `Twitter.getDirectMessages` API, which returns a list of `DirectMessage` objects. Groovy conveniently allows us to take shortcuts to any getter methods as a property access, even though the `Twitter` class is not in fact a POJO. We then list the sending user's screen name and the text of the message. We can also retrieve the time when the message was sent, and the user objects for the sender and recipient of the message.

Searching

The Twitter APIs have a powerful search capability that allows us to search for what people are commenting on at any given time. Twitter4J implements searching by passing a `Query` object to the `Twitter.search` API. Using the following code, we will search for tweets containing the keywords `Groovy` and `DSL`:

```
def twitter = TwitterFactory.singleton
// Create a query for tweets containing terms "Groovy" and "DSL"
def query = new Query("Groovy DSL")
// Search and iterate the results
twitter.search(query).tweets.each { tweet ->
    println "${tweet.user.screenName} : ${tweet.text}"
}
```

Calling the `Twitter.search` API returns a `QueryResult` object. `QueryResult.getTweets()` will return a list of tweet objects. We can use the list of tweets matching our search criteria as a Groovy collection, and iterate it through the use of the built-in `each` method. At the time of writing this book, I got the following result from running this script:

Amid this cacophony of tweets, you might see comments from `glaforge`, the Groovy project manager. We might also see comments from Graeme Rocher in this list depending on when we run the script. Graeme is the creator of the Grails project. We might be interested in seeing what Graeme is saying about Grails right now. We can then modify our query to search for messages just from Graeme about Groovy and Grails as follows:

```
// Create a query for tweets containing the terms
// "Groovy" and "Grails"
Query query = new Query("from:graemerocher Groovy Grails")
```

Running the search script with this query would have resulted in an output that contained the following comment among the tweets:

graemerocher : RT @springsource: @glaforge , @graemerocher and @cdupuis are presenting at this week's #Groovy and #Grails eXchange http://bit.ly/6Otsf ...

The `@glaforge` notation means `graemerocher` is referencing Guillaume in his comments. It's always interesting to hear what these guys are talking about, especially when they reference each other. We can search for tweets from Guillaume referencing Graeme by using the query string `from:glaforge @graemerocher`, and so on.

I've just touched upon some of the search capabilities of the Twitter APIs. The APIs allow you to use all of the same search operators that you can use in the Twitter **Search** box on the web application at `https://twitter.com/search-home`. The full list of search operators that can be used are listed at `https://dev.twitter.com/rest/public/search`.

Following

The fundamental feature of Twitter is the concept of *following* and having *followers*. You can tweet away on Twitter to your heart's content, but if no one is following your tweets, you will not be heard. When you follow someone, your Twitter client will pick up their latest tweets and display them for you. If they follow you, then your tweets will be listed in their Twitter client when they view it. The Twitter web application has two lists: for those "following" and your "followers". Confused?

The Twitter4J APIs refer to the users you follow as *friends* and those following you as *followers*. This certainly clears up the confusion a little bit. However, users on Twitter don't necessarily know, or seldom care about, who is following them. So, calling them friends who eavesdrop on all their conversations is a little like stalking. Anyway, we can use the APIs to list all of our friends or followers, or to create a new friendship (in other words follow another user):

```
def twitter = TwitterFactory.singleton
// Get a list of my followers
def friends = twitter.getFriendsList('groovydsl',-1)
friends.each { friend ->
    // Print each screen name
    println friend.screenName
}
// "Follow" the Twitter user GroovyDSL
twitter.createFriendship("GroovyDSL")
```

Here we use the `Twitter.getFriendsList` method to retrieve the list of users that we are currently following. Iterating this list, we can print the screen names of all of these users. Finally, we use the `Twitter.createFriendship` method to start stalking the user `GroovyDSL`. This is a user that I set up while writing this book and testing out these scripts. Feel free to run this script and start following me yourself. I just can't guarantee that it won't be a Twitter bot written in the Groovy DSL that updates this user!

Groovy improvements

So far we have been using Twitter4J as a vanilla API, with a smattering of Groovy, so we have not been bringing any of the Groovier features to bear. Now that we know a little bit about the API, let's try to improve our usage by using some Groovy features. In this section, we will progressively improve our usage of the Twitter4J APIs by selectively using the features that Groovy provides. One of the most obvious features to use is **closures**.

A Groovier way to find friends

In the previous examples, we iterated over our friends and printed out their details. What if we were to provide a method that takes a closure to apply to each friend or follower? In this example, we add these methods to a script, along with a `follow` method, to follow another Twitter user. We can use the `eachFollower` or `eachFriend` methods to list our current connections:

```
followersList = { user ->
    TwitterFactory.singleton.getFollowersList(user,-1)
```

```
}
friendsList = { user ->
    TwitterFactory.singleton.getFriendsList(user,-1)
}
cachedFriendsList = friendsList.memoize()

// Method to apply a closure to each friend
def eachFriend(Closure c) {
    def friends = friendsList('groovydsl')
    friends.each {
        c.call(it.screenName)
    }
}

// Method to apply a closure to each follower
def eachFollower(Closure c) {
    def followers = followersList('groovydsl')
    followers.each { follower ->
        c.call(follower.screenName)
    }
}

// Method to follow another twitter user
void follow(user) {
    TwitterFactory.singleton.createFriendship(user    )
}
```

With these methods defined, we can start writing some powerful Groovy code to act on our friends and followers. How about printing the screen names of all the users that we are following:

```
println "I'm Following"
eachFriend {
    println it
}
```

Or those who are following us:

```
println "Following me"
eachFollower {
    println it
}
```

We can write a neat auto-follow script. In the following example, we will use `eachFollower` to apply a closure to each of our followers. The closure method determines if we are already a friend of this follower simply by using the Groovy collections any, and follows the follower if we are not:

```
// Auto follow
eachFollower { follower ->
   // If any of my friends is this follower
   if (twitter.friends.any { friend ->
      friend.screenName == follower
   })
      return;
   // Otherwise follow him
   println "Following ${follower}"
   follow(twitter, follower)
}
```

Twitter throws an exception if we try to follow a user that we are already following. In the `Auto follow` closure shown in the previous code snippet, we first checked to see if any of our friends is a follower before trying to follow him or her.

Groovy searching

In the same vein, we can also add a `search` method taking a closure:

```
void search(terms, Closure c) {
   def query = new Query(terms)
   TwitterFactory.singleton.search(query).tweets.each {
      c.call(it.user.screenName,it.text)
   }
}
```

We can pass a closure to the `search` method in order to print out the details of the tweets that we find:

```
// Print all recent tweets about Groovy and DSL
search ("Groovy DSL") { from, tweet ->
   println from + " : " + tweet
}
```

Or we can use the `follow` method to follow the tweets of any user who posts about the search terms that we are interested in:

```
// Follow users that have tweeted recently about Groovy and DSL
search ("Groovy DSL") { from, tweet ->
    follow(from)
    println "Following ${from}"
}
```

Adding all of these methods together is the first step towards writing a useful and simple DSL for Twitter, but it suffers from a number of problems, which we need to address.

Removing the boilerplate

Any DSL that we develop with Groovy is referred to as an embedded DSL. In other words, it uses language features from the host language in order to build a new mini dialect that achieves a particular goal. As programmers, we can appreciate the elegance of how a closure can define a mini dialect that is embedded within our code. We are used to all of the boilerplate that goes with using a Java library.

By boilerplate, we mean all of the setup code that is needed to establish the context in which our code is running. This could be connecting to a database, establishing a connection to a remote EJB object via a JNDI lookup, and so on. It also includes all of the other code, which is superfluous to the problem at hand but is imposed by the languages and environments that we use. The requirement in Java to write all of our code within a class is a case in point. Comparing the Groovy "Hello, World" program with its Java equivalents, we can see that all but a single line of the code is boilerplate, imposed by the language:

```
// Groovy
println "Hello, World!"

// Java
class HelloWorldApp {
    public static void main(String[] args) {
        System.out.println("Hello, World!");
    }
}
```

Even the one useful line in the Java version is burdened with boilerplate. We have to explicitly write `System.out.println` to say that we are using the `System` class to print to the standard output. In Groovy, this is all just assumed. When we write Groovy, we embed mini DSLs within our code all the time, and surround it with these types of regular Groovy and Java-like structures. The fact that we are using the mini dialect of Groovy is hidden because the cool stuff gets hidden among other not-so-cool boilerplate code.

What if we would like a non-Groovy or non-Java programmer to use our DSL? Ideally, we just want to document how to use the DSL features, and not the boilerplate that goes with it. Otherwise, we would find ourselves saying to our users, "Trust me, just write this line of code and it will work... don't worry about what it does." Unfortunately, that's not what happens in practice. Boilerplate will always be a source of confusion and mistakes; so the less of it we have the better.

When we write something like the following in isolation of the boilerplate, we are actually getting towards a dialect that could be written by a non-Groovy programmer:

```
eachFriend {
    println it
}
```

The goal now should be to remove as much of the boilerplate code as possible from our scripts.

Refactoring

The next steps we take with our DSL are refactorings to remove boilerplate. Our previous examples have all implemented methods locally within the script. This clearly needs to change, so our first step will be to refactor these methods into a standalone class. This class will become the main class for our DSL. We'll call the class `GeeTwitter`.

We need to consider how we would like our users to access the methods in our class. By default, the methods that we add to a class are instance methods and are only accessible through an instance of the class. If we define `login` and `search` methods in our class, as shown in the following code, the user of the DSL must first create a new instance of the GeeTwitter class before they can use them:

```
import twitter4j.*

class GeeTwitter {
    void search(terms) {
        def query = new Query(terms)
```

```
        TwitterFactory.singleton.search(query).tweets.each {
            println it.text
        }
    }

    void search(terms, Closure c) {
        def query = new Query(terms)
        TwitterFactory.singleton.search(query).tweets.each {
            c.call(it.user.screenName,it.text)
        }
    }
}
```

We can write a script that uses these `search` methods, as follows:

```
def gTwitter = new GeeTwitter()

gTwitter.search "Groovy DSL"

gTwitter.search ("Groovy DSL") { from, tweet ->
    println "${from} : ${tweet}"
}
```

Although this is fine for most circumstances, we would like to make the ending DSL scripts as clear and to the point as possible so that a non-programmer might be able to write them. The need to create a `GeeTwitter` object before we can use the method is more unnecessary boilerplate. If, instead, we make the method static, the usage of the method is much clearer to the average user:

```
class GeeTwitter {
    static void search(terms) {
        def query = new Query(terms)
        TwitterFactory.singleton.search(query).tweets.each {
            println it.text
        }
    }

    static void search(terms, Closure c) {
        def query = new Query(terms)
        TwitterFactory.singleton.search(query).tweets.each {
            c.call(it.user.screenName,it.text)
        }
    }
}
```

To use this method, we can write the following script:

```
GeeTwitter.search ("Groovy DSL") { from, tweet ->
    println "${from} : ${tweet}"
}
```

Or even better:

```
import static GeeTwitter.*

search "Groovy DSL"
```

The classes generated by Groovy scripts are in the default package by default. In the previous examples, we didn't define a package for the GeeTwitter class, so it also resides in the default package. When we run the search script, Groovy will automatically look for any class that we use and compile it, as long as it is in the same directory as the script that we launch with.

Next, we will look at some more improvements to allow us launch our DSL scripts from the command line. First, let's fully flesh out the GeeTwitter class with more methods.

Fleshing out GeeTwitter

The following code is the fully fleshed out GeeTwitter class, with methods for sending direct messages, along with following and searching methods:

```
import twitter4j.*
import static twitter4j.TwitterFactory.*

class GeeTwitter {
    static sendMessage(user, message) {
        // Send a direct messsage to twitter user GroovyDSL
        singleton.sendDirectMessage(user, message)
    }
    // Method to apply a closure to each friend
    static eachMessage(Closure c) {
        singleton.directMessages.each {
            c.call(it.senderScreenName,it.text)
        }
    }

    // Method to apply a closure to each friend
    static void eachFriend(Closure c) {
        singleton.getFriendsList('fdearle',-1).each {
```

```
            c.call(it.screenName)
        }
    }

    // Method to apply a closure to each follower
    static void eachFollower(Closure c) {
        singleton.getFollowersList('fdearle',-1).each {
            c.call(it.screenName)
        }
    }

    // Method to follow another twitter user
    static void follow(user) {
        singleton.createFriendship(user)
    }

    static void search(terms) {
        def query = new Query(terms)
        singleton.search(query).tweets.each {
            println it.text
        }
    }

    static void search(terms, Closure c) {
        def query = new Query(terms)
        singleton.search(query).tweets.each {
            c.call(it.user.screenName,it.text)
        }
    }
}
```

Now, if we launch the GroovyConsole from the same directory as this class and add the Twitter4J JAR from the class path, we can start experimenting with our fully-fledged Twitter DSL interactively. Here we can issue a search for the terms "Groovy DSL" and see the result directly within the console output pane.

In the following snippet, we will see how the auto follow script has been reduced to one line. By removing all boilerplate and handling the follow method within our own DSL method, we can eliminate the need for the user to care about any exceptions that might be thrown. Auto follow becomes one elegant line of script:

```
import static GeeTwitter.*

eachFollower { follow it }
```

Improving search

Earlier on, in this chapter, we searched for Tweets from Guillaume LaForge to Graeme Rocher by passing the string `from:glaforge @graemerocher` to the Twitter4J Query method. We could do the same with our simple DSL `search` method:

```
search "from:glaforge @graemerocher"
```

This feels a little clunky, so let's see if there are ways we can improve this interface. You will remember from *Chapter 4, The Groovy Language*, the technique we referred to as named parameters. When we have a method signature in Groovy that includes a `Map`, we can omit the brackets around the `Map` when passing it as a parameter. Imagine we have a search method that takes a `Map` as a parameter, then we can make calls to it as follows:

```
search from: "glaforge", username: "graemerocher", "Groovy"
search "authentication", from: "alvaro_sanchez", hashtag: "codemotion_
es"
```

Named parameters allow us to intersperse the `String` search terms parameter with the named, `Map` parameters. In this case, we are using the `Map` to represent some of the extended searching features available from the Twitter search API, which we can implement as follows:

```
static void search(Map args, String terms = "") {
    def queryString = ""
    args.each { arg ->
        switch (arg.key.toString().toLowerCase()) {
            case 'from':
                queryString += "from:${arg.value} "
                break
            case 'to':
                queryString += "to:${arg.value} "
                break
            case 'hashtag':
                queryString += "#${arg.value} "
                break
            case 'username':
                queryString += "@${arg.value} "
                break
        }
    }
    queryString += terms
    def query = new Query(queryString)
        singleton.search(query).tweets.each {
            println it.text
        }
}
```

Adding a command-line interface

One more step in making our DSL roadworthy is to add a command-line interface to it. In doing so, we move from invoking the DSL directly to allowing it to be loaded by a DSL command. This gives us more control over the environment in which the DSL will run, and allows us to take care of the housekeeping, such as adding the `search` method to the `String` class.

Groovy being Groovy, adding a command line is surprisingly easy:

```
#!/usr/bin/env groovy
@Grab(group='org.twitter4j', module='twitter4j-core',
version='[4.0,)')

if (args)
    evaluate(new File(args[0]))
else
    println "Usage: GeeTwitter <script>"
```

The preceding shell script is all that we need in order to launch and run our `GeeTwitter` DSL. Being a shell script, we can run this directly on most Linux environments and Mac OS X, and on Windows if you have the Cygwin shell installed. In the script, we will test to see if we have any arguments passed, and evaluate the first argument as the name of a file containing the DSL script.

The `evaluate` method in Groovy allows us to pass a file containing Groovy code to the Groovy interpreter. Any code contained within the file is compiled and executed within the same virtual machine as the one where we are running the loading script. When the preceding script is executed from the command, the `groovy` command is invoked by the shell, which in turn launches a JVM. The `evaluate` method causes the target script to be loaded and executed in the same environment, and everything else works as if by magic.

Using the `evaluate` method means that any filename or extension can be used to contain the Twitter DSL scripts. Instead of naming all of our `GeeTwitter` scripts with the `.groovy` extension, we can decide that by convention our Twitter DSLs should have the extension `.gtwit`.

By saving the command-line script as `GTweet_1.0` in a file accessible on the command path, we now have a bona fide Twitter DSL, implemented in Groovy, and that we can invoke through a `shell` command.

We can now try out our DSL from the command line. To run a script to search for tweets about the Groovy and Grails eXchange event, we can save the following in a file called `ggx.gtwit` and invoke the `GTweet_1.0` shell script:

```
import static GeeTwitter.*

search "Groovy Grails eXchange"
```

Adding built-in methods

However simple our DSL might now look, the need to preface our method calls with `GeeTwitter` is one final piece of boilerplate code that it would be nice to remove. In some of the previous examples we have used a static import to do this, but it is still not very intuitive to a non Java/Groovy programmer why we are doing this. Since we are evaluating the DSL script ourselves, rather than allowing Groovy to do it, we still have some scope to do this.

It would certainly be nicer to be able to write:

```
eachFollower {
  sendMessage it, "Thanks for taking the time to follow me!"
}
```

This assumes that the `eachFollower` method is built in to the DSL, rather than the more verbose:

```
GeeTwitter.eachFollower {
  GeeTwitter.sendMessage (it,
        "Thanks for taking the time to follow me!")
}
```

Groovy provides two mechanisms that allow us achieve just this. Later in the book, we will look at how we can manipulate the binding to achieve this. For this chapter, we will look at a more straightforward mechanism, which exploits the compilation model for Groovy scripts.

Whenever we run a Groovy script, the script gets compiled behind the scenes into a class derived from the Groovy `Script` class (see `http://docs.groovy-lang.org/latest/html/gapi/groovy/lang/Script.html`). Most of the time, we are unaware of the fact that `Script` has just a few methods of interest to us. For instance, to access the binding of a script, we reference the `binding` property. When we do so, what we are in fact doing is calling the `Script.getBinding()` method. Similarly, when we used `evaluate` in the previous section to load and run our DSL from the launcher script, we were actually calling the `Script.evaluate()` method.

Instead of calling `Script.evaluate()` in the launch script, we can use the `GroovyScript` class to do the same thing. However, now we have the option of initializing the `GroovyScript` object that evaluates our DSL with a `CompilationConfiguration` object (See `http://docs.groovy-lang.org/latest/html/gapi/org/codehaus/groovy/control/CompilerConfiguration.html`). This now gives us control over how the compilation of the script will be handled.

`CompilationConfiguration` gives us the ability to set a number of compilation attributes, including the classpath to be used and the `PrintWriter` object to be used as a standard output. We can even add the static import for the `GeeTwitter` class. The command-line script needs to be modified as follows:

```
#!/usr/bin/env groovy
import org.codehaus.groovy.control.*
import org.codehaus.groovy.control.customizers.*

if(args) {
    def conf = new CompilerConfiguration()
    def imports = new ImportCustomizer()
    imports.addStaticStar("GeeTwitter")
    conf.addCompilationCustomizers(imports)
    def shell = new GroovyShell(this.class.classLoader,
    new Binding(), conf)
    shell.evaluate (new File(args[0]))
} else
    println "Usage: GTweet_2.0 <script>"
```

The `CompilationConfiguration` class also provides a method `CompilationConfiguration.setScriptBaseClass()`, which allows us to provide an alternative subclass of `Script` to be used for the base class of our script instance:

```
abstract class MyBaseScript extends Script {
    def builtIn ( a ) { println a }
}
```

If we provide the preceding `MyBaseScript` class as the alternate `Script` class, any script that we evaluate by using this class will have the `builtIn` method available by default. There is nothing magical here; it's now just a method of the `Script` class that gets compiled into our environment. We can now rewrite our `GeeTwitter` class to make it a subclass of `Script`. Let's call it `GeeTwitterScript`, in order to distinguish it from the original:

```
@Grab(group='org.twitter4j', module='twitter4j-core',
version='[4.0,)')
import twitter4j.*
```

```
import static twitter4j.TwitterFactory.*

abstract class GeeTwitterScript extends Script {
def sendMessage(user, message) {
    // Send a direct messsage to twitter user GroovyDSL
    singleton.sendDirectMessage(user, message)
}
// Method to apply a closure to each friend
def eachMessage(Closure c) {
    singleton.directMessages.each {
        c.call(it.senderScreenName,it.text)
    }
}


// Method to apply a closure to each friend
def eachFriend(Closure c) {
    singleton.getFriendsList('groovydsl',-1).each {
        c.call(it.screenName)
    }
}


// Method to apply a closure to each follower
def eachFollower(Closure c) {
    singleton.getFollowersList('groovydsl',-1).each {
        c.call(it.screenName)
    }
}


// Method to follow another twitter user
def follow(user) {
    singleton.createFriendship(user)
}

void search(terms) {
    def query = new Query(terms)
     singleton.search(query).tweets.each {
        println it.text
    }
}

def search(terms, Closure c) {
    def query = new Query(terms)
    singleton.search(query).tweets.each {
        c.call(it.user.screenName,it.text)
```

```groovy
        }
    }

    void search(Map args, String terms = "") {
        def queryString = ""
        args.each { arg ->
            switch (arg.key.toString().toLowerCase()) {
                case 'from':
                    queryString += "from:${arg.value} "
                    break
                case 'to':
                    queryString += "to:${arg.value} "
                    break
                case 'hashtag':
                    queryString += "#${arg.value} "
                    break
                case 'username':
                    queryString += "@${arg.value} "
                    break
            }
        }
        queryString += terms
        def query = new Query(queryString)
            singleton.search(query).tweets.each {
                println it.text
            }
    }

    def block(user) {
        singleton.createBlock(user)
    }
}
```

With this version, we will supply the name of the new subclass to the CompilerConfiguration object in the launch script. The new launch script appears as follows:

```groovy
#!/usr/bin/env groovy
  import org.codehaus.groovy.control.*

if(args) {
    def conf = new CompilerConfiguration()
    conf.setScriptBaseClass("GeeTwitterScript")
    def shell = new GroovyShell(this.class.classLoader,
        new Binding(), conf)
```

```
        shell.evaluate (new File(args[0]))
    }
    else
        println "Usage: GTweet_2.1 <script>"
```

With this final version of our DSL, we have managed to distill the code down to the barest outline that is needed to express what we want to do. Using only the preceding launcher shell script, and the GeeTwitterScript.groovy class, we can start to automate our Twitter experience from the command line. Here are some of sample GeeTwitter scripts we can try out:

- Send a direct message to a user:

```
sendMessage "GroovyDSL", "Using GeeTwitter to send you a message."
```

- Send a direct message to all of my followers:

```
eachFollower {
  sendMessage it, "Thanks for taking the time to follow
  me!"
}
```

- List all of the users that I'm following:

```
eachFriend { println it}
```

- Follow all of my followers:

```
eachFollower {
    follow it
}
```

I think you'll agree that we've built quite an elegant DSL for Twitter, and we've been able to do it with surprisingly little code. This version has limited functionality to choose from, as I did not want to clutter the text with a fully functional Twitter DSL. With a little bit more coding, we could extend this DSL to do a lot more. For example, if you've got a follower on Twitter who is following hundreds of users, but who has no followers, and who has issued only one tweet containing a link, then chances are that the follower is a spammer. Wouldn't it be nice to be able to block such a user automatically with a DSL script?

Summary

We have now built our first fully-fledged, albeit simple, Groovy DSL. We've seen how we can start with an existing Java-based API and evolve it into a simple user-friendly DSL that can be used by almost anybody. We've learned the importance of removing boilerplate code and how we can structure our DSL in such a way that the boilerplate is invisible to our DSL users.

The resulting DSL, being written in Groovy, is still an embedded DSL, but by sufficiently isolating the user scripts from its runtime and boilerplate, we have developed a DSL that could be documented in such a way that non-programming users could readily grasp how to use it. In the next chapter, we will extend our knowledge of the language further, by using some of Groovy's more advanced features, such as builders, metaprogramming, and command chains.

Power Groovy DSL Features

In this chapter, we will cover some more advanced Groovy features. Coincidentally, these are also the features that, along with closures, allow us to extend and manipulate the language in order to create DSLs. We will cover a lot of ground in this chapter, including the following important features:

- **Named parameters**: To begin, we will look at this simple but effective feature, and see how maps passed as parameters act as named parameters to a method.

- **Command chains**: We will cover how, when chaining methods together, we can omit the dot notation to give us a simple command chain DSL pattern.

- **Builders**: We will cover how to use Groovy builders to rapidly construct anything from web pages and XML to Swing UIs. While looking at Groovy builders, we will also introduce the native Groovy support for tree-based DOM structures, by looking at the built-in GPath operators in the Groovy language.

- SwingBuilder: We will add a quick and simple UI to our Twitter DSL, by using the SwingBuilder class.

- **Method pointers**: We will cover method pointers as a useful way to create aliases.

- **Meta Object Protocol**: We will cover the inner workings of Groovy's **Meta Object Protocol (MOP)**.

- **How builders work**: Once we have covered the concepts behind the MOP, we will revisit Groovy builders to understand how they are implemented using features from the MOP.

- ExpandoMetaClass: Finally, we will take a look at ExpandoMetaClass, which is one of the most interesting Groovy classes as it provides the keys to dynamically change the behavior of any existing class, including Java classes, on the fly.

Named parameters

We have touched upon the concept of named parameters already. In a previous chapter, we looked at how Groovy allows us to construct a POGO by using a default built-in constructor that accepts a `Map` argument. We can construct a POGO by passing an inline `Map` object to the constructor. Groovy uses the map object to initialize each property of the POGO in turn. The map is iterated and the corresponding setter is invoked for each map element that is encountered:

```
class POGO {
    def a = 0
    def b = 0
    def c = 0
}

given:
    def pogo1 = new POGO(a:1, b:2, c:3)
    def pogo2 = new POGO( b:2, c:3)
    def pogo3 = new POGO(b:2, a:3)
expect:
    pogo1.a == 1
    pogo1.b == 2
    pogo1.c == 3
and:
    pogo2.a == 0
    pogo2.b == 2
    pogo2.c == 3
and:
    pogo3.a == 3
    pogo3.b == 2
```

When we pass a `Map` object to a constructor, the parentheses [] can be left out. We can also list the property values in any order we like. If a property is excluded, the corresponding setter will not be called, so its default value will be preserved.

Groovy also allows the same parameter-passing scheme to be used with method calls. If we invoke a method and pass a list of map elements in the same fashion, as shown in the preceding code, Groovy will collect the map elements into a `Map` object and pass this to the method as the first parameter. Parameters passed in this way are generally known as **named parameters**. The key that we use for each parameter provides a name for the parameter, which otherwise is anonymous.

```
def namedParamsMethod1(Map params) {
assert params.a == 1
assert params.b == 2
assert params.c == 3
true
}
```

```
expect: "We can pass named parameters in any order"
    namedParamsMethod1(a:1, b:2, c:3)
    namedParamsMethod1(b:2, c:3, a:1)
    namedParamsMethod1(c:3, a:1, b:2)
```

If the method has other parameters, Groovy allows the map entries to be placed before or after the other parameters. The map entries will still get collected and passed as the first argument:

```
def namedParamsMethod2(Map params, String param2, String param3) {
assert params.a == 1
assert params.b == 2
assert params.c == 3
assert param2 == "param2"
assert param3 == "param3"
true
}
```

```
expect: "We can mix named and regular parameter in any order"
    namedParamsMethod2(a:1, b:2, c:3, "param2", "param3")
    namedParamsMethod2("param2", b:2, "param3", c:3, a:1)
    namedParamsMethod2(c:3, "param2", a:1, "param3", b:2)
```

In fact, the map entries can be interspersed among the other parameters in any order we like. Groovy will collect the map entries and pass them as the first parameter. It will then scan the rest of the parameters from left to right and assign them to the subsequent parameters of the method. We can also drop the method call parentheses, which allows us to invoke the method call as follows:

```
expect: "We can leave out parentheses"
    namedParamsMethod2 a:1, b:2, c:3, "param2", "param3"
    namedParamsMethod2 "param2", b:2, "param3", c:3, a:1
    namedParamsMethod2 c:3, "param2", a:1, "param3", b:2
```

These features combine neatly together for use in a DSL. Consider a method call to transfer funds from one account to another for a customer. The conventional way to lay out parameters to a method is in the order of their importance from a programming logic point of view. So we declare the `customer` parameter as the first parameter, as this is the primary object that we are operating on. We follow this with the accounts we are operating on, and finish up with the amount to transfer:

```
def transfer( customer, from_account, to_account, amount) {
    println """debiting ${amount} from ${from_account} account,
crediting ${to_account} account for ${customer}"""
}
transfer("Joe Bloggs", "checking", "savings", 100.00)
```

Reading the method call does not provide any immediate clarity as to the function of all of the parameters. So we will only know for sure that `savings` is the receiving account by checking the method documentation to see that the third parameter is the receiving account. What if we make a small change to this method and have it accept named parameters instead?

```
def transfer( transaction, amount) {
    println """debiting ${amount} from ${transaction.from} account,
crediting ${transaction.to} for ${transaction.for}"""
}

transfer 100.00, from: "checking", to: "savings", for: "Joe Bloggs"
transfer for: "Joe Bloggs", 200.00, from: "checking", to: "savings"
```

Now our method call is starting to look like English. We also have a good degree of flexibility over the order in which we place the named parameters and where we place the `amount` parameter, so if we like, we can turn the call into something that looks like English:

```
transfer 100.00, from: "checking", to: "savings", for: "Joe Bloggs"
```

Named parameters in DSLs

Being able to clarify exactly what a parameter means is a very useful technique to use in a DSL. Not only does it improve the readability of the DSL, but it can also remove potential ambiguities. Looking back at our `GeeTwitter` DSL from the last chapter, we had a `sendMessage` call, which sends a text message to a Twitter user. Both the `message` parameter and the user `id` parameter were defined as strings, which of course could lead to ambiguity in the calling sequence:

```
static String sentMessage
static def sendMessage1(id, message) {
    sentMessage = "Sending (${message}) to ${id}"
}

given:
    sendMessage1 "GroovyDSL", "Hi from GeeTwitter"
expect: "message sent correctly"
    sentMessage == "Sending (Hi from GeeTwitter) to GroovyDSL"
when:
    sendMessage1 "Hi from GeeTwitter", "GroovyDSL"
then: "message sent incorrectly"
    ! (sentMessage == "Sending (Hi from GeeTwitter) to GroovyDSL")
```

The second invocation here would, of course, cause an exception in the real GeeTwitter as we try to send a message to a user called "Hi from GeeTwitter" instead of to GroovyDSL. A small change removes this ambiguity and improves the readability of the DSL:

```
static def sendMessage2(Map params, message) {
    sentMessage = "Sending (${message}) to ${params.to}"
}
when:
    sendMessage2 to: "GroovyDSL", "Hi from GeeTwitter"
then: "message sent correctly"
    sentMessage == "Sending (Hi from GeeTwitter) to GroovyDSL"

when:
    sendMessage2 "Hi from GeeTwitter", to: "GroovyDSL"
then: "message sent incorrectly"
    sentMessage == "Sending (Hi from GeeTwitter) to GroovyDSL"
```

It might seem a little redundant or inefficient, from a programming point of view, to package a single value in a map. However, even though we are only going to pass the single value to a parameter along with a message parameter, naming this to parameter adds significantly to the resulting DSL script in terms of legibility.

Command chains

We already knew that Groovy allows us to leave out parentheses when calling methods. Another neat trick introduced in Groovy 1.8 is the ability to leave out the dot when we chain method calls. Using this feature, we can further improve the readability of our DSLs by adding constructs that mimic natural language. Take the following chained method calls:

```
deposit (100.00).currency(USD).to(savings)
```

By leaving out the parentheses on these calls and the intervening dots we can express this chain as follows:

```
deposit 100.00 currency GBP to savings
```

Building this mini DSL is relatively straightforward. First we need an `enum` for currencies, which we statically import. We also define two method calls, `convert` and `deposit`:

```
enum Currency { USD, GBP, EUR }

class Account {
    double balance
}

static def convert ( currency, amount) {
    def result
    switch (currency) {
    case Currency.USD: result = amount
        break
    case Currency.GBP: result = amount * 1.3
        break
    case Currency.EUR: result = amount * 1.1
    }
    result
}

static def deposit (double amount) {
    [
        currency: { Currency currency ->
            [to: { account ->
                account.balance += convert( currency , amount )
                }
            ]

        }
    ]
}
```

The breakdown of the calling sequence is then as follows:

- Calling `deposit` returns a `Map` with an entry `currency`, which is a closure
- Calling `currency` returns another `Map` with an entry `to` which is a closure that can be called just like a method, as described earlier
- Calling `to` does the conversion based on the parameters passed to `deposit` and `currency` and sets the `balance` on the `Account` passed to itself:

```
given:
Account savings = new Account()

when:
deposit (100.00).currency(USD).to(savings)
deposit 100.00 currency GBP to savings

then:
savings.balance == 230.0
```

Builders

Much of what we do in writing software involves construction or assembly of some sort or other. It could be building a graphical user interface, constructing a file to be saved on disk, or structuring a response to be sent to another system through a web services request. A lot of coding effort is dedicated to getting the structure of what we are building correct. Web pages need to be structured correctly in order to be displayed in a browser. XML-based files and responses to service requests need to be well-formed or they will cause validation exceptions. Building rich client UIs is an art in itself, with each client framework—such as Swing or SWT—having its own arcane API to work with.

Beyond the complexities of the structures that we build, the pattern of construction and the order of initialization imposed by different APIs bring their own constraints. This alone will often obfuscate the structure of what we are building by burying it deep within boilerplate code. In addition to this, the classes of object that we need to construct may be of a similar nature and have different means of construction.

The builder design pattern

It would be useful to have a means of constructing objects such that the method of construction was hidden. Enter the builder design pattern. The concept of a design pattern comes originally from the architectural profession in the late 1970s. In building architecture, a design pattern refers to the reuse of design solutions for similar problems. In office complexes, the locating of stairwells, elevators, and bathrooms around central service columns is a typical design pattern.

Using such a design pattern, architects designing large office buildings can quickly lay out floor after floor of the building by repeating the layouts around the service columns on each floor. This leaves more time and effort to be expended on developing the functional work areas and aesthetics of the building. This not only benefits the architect but also benefits the user of the building.

No matter where we travel, whether it is to Bangkok, San Francisco, Paris, or London, it's usually not too difficult to find a bathroom, presuming we can remember how to find our way back to the elevator that we came up in. When we do, we are benefiting from the application of a design pattern.

Design patterns are seldom invented. Instead, they are usually observed in existing buildings and catalogued. Good design evolves over time and is repeated again and again. By exploiting existing design patterns, the architect can rely on the experience of generations of previous building projects and be sure that at least these elements of the building will work as expected.

Design patterns began to be observed and catalogued in software engineering in the late eighties. Ward Cunningham and Kent Beck wrote one of the first conference papers on the subject at OOPSLA 1987. By 1994, the seminal work by Eric Gamma, Richard Helm, Ralph Johnson, and John Vlissides, also known as the Gang of Four — *Design Patterns: Elements of Reusable Object-Oriented Software, Addison Wesley* — was published, which catalogued over 20 reusable design patterns, including the **Model View Controller (MVC)**, and Factory and Builder patterns.

These authors were not claiming to have invented all of these patterns. For each of the patterns, they listed source systems where the patterns could be observed in use. Some came from ET++, an object-oriented framework developed by Gamma and others at Taligent. Many of the patterns, including MVC and Builder, originated from the Smalltalk language and framework.

In fact, I can claim to have come up with one of the patterns myself. In 1989, while working for Glockenspiel on a Cross GUI class library for C++, I was struggling for a way to accommodate multiple library implementations in a single class library header file. I proposed a solution to the company's founder and C++ guru, John Carolan. John immediately christened the pattern, the Cheshire Cat. The Bridge pattern in the GOF book also quotes this name for the pattern.

Using Groovy builders

An important and powerful part of Groovy is its implementation of the builder design pattern. We implement design patterns in Java via Java classes and interfaces. The Groovy implementation of Builder goes beyond this by providing a mini DSL, which appears to embed the building process right into the language.

This style of markup is known as GroovyMarkup, and the code looks more like a customized markup script than a regular Groovy script. This is due to the clever use of Groovy's **Meta Object Protocol (MOP)** and closures.

At first glance, Groovy's builders defy our understanding of how things should work in an object-oriented language. We no longer seem to be creating objects and invoking methods as we would expect. For this section, let's suspend our disbelief and just enjoy the power that Groovy builders provide.

Here we will just try to understand how to use GroovyMarkup to build things. Later on in the chapter, we will cover how the MOP works, and it will become clear what tricks are being employed by the Groovy designers in order to give us a very neat way of constructing complex objects.

The best way to illustrate the GroovyMarkup feature is by way of an example. We'll start with something simple. Suppose that we need to export customer records from our e-commerce package in such a way that they can be used to initialize the customer database of a new CRM system that has been installed by us. The CRM system accepts customer records formatted in XML with customer IDs, names, and addresses. The XML required might look like this:

```
<customers>
  <customer id='1001'>
    <name firstName='Fred' surname='Flintstone' />
    <address street='1 Rock Road' city='Bedrock' />
  </customer>
  <customer id='1002'>
    <name firstName='Barney' surname='Rubble' />
    <address street='2 Rock Road' city='Bedrock' />
  </customer>
</customers>
```

Constructing this simple snippet of XML in Java requires numerous method calls to create XML elements and to set the attributes of these elements. The nested structure of the document would need to be explicitly constructed by appending some elements as children of other elements. By the time that we are done coding, the procedural nature of the construction process means that the code doing the markup bears no resemblance to the end result XML.

MarkupBuilder

Consider the GroovyMarkup equivalent. In the following code, we use a Groovy MarkupBuilder class to construct the same snippet of XML as in the previous section. The xmlIsIdentical method uses XMLUnit to test whether both XML snippets are the same:

```
given:
def writer = new StringWriter()
def builder = new groovy.xml.MarkupBuilder(writer)
when:

def customers = builder.customers {
    customer(id:1001) {
        name(firstName:"Fred",surname:"Flintstone")
        address(street:"1 Rock Road",city:"Bedrock")
    }
    customer(id:1002) {
        name(firstName:"Barney",surname:"Rubble")
        address(street:"2 Rock Road",city:"Bedrock")
    }
}
then:
    xmlIsIdentical (writer.toString(), "customers.xml" )
```

The striking thing about the previous code snippet is that, unlike the Java code required to do the same, this snippet is remarkably similar in structure to the XML that is output. In this example, we are using the MarkupBuilder class from the groovy.xml package. MarkupBuilder is one of several builder classes provided out of the box as part of the Groovy JARs. MarkupBuilder can be used to effortlessly build XML- and HTML-formatted output. What we are in fact looking at is a series of nested closures, one within the other. The nesting of the closures exactly matches the tree-like structure of the desired XML output.

Namespaced XML

What if we would like to create namespaced XML? In `GroovyMarkup`, tags conform to the method call syntax. So how can we do that if `namespace:tag` is not a valid Groovy method name? Fortunately, there is a way around this. In order to insert the colon into a tag name, we simply surround the element name in quotes. Groovy allows us to invoke a method by using a string in place of the method name, so `"myMethod"()` is treated the same as `myMethod()`:

```
given:
def writer = new StringWriter()
def xml = new groovy.xml.MarkupBuilder(writer)

def params = [:]

when:
params."xmlns:bk" = "urn:loc.gov:books"
params."xmlns:isbn" = "urn:ISBN:0-393-36341-6"

def bk_tag = "bk:book"
xml."bk:book"(params) {
    "bk:title"("Cheaper by the Dozen")
    "isbn:number"(1568491379)
}

then:
    xmlIsIdentical writer.toString(), "book1.xml"
```

Here we are using the strings' references to set the `xmlns` namespaces for `bk` and `isbn`. Then we use strings to declare the element names in our markup. All of this results in the following output:

```
<bk:book xmlns:bk='urn:loc.gov:books' xmlns:isbn='urn:ISBN:0-393-
36341-6'>
  <bk:title>Cheaper by the Dozen</bk:title>
  <isbn:number>1568491379</isbn:number>
</bk:book>
```

This technique is not limited to namespaces. We can use it anywhere that we need to output a character in a tag name, which would otherwise not be valid as a Groovy method name (for instance, hyphenated element names). Any Groovy string can be used as an element name, so the following is also valid, where we use `${book_title}` to paste the tag name into the markup from a local variable:

```
given:
def writer = new StringWriter()
def xml = new groovy.xml.MarkupBuilder(writer)

def book = "bk-book"
def book_title = "bk-title"

when:
xml."${book}" {
    "${book_title}"("Cheaper by the Dozen")
    "isbn_number"(1568491379)
}
then:
    xmlIsIdentical writer.toString(), "book2.xml"
```

The `MarkupBuilder` class will slavishly emit whatever we ask it to. In the previous code snippet, we are creating namespaces by using standard markup with the `MarkupBuilder` class. A more elegant way of creating namespaced XML is by using the `StreamingMarkupBuilder` class, which has built-in support for namespaces.

`StreamingMarkupBuilder` decouples the output of the markup from the creation of the markup closure. We then `bind` the closure to `StreamingMarkupBuilder` at the time at which we want the output to take place:

```
given:
def xml = new groovy.xml.StreamingMarkupBuilder()

when:
def markup = {
    customers {
        customer(id:1001) {
            name(firstName:"Fred",surname:"Flintstone")
            address(street:"1 Rock Road",city:"Bedrock")
        }
        customer(id:1002) {
            name(firstName:"Barney",surname:"Rubble")
            address(street:"2 Rock Road",city:"Bedrock")
        }
    }
}

then:
    xmlIsIdentical xml.bind( markup ).toString(), "customers.xml"
```

Within the closure, we can reference a variable, `mkp`, which allows us to give instructions to the builder in order to control XML generation. Two handy methods we can invoke are `xmlDeclaration()`, which causes the XML declaration header to be output, and `declareNamespace()`, which sets up a namespace:

```
given:
    def xml = new groovy.xml.StreamingMarkupBuilder().bind {
        mkp.xmlDeclaration()
        mkp.declareNamespace('bk':'urn:loc.gov:books')
        mkp.declareNamespace('isbn':'urn:ISBN:0-393-36341-6')

        bk.book {
            bk.title("Cheaper by the Dozen")
            isbn.number(1568491379)
        }
    }

expect:
    xmlIsIdentical xml.toString(), "book1.xml"
```

Once we have made the builder aware of our namespaces, we can utilize them in the markup code by using suffix notation. So `namespace.tag` will be output in the XML as `namespace:tag`, as follows:

```
<?xml version='1.0'?>
<bk:book xmlns:bk='urn:loc.gov:books' xmlns:isbn='urn:ISBN:0-393-
36341-6'>
  <bk:title>Cheaper by the Dozen</bk:title>
  <isbn:number>1568491379</isbn:number>
</bk:book>
```

The GroovyMarkup syntax

`GroovyMarkup` is nothing more than method call syntax combined with closures and named parameters. But, in effect, these Groovy syntactical features are combined to produce a new DSL syntax for `GroovyMarkup` with its own rules. Let's look in detail at the syntax from the previous examples:

```
def customers = builder.customers {
    ...
```

To begin with, we define the root node of our XML by invoking
`MarkupBuilder.customers()` on the `builder` object. This causes a root
`customers` tag to be output into the XML stream and the code. The tag is not closed
off until the following closure is executed. This looks and behaves like a `customer`
method taking a closure as a parameter even though there is no such method.

Nested within the closure we come across more methods, such as calls to `customer`,
`title`, `name`, and `address`:

```
customer(id:1001) {
    ...
```

This method call will cause a new nested `customer` tag to be output into the XML
stream with an `id` attribute set to `1001`. Once again, the tag is not closed off until the
closure is executed, during which more method-like calls are encountered:

```
title("Mr")
name(firstName:"Fred",surname:"Flintstone")
address(street:"1 Rock Road",city:"Bedrock")
```

No methods exist for `customers`, `customer`, `title`, `name`, or `address`.
`MarkupBuilder`, in conjunction with its base `BuilderSupport` class, uses the Groovy
MOP to make all of this work as if by magic. The beauty of this approach is how
intuitive the resulting code is, because it closely reflects the resulting markup. All we
need to remember is that pseudo-method call syntax will create a tag, and named
parameters will be inserted as attributes in the resulting output.

The parameters passed follow the same conventions that we discussed earlier in
relation to named parameters. In this case, all named parameters are collected and
become the attributes of the element. We should only pass one additional parameter,
which is used as the body of the tag or element.

GroovyMarkup and HTML

With `MarkupBuilder`, it's just as easy to build HTML pages. Here we generate a
simple HTML page:

```
given:
def writer = new StringWriter()
def html = new groovy.xml.MarkupBuilder(writer)

when:
html.html {
    head {
        title "Groovy Builders"
```

```
        }
        body {
            h1 "Groovy Builders are cool!"
        }
    }
```

```
    then:
    xmlIsIdentical writer.toString(), "simple.html"
```

In the next example, we build a more complex HTML page containing **nested tables**. `MarkupBuilder` will close all tags correctly so that they are well-formed. A classic mistake when working with nested tag formats is to misplace or unbalance the closing of tags. The HTML `<table>` tag and its nested `<tr>` and `<td>` tags are highly prone to error when hand-coded. Assume that we want to generate HTML to display the names of the various Groovy builder and `ConcreteBuilder` classes in a nested table.

The HTML to produce this table would be something like the following:

```
<html>
  <head>
    <title>Groovy Builders</title>
  </head>
  <body>
    <table style='border: 1px solid black;'>
      <tr>
        <th>Builder class</th>
        <th>Concrete class</th>
      </tr>
      <tr>
        <td>groovy.util.BuilderSupport</td>
        <td>
          <table>
            <tr>
              <td>groovy.util.AntBuilder</td>
            </tr>
            <tr>
              <td>groovy.xml.MarkupBuilder</td>
            </tr>
          </table>
        </td>
      </tr>
      <tr>
        <td>groovy.util.FactoryBuilderSupport</td>
        <td>
```

```
            <table>
              <tr>
                <td>groovy.util.NodeBuilder</td>
              </tr>
              <tr>
                <td>groovy.swing.SwingBuilder</td>
              </tr>
            </table>
          </td>
        </tr>
      </table>
    </body>
</html>
```

Although the preceding HTML code looks correct, one of the table tags is incorrectly terminated as </td>. Displaying the preceding code in a browser would show an extra layer of nesting in the table tag that was not intended. The same HTML can be generated using MarkupBuilder, as shown in the following listing:

```
given:
def writer = new StringWriter()
def html = new groovy.xml.MarkupBuilder(writer)

when:
html.html {
  head {
    title "Groovy Builders"
  }
  body {
    table(style:"border: 1px solid black;") {
      tr {
        th "Builder class"
        th "Concrete class"
      }
      tr {
        td "groovy.util.BuilderSupport"
        td {
          table {
            tr {
              td "groovy.util.AntBuilder"
            }
            tr {
              td "groovy.xml.MarkupBuilder"
            }
          }
```

```
              }
          }
        tr {
          td "groovy.util.FactoryBuilderSupport"
          td {
            table {
              tr {
                td "groovy.util.NodeBuilder"
              }
              tr {
                td "groovy.swing.SwingBuilder"
              }
            }
          }
        }
      }
    }
  }
}
then:
xmlIsIdentical writer.toString(), "table.html"
```

In the Groovy version, all of the tags that are produced are guaranteed to be correct with respect to nesting and balancing. The Groovy version also looks much less cluttered and readable. In fact, it is impossible for us to make the same type of errors with the Groovy version, as the compiler will insist that all parentheses are properly balanced.

Using program logic with builders

So far we have just used Groovy builders as straightforward markup code. In spite of the unusual syntax, GroovyMarkup programs are still just plain Groovy code, so there is nothing stopping us from mixing the construction process with regular program logic if we please. Here we iterate over a list of customer data while generating XML from the customer records that we find:

```
given:
def writer = new StringWriter()
def builder = new groovy.xml.MarkupBuilder(writer)

def fred = new Customer(id:1001,firstName:"Fred",
surname:"Flintstone",
street:"1 Rock Road",city:"Bedrock")
def barney = new Customer(id:1002,firstName:"Barney",
surname:"Rubble",
```

```
        street:"2 Rock Road",city:"Bedrock")
        def customerList = [ fred, barney]

when:
builder.customers {
    for (cust in customerList) {
        customer(id:cust.id) {
            name(firstName:cust.firstName,surname:cust.surname)
            address(street:cust.street, city:cust.city)
        }
    }
}

then:
xmlIsIdentical writer.toString(), "customers.xml"
```

Builders for every occasion

Out of the box, the Groovy libraries include a suite of builders for most of the common construction tasks that we might encounter. Here is a list of some of them:

- `MarkupBuilder`: This we have already seen. It can be used to generate any XML-style tagged output. Class: `groovy.xml.MarkupBuilder`.

- `NodeBuilder`: This is a useful builder for building tree-like structures of node instances in memory. Class: `groovy.util.NodeBuilder`.

- `DOMBuilder`: This builder will construct a WC3 DOM tree in memory from the `GroovyMarkup` that we provide. Class: `groovy.xml.DOMBuilder`.

- `SAXBuilder`: This is very similar to the `DOMBuilder` insofar as the end result is a WC3 DOM in memory. The difference is that it works with an existing SAX `ContentHandler` class and fires SAX events to it as the `GroovyMarkup` is executed. Class: `groovy.xml.SAXBuilder`.

- `JMXBuilder`: Also in the same vein as `AntBuilder` is the `JMXBuilder` class, which can be used to deploy JMX management beans by using simple markup-style syntax. `JMXBuilder` is a Groovy-based DSL for declaratively exposing services, POJOs, POGOs, and so on, via the **Java Management Extensions (JMX)**. Class: `groovy.jmx.builder.JMXBuilder`.

- `SwingBuilder`: Next we'll cover `SwingBuilder` in detail with an example. This builder constructs Swing-based UIs. Class: `groovy.swing.SwingBuilder`.

NodeBuilder

NodeBuilder is used to build tree structures of node instances in memory. We use exactly the same GroovyMarkup syntax as before. Here we build up a tree structure in memory from customer data, using the same structure as with MarkupBuilder. All that needs to change to construct a node-based tree in memory is to replace the builder instance created with an instance of NodeBuilder. Once the markup code has been executed, the customers field contains the tree structure, which can be accessed by using Groovy's XPath-like syntax, GPath:

```
given:
def builder = new groovy.util.NodeBuilder()

def fred = new Customer(id:1001,firstName:"Fred",
surname:"Flintstone",
    street:"1 Rock Road",city:"Bedrock")
def barney = new Customer(id:1002,firstName:"Barney",
surname:"Rubble",
    street:"2 Rock Road",city:"Bedrock")
def wilma = new Customer(id:1003,firstName:"Wilma",
surname:"Flintstone",
    street:"1 Rock Road",city:"Bedrock")
def betty = new Customer(id:1004,firstName:"Betty", surname:"Rubble",
    street:"2 Rock Road",city:"Bedrock")
def customerList = [ fred, barney,wilma,betty]

when:
def customers = builder.customers {
    for (cust in customerList) {
        customer(id:cust.id) {
            name(firstName:cust.firstName,surname:cust.surname)
            address(street:cust.street, city:cust.city)
        }
    }
}

then:
customers.customer[0].'@id' == 1001
customers.customer[1].'@id' == 1002
customers.customer[0].address[0].'@street' ==
                    customers.customer[2].address[0].'@street'
customers.grep{
    it.name.any{it.'@surname' == "Rubble"}
}.size == 2
customers.grep{
    it.name.any{it.'@surname' == "Rubble"}
}.address.every{ it.'@street'[0] == "2 Rock Road"}
```

Using GPath to navigate a node tree

We've used GPath in the preceding code to access the node structure created from our markup. To make sense of how the GPath syntax works, we must visualize it as a tree structure where customers is the root node. Node attributes are accessible as map entries, so element.'@attribute' is used to access the attribute values:

```
assert customers.customer[0].'@id' == 1001
assert customers.customer[1].'@id' == 1002
```

The following is the root customers node. Each node can have 1 to *n* leaf nodes, so customer is always returned as a list object even if only one item is contained in the list. We access individual elements by using array syntax (customer[1]) but any list method can be used. The following snippet will list the first names of all customers in the tree:

```
customers.customer.each {
    println it.name[0].'@firstName'
}
```

As we index deeper into the tree, we still need to use array syntax to access the lower nodes, even if the elements at these levels are singletons. Here we assert that Fred and Wilma live at the same address:

```
assert customers.customer[0].address[0].'@street'
  == customers.customer[1].address[0].'@street'
```

Finally, we can use a more complex GPath query to assert that all the Rubbles live at 2 Rock Road. This is quite a complex query, so we will decompose it, as shown in the following snippet. First, we use grep on the root customers node to produce a tree of all customers whose surname is Rubble. This tree should have two nodes: one for Barney and one for Betty:

```
def rubbles = customers.grep{ it.name.any{it.'@surname' == "Rubble"}}
```

Now we can assert that every Rubble lives at 2 Rock Road:

```
assert rubbles.address.every{ it.'@street'[0] == "2 Rock Road"}
```

SwingBuilder

Most Java developers I know hate Swing UIs with a passion. The reason people hate Swing is because of the APIs. Let's face it, Swing UIs are a chore to build and maintain, due to the unwieldy nature of the Swing APIs.

Any Swing app I've ever worked on has been a mess of component initialization code, intermingled with anonymous inner classes for event handling. Each Swing component, however small or insignificant, has to be renewed and given a name. Figuring out how all of the components nest together, when some such as button groups and panels may not even be visible, is an endless chore.

The following is a UI built with SwingBuilder that puts a simple UI onto the GeeTwitter searching DSL from the last chapter. You can see in the forthcoming screenshot how the markup mirrors the actual layout in the UI. Closures are used in place of anonymous inner classes for events such as actionPerformed on the **Exit** menu. This took less than five minutes to throw together, and unlike a pure Swing API version, it is production-ready as soon as we remove the **Napkin Look and Feel** line from the code:

```
@Grab(group='net.sf.squirrel-sql.thirdparty-non-maven',
module='napkinlaf', version='[1.2,)')
import groovy.swing.SwingBuilder
import javax.swing.*
import java.awt.*
import net.sourceforge.napkinlaf.*

data = []

def results
swing = new SwingBuilder()
swing.lookAndFeel(new NapkinLookAndFeel())
frame = swing.frame(title:'Twitter Search') {
  menuBar {
    menu('File') {
      menuItem 'Exit', actionPerformed: { System.exit(0) }
    }
  }
  panel(layout: new BorderLayout()) {
    panel (constraints:BorderLayout.NORTH) {
      label 'Search for Tweets'
      textField(columns:10, actionPerformed: { event ->
          println "Search for Event ${event.source.text}"
          data = GeeTwitter.search(event.source.text)
          results.model = tableModel(list:data) {
            propertyColumn(header:'Sender',
                        propertyName:'from',preferredWidth:20)
            propertyColumn(header:'Tweet',
                        propertyName:'tweet',preferredWidth:140)
          }
```

```
        })
      }
      scrollPane (constraints:BorderLayout.SOUTH){
        results = table() {
          tableModel(list:[]) {
            propertyColumn(header:'Sender',
                          propertyName:'from',preferredWidth:20)
            propertyColumn(header:'Tweet',
                          propertyName:'tweet',preferredWidth:140)
          }
        }
      }
    }
  }
  frame.pack()
  frame.show()
```

The GroovyMarkup that we use for SwingBuilder is pretty much identical to what we've seen before, with a few differences. Unlike MarkupBuilder and NodeBuilder, we can't simply invent tags to insert into GroovyMarkup, as this would not make sense. The tags must correspond to real UI widgets or controls that can be placed into the UI. In the preceding code, we use frame, menuBar, panel, and textField, among others. There are other non-widget tags, such as tableModel, that must be used in conjunction with a table tag and others.

In the preceding example, we start with a frame tag. The SwingBuilder class takes care of creating a JFrame widget for this frame, and maintaining it. Any further widgets declared in the nested closure later in this frame will be added to the frame. Take the preceding scrollPane, for example. Widgets that are nested below this will be added to the scrollPane, and so on. The nesting of the closure code that we use to declare the components dovetails exactly with how these components are nested in the UI. Declaring a widget returns the corresponding Swing widget; so the frame variable in the preceding code contains a JFrame instance that allows us to call the regular swing pack() and show() methods to display the UI.

SwingBuilder handles the Swing event loop and dispatches any event that occurs. All we need to do is supply a closure for the actionPerformed attribute of any widget that we want to provide event handling for. This is far neater than the anonymous classes that regular Swing code is usually littered with.

The following result is a quick and nasty UI for Twitter searching:

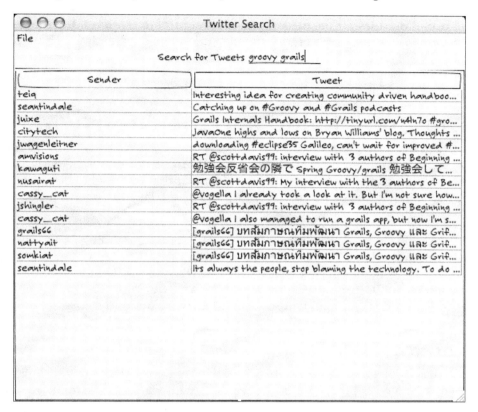

Method pointers

Groovy allows you to assign a method to a closure by using the & syntax. The closure returned is often referred to as a **method pointer**. Method pointers can be assigned by dereferencing the method name from any object instance, for example:

```
given:
def list = ["A", "B", "C"]

when:
def addToList = list.&add

and:
addToList "D"

then:
list == ["A", "B", "C", "D"]
```

The difficulty with method pointers to instance methods is being sure what instance the method pointer is referencing. In essence, an instance method pointer violates the encapsulation rules for the object by passing control to an object that is outside the direct control of a class. So I recommend caution when using them. However, method pointers when applied to static methods can be a very useful way to create DSL shortcut keywords.

Metaprogramming and the Groovy MOP

In a nutshell, the term **metaprogramming** refers to writing code that can dynamically change its behavior at runtime. A **Meta-Object Protocol** (**MOP**) refers to the capabilities in a dynamic language that enable metaprogramming. In Groovy, the MOP consists of four distinct capabilities within the language: reflection, metaclasses, categories, and expandos.

The MOP is at the core of what makes Groovy so useful for defining DSLs. The MOP is what allows us to bend the language in different ways in order to meet our needs, by changing the behavior of classes on the fly. This section will guide you through the capabilities of MOP and, based on what we learn, we will later dissect some builder code in order to understand how builders work under the covers.

Reflection

To use Java reflection, we first need to access the `Class` object for any Java object in which we are interested through its `getClass()` method. Using the returned `Class` object, we can query everything from the list of methods or fields of the class, to the modifiers that the class was declared with. In the following code, we see some of the ways that we can access a `Class` object in Java and the methods we can use to inspect the class at runtime:

```
import java.lang.reflect.Field;
import java.lang.reflect.Method;

public class Reflection {
  public static void main(String[] args) {
    String s = new String();
    Class sClazz = s.getClass();
    Package _package = sClazz.getPackage();
    System.out.println("Package for String class: ");
    System.out.println("    " + _package.getName());
    Class oClazz = Object.class;
    System.out.println("All methods of Object class:");
    Method[] methods = oClazz.getMethods();
    for(int i = 0;i < methods.length;i++)
      System.out.println("    " + methods[i].getName());
```

```
    try {
      Class iClazz = Class.forName("java.lang.Integer");
      Field[] fields = iClazz.getDeclaredFields();
      System.out.println("All fields of Integer class:");
      for(int i = 0; i < fields.length;i++)
        System.out.println("    " + fields[i].getName());
    } catch (ClassNotFoundException e) {
      e.printStackTrace();
    }
  }
}
```

We can access the Class object from an instance by calling its Object.getClass() method. If we don't have an instance of the class to hand, we can get the Class object by using .class after the class name, for example, String.class. Alternatively, we can call the static Class.forName, passing to it a fully qualified class name.

Class has numerous methods, such as getPackage(), getMethods(), and getDeclaredFields() that allow us to interrogate the Class object for details about the Java class under inspection. The preceding example will output various details about String, Integer, and Double:

```
ChapterSeven — bash — 65×26
Big-Mac:ChapterSeven fdearle$ java Reflection
Package for String class:
    java.lang
All methods of Object class:
    wait
    wait
    wait
    equals
    toString
    hashCode
    getClass
    notify
    notifyAll
All fields of Integer class:
    MIN_VALUE
    MAX_VALUE
    TYPE
    digits
    DigitTens
    DigitOnes
    sizeTable
    value
    SIZE
    BYTES
    serialVersionUID
Big-Mac:ChapterSeven fdearle$ []
```

Groovy reflection shortcuts

Groovy, as we would expect by now, provides shortcuts that let us reflect classes easily. In Groovy, we can shortcut the `getClass()` method as a property access `.class`, so we can access the class object in the same way whether we are using the class name or an instance. We can treat `.class` as a string and print it directly without calling `Class.getName()`, as follows:

The variable `greeting` is declared with a dynamic type, but has the type `java.lang.String` after the `Hello` string is assigned to it. Classes are first class objects in Groovy so we can assign a string to a variable. When we do this, the object that is assigned is of the type `java.lang.Class`. However, it describes the `String` class itself, so printing will report `java.lang.String`.

Groovy also provides shortcuts for accessing packages, methods, fields, and just about all the other reflection details that we need from a class. We can access these straight off the class identifier, as follows:

```
println "Package for String class"
println "    " + String.package
println "All methods of Object class:"
Object.methods.each { println "    " + it }
println "All fields of Integer class:"
Integer.fields.each { println "    " + it }
```

Incredibly, these six lines of code do all of the same work as the 30 lines in our Java example. If we look at the preceding code, it contains nothing that is more complicated than it needs to be. Referencing `String.package` to get the Java package of a class is as succinct as you can make it. As usual, `String.methods` and `String.fields` return Groovy collections, so we can apply a closure to each element with the `each` method. What's more, the Groovy version outputs a lot more useful detail about the package, methods, and fields.

When using an instance of an object, we can use the same shortcuts through the `class` field of the instance:

```
given:
    def greeting = "Hello"
expect:
    greeting.class.package == String.package
    String.package.toString().contains "package java.lang"
```

Expandos

An `Expando` is a dynamic representation of a typical Groovy bean. Expandos support typical `get` and `set` style bean access but, in addition to this, they accept gets and sets to arbitrary properties. If we try to access a non-existing property, the `Expando` does not mind and, instead of causing an exception, it will return `null`. If we set a non-existent property, the `Expando` will add that property and set the value. In order to create an `Expando`, we instantiate an object of class `groovy.util.Expando`:

```
given:
    def customer = new Expando()

expect:
    customer.properties == [:]
    customer.id == null
    customer.properties == [:]

when:
    customer.id = 1001
    customer.firstName = "Fred"
    customer.surname = "Flintstone"
    customer.street = "1 Rock Road"

then:
    customer.id == 1001

    customer.properties == [
        id:1001, firstName:'Fred',
        surname:'Flintstone', street:'1 Rock Road']
```

The `id` field of `customer` is accessible on the `Expando` shown in the preceding example even when it does not exist as a property of the bean. Once a property has been set, it can be accessed by using the normal field getter, for example, `customer.id`. Expandos are a useful extension to normal beans when we need to be able to dump arbitrary properties into a bag and we don't want to write a custom class to do so.

A neat trick with expandos is what happens when we store a closure in a property. As we would expect, an `Expando` closure property is accessible in the same way as a normal property. However, because it is a closure, we can apply function call syntax to it to invoke the closure. This has the effect of seeming to add a new method on the fly to the `Expando`:

```
customer.prettyPrint = {
    println "Customer has following properties"
    customer.properties.sort {it.key} .each {
        if (it.key != 'prettyPrint')
            println "    " + it.key + ": " + it.value
    }
}

customer.prettyPrint()
```

Here we appear to be able to add a `prettyPrint()` method to the `customer` object, which outputs to the console:

```
Customer has following properties
    surname: Flintstone
    street: 1 Rock Road
    firstName: Fred
    id: 1001
```

Categories

Adding a closure to an `Expando` to give a new method is a useful feature, but what if we need to add methods to an existing class on the fly? Groovy provides another useful feature—**categories**—for this purpose. A `Category` can be added to any class at runtime, by using the `use` keyword.

We can create `Category` classes that add methods to an existing class. To create a `Category` for a class, we define a class containing static methods that take an instance of the class that we want to extend as their first parameter. By convention, we name this parameter as `self`. When the method is invoked, `self` is set to the object instance that we are extending. The `Category` can then be applied to any closure by using the `use` keyword.

Here we create a `CustomerPrinter` class that pretty prints a customer object. We can then make use of this class's methods in a use block and apply them to a `Customer` object:

```
class Customer {
    int id
    String firstName
    String surname
    String street
    String city
}

class CustomerPrinter {
    static void prettyPrint(Customer self) {
        println "Customer has following properties"
        self.properties.sort { it.key }.each {
            if (it.key != 'prettyPrint' && it.key != 'class')
                println "    " + it.key + ": " + it.value
        }
    }
}

given:
def fred = new Customer(id:1001,firstName:"Fred",
surname:"Flintstone",
    street:"1 Rock Road",city:"Bedrock")
def barney =  new Customer(id:1002,firstName:"Barney",
surname:"Rubble",
    street:"2 Rock Road",city:"Bedrock")

def customerList = [ fred, barney]

when:
use (CustomerPrinter) {
    for (customer in customerList)
        customer.prettyPrint()
}
then:
        """Customer has following properties
    city: Bedrock
    firstName: Fred
```

```
            id: 1001
            street: 1 Rock Road
            surname: Flintstone
    Customer has following properties
            city: Bedrock
            firstName: Barney
            id: 1002
            street: 2 Rock Road
            surname: Rubble""" == output()
```

Java libraries are full of classes that have been declared `final`. The library designers in their wisdom have decided that the methods they have added are all that we will ever need. Unfortunately, that is almost never the case in practice. Take the Java `String` class, for example. There are plenty of useful string manipulation features that we might like to have in the `String` class. Java has added methods progressively to this class over time, for instance, `match` and `split` in Java 1.4, with `replace` and `format` being added in Java 1.5.

If we needed these style methods before Sun got around to adding them, we could not do it ourselves because of the `final` modifier. So the only option has been to use classes from add-on libraries such as commons `StringUtils`. The **Apache Commons Lang** component class contains a slew of useful classes that augment the basic capabilities of Java classes, including `BooleanUtils`, `StringUtils`, `DateUtils`, and so on. All of the `util` class methods are implemented as static, taking `String` as the first parameter. This is the typical pattern used in Java when we need to mix in extra functionality to an existing class:

```
@Grab(group='org.apache.commons', module='commons-lang3',
version='3.0')
import org.apache.commons.lang3.StringUtils;

public class StringSplitter {

    public static void main(String[] args) {
        if (!args) {
            System.out.println("USAGE : StringSplitter string
seperator");
            System.exit(0);
        }
        String [] splits = StringUtils.split(args[0], args[1]);

        for (int i = 0; i < splits.length; i++) {
            System.out.println("token : " + splits[i]);
        }
    }
}
```

Conveniently, this pattern is the same as the one used in Groovy categories, which means that the Apache Commons Lang Util classes can all be dropped straight into a use block. So all of these useful utility classes are ready to be used in your Groovy code as categories:

```
import org.apache.commons.lang.StringUtils

expect:
    use (StringUtils) {
        "org.apache.commons.lang3".split(".") ==
            ["org", "apache", "commons", "lang3"]
    }
```

 You can also use the @Category annotation in association with a class.

Traits

A recent and very useful addition to the Groovy language is the concept of a trait. A trait is a reusable set of methods and properties that can be applied to any class without the need for multiple inheritance. Earlier in the chapter, we implemented a pretty print class for the Customer class. In the following example we implement the PrettyPrintable class as a trait. This trait can be applied to any class to give it the ability to pretty print its properties:

```
trait PrettyPrintable {
    void prettyPrint() {
        this.properties.sort { it.key }.each {
            if (it.key != 'prettyPrint' && it.key != 'class')
                println it.key + ": " + it.value
        }
    }
}
class Customer implements PrettyPrintable {
    int id
    String firstName
    String surname
    String street
    String city
}
```

```
given:
def fred = new Customer(id:1001,firstName:"Fred",
    surname:"Flintstone",
    street:"1 Rock Road",city:"Bedrock")
def barney = new Customer(id:1002,firstName:"Barney",
    surname:"Rubble",
    street:"2 Rock Road",city:"Bedrock")

def customerList = [ fred, barney]

when:
for (customer in customerList)
    customer.prettyPrint()
then:
        """city: Bedrock
firstName: Fred
id: 1001
street: 1 Rock Road
surname: Flintstone
city: Bedrock
firstName: Barney
id: 1002
street: 2 Rock Road
surname: Rubble""" == output()
```

MetaClass

In addition to the regular Java `Class` object that we saw earlier when looking at reflection, each Groovy object also has an associated `MetaClass` object. All Groovy classes secretly implement the `groovy.lang.GroovyObject` interface, which exposes a `getMetaClass()` method for each object:

```
public interface GroovyObject {
    /**
     * Invokes the given method.
     */
    Object invokeMethod(String name, Object args);

    /**
     * Retrieves a property value.
     */
    Object getProperty(String propertyName);
```

```
/**
 * Sets the given property to the new value.
 */
void setProperty(String propertyName, Object newValue);

/**
 * Returns the metaclass for a given class.
 */
MetaClass getMetaClass();

/**
 * Allows the MetaClass to be replaced with a
 * derived implementation.
 */
void setMetaClass(MetaClass metaClass);
}
```

Pure Java classes used in Groovy do not implement this interface, but they have a MetaClass assigned anyway. This MetaClass is stored in the MetaClass registry. The MetaClass of any class can be found by accessing its .metaClass property:

```
class Customer {
    int id
    String firstName
    String surname
    String street
    String city
}

// Access Groovy meta class
def groovyMeta = Customer.metaClass

// Access Java meta class
def javaMeta = String.metaClass
```

Metaclasses are the secret ingredients that make the Groovy language dynamic. MetaClass maintains all of the metadata about a Groovy class. This includes all of its available methods, fields, and properties. Unlike the Java Class object, the Groovy MetaClass allows fields and methods to be added on the fly. So while the Java class can be considered as describing the compile time behavior of the class, MetaClass describes its runtime behavior. We cannot change the Class behavior of an object but we can change its MetaClass behavior by adding properties or methods on the fly.

The Groovy runtime maintains a single MetaClass per Groovy class, and these operate in close quarters with the GroovyObject interface. GroovyObject implements a number of methods, which in their default implementations are just facades to the equivalent MetaClass methods. The most important of these to understand is the invokeMethod() method.

Pretended methods – MetaClass.invokeMethod

An important distinction between Java and Groovy is that, in Groovy, a method call never invokes a class method directly. A method invocation on an object is always dispatched in the first place to the GroovyObject.invokeMethod() method of the object. In the default case, this is relayed onto the MetaClass.invokeMethod() method for the class and MetaClass is responsible for looking up the actual method. This indirect dispatching is the key to how a lot of Groovy power features work as it allows us to hook ourselves into the dispatching process in interesting ways:

```
class Customer {
    int id
    String firstName
    String surname
    String street
    String city

    Object invokeMethod(String name, Object args) {
        if (name == "prettyPrint") {
            println "Customer has following properties"
            this.properties.sort { it.key }.each {
                if (it.key != 'class')
                println "    " + it.key + ": " + it.value
            }
        }
    }
}

given:
def fred = new Customer(id:1001,firstName:"Fred",
    surname:"Flintstone",
    street:"1 Rock Road",city:"Bedrock")
def barney = new Customer(id:1002,firstName:"Barney",
    surname:"Rubble",
    street:"2 Rock Road",city:"Bedrock")
```

```
def customerList = [ fred, barney]

when:
for (customer in customerList)
    customer.prettyPrint()
then:
        """Customer has following properties
    city: Bedrock
    firstName: Fred
    id: 1001
    street: 1 Rock Road
    surname: Flintstone
Customer has following properties
    city: Bedrock
    firstName: Barney
    id: 1002
    street: 2 Rock Road
    surname: Rubble""" == output()
```

In the preceding code, we added a `Customer.invokeMethod()` method to the `Customer` class. This allows us to intercept method invocations and respond to calls to `Customer.prettyPrint()` even though this method does not exist. Remember how in `GroovyMarkup` we appeared to be calling methods that did not exist? This is the core of how `GroovyMarkup` works. The `Customer.prettyPrint()` method in the previous code snippet is called a **pretended method**.

Understanding this, delegate, and owner

Like Java, Groovy has a `this` keyword that refers to the current or enclosing Java object. In Java, we don't have any other context in which we can execute code except in a `class` method. In an instance method, `this` will always refer to the instance itself. In a static method, `this` has no meaning as the compiler won't allow us to reference this in a static context.

In addition to the instance methods, Groovy has three additional execution contexts to be aware of:

- Code running directly within a script where the enclosing object is the script
- Closure code where the enclosing object is either a script or an instance object
- Closure code where the enclosing object is another closure

In addition to the `this` keyword, Groovy has two other keywords that are referred only in the context of a closure—`owner` and `delegate`:

- The `owner` keyword refers to the enclosing object, which in the majority of cases is the same as `this`, the only exception being when a closure is surrounded by another closure.

- The `delegate` keyword refers to the enclosing object and is usually the same as `owner` except that `delegate` is assignable to another object. Closures relay method invocations that they handle themselves back to their `delegate` keywords. This is how the methods of an enclosing class become available to be called by the closure as if the closure was also an instance method. We will see later that one of the reasons builders work the way they do is because they are able to assign the delegate of a closure to themselves.

[The `delegate` keyword will initially default to `owner`, except when we explicitly change the `delegate` keyword to something else through the `Closure.setDelegate` method.]

The following example illustrates `this`, `owner`, and `delegate` working under various different contexts. This example is necessarily complex, so take the time to read and understand it:

```
class Clazz {
    def method() {
        this
    }

    def methodDelegate() {
        delegate
    }

    def methodOwner() {
        owner
    }
    def closure = {
        [this, delegate, owner]
    }

    def closureWithinMethod() {
        def methodClosure = {
            [this, delegate, owner]
        }
        methodClosure()
```

```
        }
    }
given: "A class with an Instance method"
def clazz = new Clazz()

when: "In a class instance method 'this' is the "
def methodThis = clazz.method()

then:
methodThis == clazz

when: "we try to access delegate from a method"
def methodDelegate = clazz.methodDelegate()

then:
thrown(MissingPropertyException)
methodDelegate == null

when: "we try to access owner from a method"
def methodOwner = clazz.methodOwner()

then:
thrown(MissingPropertyException)
methodOwner == null

when: "we get this, delegate and owner for a closure"
def (closureThis, closureDelegate, closureOwner) = clazz.closure()

then: "this, delegate and owner are the class instance"
closureThis == clazz
closureDelegate == clazz
closureOwner == clazz

when: "get this, delegate and owner for a closure in method"
def (closureInMethodThis, closureInMethodDelegate,
    closureInMethodOwner) = clazz.closureWithinMethod()

then: """this, delegate and owner are the class instance not the
        enclosing closure"""
closureInMethodThis == clazz
closureInMethodDelegate == clazz
closureInMethodOwner == clazz
closureInMethodThis != clazz.closure
closureInMethodDelegate != clazz.closure
closureInMethodOwner != clazz.closure
```

Running the preceding code will output the following text:

```
Class method this is : class Clazz
Closure this is : class ConsoleScript1
Closure Closure this is : class ConsoleScript1
Method Closure this is : class Clazz
Script this is : class ConsoleScript1
```

So, the rules for resolving `this`, `owner`, and `delegate` in the various contexts are:

- In a class `instance` method, `this` is always the instance object. `owner` and `delegate` are not applicable and will be disallowed by the compiler

- In a class `static` method, `this`, `owner`, and `delegate` references will be disallowed by the compiler

- In a closure defined within a script, `this`, `owner`, and `delegate` all refer to the `Script` object unless `delegate` has been reassigned

- In a closure within a method, `this` and `owner` refer to the instance object of the enclosing class; as will `delegate`, unless it has been reassigned to another object

- In a script, `this` is the `Script` object, and `owner` and `delegate` are not applicable

How builders work

Earlier, when we looked at the `MarkupBuilder` code, the unfamiliar syntax must have seemed strange. Now that we have an understanding of how the MOP and pretended methods work, let's take a quick look again at some builder code and see if we can figure out what might be happening. `MarkupBuilder` is derived from the `BuilderSupport` class. When describing how `MarkupBuilder` works, I won't make a distinction between `BuilderSupport` and `MarkupBuilder`. Most of the mechanisms described here are in fact implemented by `BuilderSupport` and are shared with other `Builder` classes:

```
def customers = builder.customers {
    customer(id:1001) {
        name(firstName:"Fred",surname:"Flintstone")
        address(street:"1 Rock Road",city:"Bedrock")
    }
    customer(id:1002) {
        name(firstName:"Barney",surname:"Rubble")
        address(street:"2 Rock Road",city:"Bedrock")
    }
}
```

No matter how far you look in the documentation for `MarkupBuilder`, you won't find anything about it having a `customers` method. So what's happening when we write:

```
def customers = builder.customers {
...?
```

The answer is that `MarkupBuilder` is pretending to have a method with the signature: `MarkupBuilder.customers(Closure c)`. In the next line of code, things get a little more interesting. This line of code is defined within the body of the closure itself:

```
customer(id:1001) {
...
```

To explain this, we need to understand how closures handle method calls. When a closure encounters a method call that it cannot handle itself, it automatically relays the invocation to its `owner` object. If this fails, it relays the invocation to its `delegate`. Normally, the `delegate` would be the enclosing script or class, but `MarkupBuilder` sets the `delegate` object to itself. The closure relays the customer method invocation to `MarkupBuilder`, which has an `invokeMethod()` implementation that pretends to have a method `MarkupBuilder.customer(Map m, Closure c)`.

Method invocation and property lookup are governed by the `resolve` strategy of the `Closure`. The resolve strategy tells `Closure` what objects it should look at when attempting to resolve a method or property reference. By default, the resolve strategy is set to `OWNER_FIRST`, which means that the first place we look is in `owner`. If this lookup fails, then the search continues to the `delegate` object.

`MarkupBuilder` relies on the default resolve strategy, but we can change the resolve strategy as the need arises. The full list of resolve strategies is as follows:

- `OWNER_FIRST` (the default): This resolves methods and properties in `owner` first followed by `delegate` if not found.

- `DELEGATE_FIRST`: This resolves in `delegate` first and then searches `owner` if not found.

- `OWNER_ONLY`: This resolves in `owner` only and doesn't search `delegate`.

- `DELEGATE_ONLY`: This resolves in `delegate` only with no search of `owner`.

- `TO_SELF`: This is a special case to allow `getProperty` of `Closure` itself to be overridden. With this resolve strategy, the closure calls `getProperty` on itself first before continuing the lookup through the normal lookup process.

Coming back to our markup processing, the next line of code is in the context of a closure within a closure:

```
name(firstName:"Fred",surname:"Flintstone")
```

At this level of nesting, `delegate` would normally refer to the enclosing script or instance object. Once again `MarkupBuilder` has reassigned `delegate` to refer to itself. With this, `Closure` relays the invocation up to its delegate, `MarkupBuilder.invokeMethod()` handles it and again pretends it has a method `MarkupBuilder.name(Map m, Closure c)`.

With each of these pretended methods, `MarkupBuilder` outputs a tag with the name of the method and attributes set according to the named parameters, and then calls the closure. As with most things in Groovy, building your own builder is surprisingly easy when you know how to do it:

```
class PoorMansTagBuilder {
    int indent = 0
    Object invokeMethod(String name, Object args) {
        indent.times {print "    "}
        println "<${name}>"
        indent++
        args[0].delegate = this // Change delegate to the builder
        args[0].call()
        indent--
        indent.times {print "    "}
        println "</${name}>"
    }
}

given:
def builder = new PoorMansTagBuilder ()

when:
builder.root {
        level1{
         level2 {
         }
      }
   }
```

```
then:
        """<root>
    <level1>
        <level2>
        </level2>
    </level1>
</root>""" == output()
```

In order to illustrate the builder mechanism shown in the previous code snippet, we are conveniently ignoring any parameter passing, and assuming that args just contains a first parameter of the type Closure. However, this short example does illustrate method pretending through the invokeMethod(), and method relaying by assigning delegate.

ExpandoMetaClasses

We briefly touched on metaclasses when building our Twitter DSL in *Chapter 4, The Groovy Language*. In the coming example, we've used String.metaClass to dynamically add a method to the String class for Twitter searching. Let's look at what is happening here:

```
String.metaClass.search = { Closure c ->
    GeeTwitter.search(delegate,c)
}
```

From the earlier section on expandos, we understand how an Expando allows us to dynamically add a property to a class. That's all that is happening here. In the preceding code, we are dynamically adding a property to MetaClass for String in the same way as we added properties to Expando. This property happens to be a Closure, and the object happens to be the MetaClass of String, so it has the effect of adding a new method to the String class.

Adding a regular property to MetaClass can be achieved in the same way as with expandos. There is only a single MetaClass per Groovy or Java class, so this is useful only if we have a new property that is relevant across all instances of a class. In practice, this will rarely happen. Apart from adding properties and methods, there are a whole bunch of other interesting things that we can do with ExpandoMetaClass. We will go through a selection of them here.

Replacing methods

The technique that we use to add a method can also be used to replace an existing method. When doing so, we can subvert the existing logic of a class. Wouldn't it be nice if we could change all bank managers' minds as easily as this?:

```
class BankManager {

    boolean approveLoan() {
        return false
    }
}

given:
def myBankManager = new BankManager()

expect:
myBankManager.approveLoan() == false

when:
BankManager.metaClass.approveLoan = { true }
myBankManager = new BankManager()

then:
myBankManager.approveLoan() == true
```

Any method can be overridden or added. This includes any of the operator methods, such a plus(), minus(), multiply(), divide(), and so on. If need be, we can add operator semantics to any class, even if we have not written it ourselves.

Adding or overriding static methods

To add or override a static method of a class, we just insert the static keyword before the method name. In this example, we have a BusinessService class with static methods. If we try to run with this service as a unit test, then the remoteService object is not wired in and is null. We can get around this by adding a isRemoteServiceLive method that returns true. This turns out to be a great way to mock service methods in unit tests:

```
class BusinessService {
    static def remoteService
    static boolean isRemoteServiceLive() {
        remoteService.isLive()
    }
}
```

```
when:
    BusinessService.isRemoteServiceLive()
then:
    thrown NullPointerException

when:
    BusinessService.metaClass.static.isRemoteServiceLive =
{ true }
    def live = BusinessService.isRemoteServiceLive()

then:
    notThrown NullPointerException
    live == true
```

Dynamic method naming

We can use GStrings to name methods as we add or override them in a class. This means that we can dynamically generate method names on the fly. In the following example, we iterate all of the properties in the Customer class. We can exclude the class and metaClass properties with the find operator it =~ /lass/ so that we just add methods for the properties that we want:

```
class Customer {
    int id
    String firstName
    String surname
    String street
    String city
}

given:
def c = new Customer()
c.properties.keySet().findAll { !(it =~ /lass/)}.each {
    Customer.metaClass."idFor${it.capitalize()}" = { ->
        delegate."$it".toString().toLowerCase().tr(' ', '_')
    }
}
when:
def cust = new Customer(firstName:"Fred",
                    surname:"Flintstone",
                    street:"Rock Road",
                    city:"Bedrock")
```

```
then:
cust.idForFirstName() == "fred"
cust.idForSurname() == "flintstone"
cust.idForStreet() == "rock_road"
```

Adding overloaded methods

Whenever we add a method to the `ExpandoMetaClass` that has the same signature as an existing method, the original method is overridden. In the following snippet, we can see that it is the last *String blanked* method that is in place after we override on subsequent occasions:

```
given:
String.metaClass.blanks { delegate.replaceAll(/./) {'%'}}
String.metaClass.blanks { delegate.replaceAll(/./) {'@'}}
String.metaClass.blanks { delegate.replaceAll(/./) {'*'}}
expect:
"A String".blanks() == "********"
```

To add overloaded versions of methods, we can continue to add new methods. As long as the signatures are different from the last `each` method, it will be added as an overloaded method:

```
given:
String.metaClass.static.valueAndType = { double d ->
    "${d.class.name}:${valueOf(d)}"
}
String.metaClass.static.valueAndType = { float f ->
    "${f.class.name}:${valueOf(f)}"
}
String.metaClass.static.valueAndType = { int i ->
    "${i.class.name}:${valueOf(i)}"
}
String.metaClass.static.valueAndType = { long l ->
    "${l.class.name}:${valueOf(l)}"
}

expect:
String.valueAndType(1.0) == "java.lang.Double:1.0"
String.valueAndType(3.333f) == "java.lang.Float:3.333"
String.valueAndType(101) == "java.lang.Integer:101"
String.valueAndType(1000000L) == "java.lang.Long:1000000"
```

When we are overloading subsequent methods with different signatures, we can make use of the append operator <<:

```
given:
  String.metaClass.static.valueAndType << { double d ->
      "${d.class.name}:${valueOf(d)}"
  }
  String.metaClass.static.valueAndType << { float f ->
      "${f.class.name}:${valueOf(f)}"
  }
  String.metaClass.static.valueAndType << { int i ->
      "${i.class.name}:${valueOf(i)}"
  }
  String.metaClass.static.valueAndType << { long l ->
      "${l.class.name}:${valueOf(l)}"
  }

expect:
String.valueAndType(1.0) == "java.lang.Double:1.0"
String.valueAndType(3.333f) == "java.lang.Float:3.333"
String.valueAndType(101) == "java.lang.Integer:101"
String.valueAndType(1000000L) == "java.lang.Long:1000000"
```

Adding constructors

Constructors can be added to a class by using the constructor property of metaclass. Just be wary when doing this so as not to call the default constructor. The mechanism used by metaclass to call the constructor will cause a stack overflow, if you do:

```
given:
Customer.metaClass.constructor = {
    String first, String last -> new Customer(
        firstName:first,
        surname:last)
}

when:
def c = new Customer("Fred", "Flintstone" )

then:
c.firstName == "Fred"
c.surname == "Flintstone"
```

Summary

We have covered a lot of ground in this chapter. We have now covered most of the important features of the Groovy language, and looked in depth at how some of these features can be applied to developing DSLs. We now have an appreciation of what can be achieved by using features in the MOP, and how using the MOP enables other powerful features, such as `GroovyMarkup`.

Using the MOP, we have learned how we can modify our program's behavior at runtime. In the next chapter we will explore features in the Groovy language that allow us to hook in the actual compilation process. We will see how AST transformations allow us a much greater degree of control over our DSL by manipulating our program code at compile time.

8
AST Transformations

In this chapter, we will take a look at Groovy **abstract syntax tree (AST)** transformations. AST transformations are a mechanism for us to hook the Groovy compilation process. Up to now, we have looked at Groovy's runtime metaprogramming abilities. Here, we will look at compile time metaprogramming and see how we can use AST transformations to build code on the fly during the compilation process. This is a complex subject, for which we will focus on the following aspects in detail:

- **Local AST transformations**: We will look at how we can use a local AST transformation to implement an annotation

- **Manipulating the AST**: We will look at the various mechanisms for adding code to our programs using the `ASTNode` APIs and the `ASTBuilder` class

- **Global AST transformations**: We will build one complete DSL based on a Global AST transformation

- **Compilation errors**: We will learn how to add our own compilation errors

- **Packaging an AST transformation**: We will learn how to package an AST transformation so that it can be shared

What is an AST

The acronym AST is shorthand for the abstract syntax tree. During the compilation process, the Groovy compiler `groovyc` will generate interim data structures that represent the code that is being compiled. The main data structure that the complier produces is the AST. The AST is quite literally an abstract syntax tree. In other words, it is a tree structure in memory that describes the syntax of the code being compiled. To illustrate this, let's take a simple example:

```
class Foo {
    def barValue

    def bar() {
        return barValue
    }
}
```

The compiler will parse this code and turn it into a tree structure to represent the syntax of the code. At the top of the tree is a node, which represents the class declaration. This node is represented by the Groovy AST class `ClassNode`. The class node will have several child nodes of the type `ConstructorNode`, `MethodNode`, `FieldNode`, and `PropertyNode` depending on what phase of compilation we are at.

> The major elements of Groovy AST are represented by objects of the type `ASTNode` and its subclasses. As you drill down the tree, you will encounter elements that represent the expressions in the code represented by the statement and its subclasses. You will encounter a lot of these in the examples in this chapter. For more information, see the class documentation for the `ast` package and its subpackages at `http://docs.groovy-lang.org/latest/html/api/org/codehaus/groovy/ast/package-summary.html`.

The method node for the bar method will have a block statement node, which represents the block of code within the body of the method. As it happens, this block of code is only a single statement, so the only child of the block statement is a return statement node and the only child of the return statement is a variable expression node.

The best way to explore the AST is via the `groovyConsole` tool. Type the preceding code snippet into `groovyConsole` and view the AST in the AST viewer, accessible via the script menu. By selecting the semantic analysis phase of compilation, we will see the following tree of AST nodes are generated at this phase of compilation. More and more detail is compiled into the class as the compiler reaches later phases. Let's take a more detailed look at the phases of the Groovy compiler.

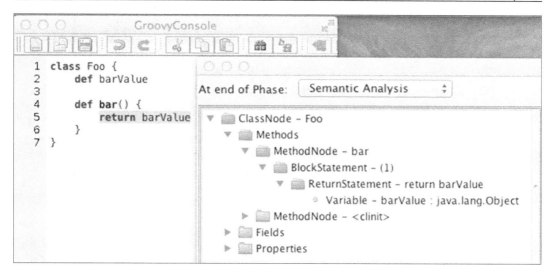

Compiler phases

As the compiler works through the different phases, it adds detail to the AST. In all the examples we will work on in this chapter, we will have sufficient detail for our transformations to work on in the semantic analysis phase of compilation. It is worth understanding the compiler phases and what additional information is added to the AST at each phase.

The AST viewer is a useful tool for exploring this. The preceding screenshot is the panel where the AST tree is displayed; the AST viewer also maintains a source view. This view is also augmented to reflect what nodes have been added to the AST. Try switching phases in the view, and you will see this happen. Now, let's look at the individual compiler phases:

- **Initialization**: In this phase, the compiler opens up all source files and configures its environment. If we are using `CompilerConfiguration` with the `GroovyShell` class, this is where that object is opened and interrogated. You will notice in the AST viewer that the AST is empty at this point. AST generation takes place later.

- **Parsing**: The Groovy grammar is used to produce a tree of tokens representing the source code. The Groovy grammar is implemented using Apache Antlr, see `http://www.antlr.org`. Note that the tokens generated at this phase are not yet an AST, so the tree view in AST viewer will still be empty.

- **Conversion**: In this phase, the token tree is converted into an AST. This is the very first time that we have access to an AST. In the AST viewer, we will see an AST representation of the code for the first time when we select this phase.

- **Semantic analysis**: The compiler performs consistency checks and validity checks on the AST that cannot be detected by the grammar. This is generally the first phase at which we would normally consider attaching our own AST transformation. If we were to hook a transform into conversion for instance, we risk operating on code that may fail the consistency and validity checks. This is the first point at which we can be confident that the code being compiled is syntactically correct. This is also the phase at which outside references are resolved to classes, static imports and the like.

- **Canonicalization**: Access from inner classes to surrounding scope is resolved. This also completes what are considered the frontend phases of the compiler. The following phases are called the backend phases and are more involved in generating the final byte code.

- **Instruction selection**: This is the point at which the instruction set is selected. Java class files are only forward compatible. This means that while a class compiled for a specific version of JVM will still work on later versions the converse is not necessarily true. For instance, early prerelease versions of JDK 5 implemented varargs, enums, and generics using the JDK 4 bytecode; however, the release version of the JDK implemented new class file attributes, so classes compiled for JDK 5, which use these features, are no longer backward compatible. This is the phase of the compilation process that selects which bytecode instruction set to use. You will note in the AST viewer that no new AST nodes are added at this point.

- **Class generation**: This is the point at which the final Java version of the Groovy class is generated. In the AST viewer, you will see the AST augmented with Groovy bean methods for property getter and setter methods. You will also see the introduction of the `metaClass` property and the `invokeMethod` method. It's also the first phase at which we can observe the generation of the bytecode. In the AST viewer, select a method or constructor and look at the bytecode tab.

- **Output**: As the name suggests, this is the phase at which the `.class` files are written out to disk with the bytecode that has been generated.

- **Finalization**: This is the bookend to the initialization phase. Files are closed, resources released, and other general housekeeping is performed. Nothing new is added to the AST at this point.

Local AST transformations

When discussing AST transformations in Groovy, we refer to local and global AST transformations. A local transformation is one that is targeted at a specific "local" piece of code. Currently, the only way to tell the Groovy compiler to implement a local transformation is to use an annotation. The annotation gives the compiler the clue as to what part of the compiled code should be transformed. Annotations can be placed next to any part of the Groovy source code, but are typically bound to a class, field, or method.

Let's start out by implementing a very simple annotation based on an AST transformation. Ultimately, we will evolve this example into an AST that implements the pretty printing functionality we built back in *Chapter 7, Power Groovy DSL Features*, as both an `Expando` closure method and via a trait. However, let's start simple and just add a method to a class that prints a string.

The functionality we want to implement can be captured in the following Spock specification. Assuming we have an annotation called `@PrettyBasic`, then adding this annotation to a class as follows will add a `prettyPrint` method to the class:

```
@PrettyBasic class Basic {
}

given:
    def target = new Basic()

when:
    target.prettyPrint()
then:
    "I'm so pretty. Oh so pretty!" == output()
```

 The examples in this chapter are relatively complex. In many cases, you are seeing sections of class files described here rather than the fully worked source. Many dependent imports are omitted for brevity and long package names are excluded. You should download the source pack instead of typing these examples in yourself. The source pack contains the full sources and dependencies.

So we are expecting a new method to be added that prints the expected string. Not very useful for now, but let's see how we implement this annotation using an AST transformation. We will start out by declaring an interface for the `PrettyPrint` annotation itself as follows:

```
import org.codehaus.groovy.transform.GroovyASTTransformationClass
import java.lang.annotation.ElementType
import java.lang.annotation.Retention
import java.lang.annotation.RetentionPolicy
import java.lang.annotation.Target

@Target([ElementType.TYPE])
@Retention(RetentionPolicy.SOURCE)
@GroovyASTTransformationClass(["PrettyBasicASTTransformation"])
public @interface PrettyBasic {
}
```

This annotation interface uses several annotations to the compiler itself, to associate a transformation with the `@PrettyBasic` annotation. The `@Target` annotation tells the compiler that this particular transformation operates on types, so the transformation will only be applied to these AST nodes during compilation. The `@RetentionPolicy` annotation tells the compiler whether to retain the annotation in the class after compilation. Our transformation only applies to the compilation phase, so we use `RetentionPolicy.SOURCE` to indicate that it should be discarded after compilation. We associate the implementing `PrettyBasicASTTransformation` class using, `@GroovyASTTransformationClass`.

The transformation class itself is in the following code. We use the `@GroovyASTTransformation` annotation to indicate that this is a class that implements an AST transformation and specify which compiler phase that the transformation should be applied to. In this case, we will select `CompilePhase.SEMANTIC_ANALYSIS`, which is the earliest phase that we can apply a local transformation.

To implement a transformation, we overload the visit method of `GroovyASTTransformation`. As you read the following code, you will notice the first lines are all defensive. Historically, the AST transformation aspects of Groovy have changed a lot from language version to version. This can make your AST transformations a little brittle on language upgrades. The convention has therefore evolved to defensively program around any assumptions you intend to make about what part of the AST you will be handed. We expect that the second AST node we are handed will be a `ClassNode` object, and we will be calling `addMethod` on it so that we ensure that only invocations that contain the expected nodes are transformed:

```groovy
@GroovyASTTransformation (phase = CompilePhase.SEMANTIC_ANALYSIS)
class PrettyBasicASTTransformation implements ASTTransformation {
    void visit(ASTNode[] nodes, SourceUnit source) {
        if (!nodes) return
        if (!(nodes[0] instanceof AnnotationNode)) return
        if (!nodes[1] && !(nodes[1] instanceof ClassNode)) return
        ClassNode classNode = nodes[1]

        def methodStatement = new ExpressionStatement(
                new MethodCallExpression(
                    new VariableExpression("this"),
                    new ConstantExpression("println"),
                    new ArgumentListExpression(
                        new ConstantExpression(
"I'm so pretty. Oh so pretty!")
                    )
                )
            )
        def methodNode = new MethodNode(
                'prettyPrint',
                Modifier.PUBLIC,
                null,
                new Parameter[0],
                null,
                methodStatement
        )
        classNode.addMethod(methodNode)
    }
}
```

Once we have verified that we are dealing with a class node of the AST, it's time to decide what we want to do with it. In this case, we will add a node below the class node for a new method called `prettyPrint`. This method node (`MethodNode` class) contains a single expression statement (the `ExpressionStatement` class), which in turn is comprised of a method call expression (the `MethodCallExpression` class), and so on.

In effect, what we are programmatically doing is building the AST nodes that would represent the following code:

```groovy
public void prettyPrint() {
    return this.println ( "I'm so pretty, Oh so pretty!")
}
```

This is not really what we want yet for a proper `PrettyPrint` transformation, but it is a fully functioning AST transformation implementing an annotation `@PrettyBasic`. If we apply this transformation to a class, we can see it in action. The Spock test we wrote earlier should now be working.

Using ASTBuilder

In the previous example, we used methods on the AST nodes themselves such as `addMethod` to build up the new code in the AST. This can get laborious if we try and add any more sophisticated code. Even the simple `prettyPrint` method would be quite difficult to implement with this mechanism. Fortunately, there are other options that will make our lives a bit easier.

Build from code

Let's build another AST transformation, which uses a useful helper class `ASTBuilder` to add the `prettyPrint` method to our class. Once again we will need to define an interface for our annotation class and the AST transformation class itself:

```
@Target([ElementType.TYPE])
@Retention(RetentionPolicy.SOURCE)
@GroovyASTTransformationClass(["PrettySimpleASTTransformation"])
public @interface PrettySimple {
}

@GroovyASTTransformation (phase = CompilePhase.SEMANTIC_ANALYSIS)
class PrettySimpleASTTransformation implements ASTTransformation {

    void visit(ASTNode[] nodes, SourceUnit source) {
  ClassNode classNode = nodes[1]

        def astNodes = new AstBuilder().buildFromCode {
            this.properties.sort { it.key }.each {
                if (it.key != 'prettyPrint' && it.key != 'class')
                    println it.key + ": " + it.value
            }
        }
        def methodStatement = astNodes[0]
        def methodNode = new MethodNode(
                'prettyPrint',
                Modifier.PUBLIC,
                null,
                new Parameter[0],
```

```
                null,
                methodStatement
        )
        classNode.addMethod(methodNode)
    }
}
```

The main difference you will notice here is the use of the `ASTBuilder` class to help us build the method statement for our new method. In this case, we use the `buildFromCode` method of `ASTBuilder`. This convenience function allows us to convert a closure into the AST nodes we need. `ASTBuilder` will interrogate the closure code and turn that into the equivalent nodes from the following code:

```
this.properties.sort { it.key }.each {
    if (it.key != 'prettyPrint' && it.key != 'class')
    println it.key + ": " + it.value
}
```

There are significant benefits to using this instead of the previous method. Firstly, it is much clearer what code is being added by the transform. You don't need to understand all the arcane `ASTNode` subtypes, and how they need to be structured. You can already see whether your code is syntactically correct because the IDE will show you. One disadvantage is, however, that not all code can be built using a closure. For instance, you cannot formulate a class field expression using a closure. It's perfect, however, for where you want to add a whole method block or to insert a block of code into an existing method.

Build from Spec

The `ASTBuilder` class also provides a rich builder style DSL for building the AST. In the next example, we will use `ASTBuilder.buildFromSpec` to build the entire `prettyPrint` method node:

```
@Target([ElementType.TYPE])
@Retention(RetentionPolicy.SOURCE)
@GroovyASTTransformationClass(["PrettyAdvancedASTTransformation"])
public @interface PrettyAdvanced {

}

@GroovyASTTransformation (phase = CompilePhase.SEMANTIC_ANALYSIS)
class PrettyAdvancedASTTransformation implements ASTTransformation {

    void visit(ASTNode[] nodes, SourceUnit source) {
        if (!nodes) return
```

```
                  if (!(nodes[0] instanceof AnnotationNode)) return
                  if (!nodes[1] && !(nodes[1] instanceof ClassNode)) return
                  ClassNode classNode = nodes[1]

                  def astNodes = new AstBuilder().buildFromSpec {
                      method( 'prettyPrint', Opcodes.ACC_PUBLIC, String) {
                          parameters {}
                          exceptions {}
                          block {
                              owner.expression.addAll
    new AstBuilder().buildFromCode {
                                  this.properties.sort { it.key }.each {
                                      if (it.key != 'prettyPrint' &&
    it.key != 'class')
                                          println it.key + ": " + it.value
                                  }
                              }
                          }
                          annotations {}
                      }
                  }
                  def methodNode = astNodes[0]

                  classNode.addMethod(methodNode)
          }

  }
```

Using this AST DSL, you can build almost any AST element you need. One disadvantage, however, is that the DSL is poorly documented, and it also tends to be subject to change between major Groovy versions. The best way that I've found of working with this DSL is to dig into the unit tests for the DSL itself. The tests demonstrate most of the capabilities of the DSL and will give you an insight into how to use them. See `https://github.com/groovy/groovy-core/blob/master/src/test/org/codehaus/groovy/ast/builder/AstBuilderFromSpecificationTest.groovy`.

Traits to the rescue

In the previous chapter, we encountered traits. We used a trait to apply pretty printing capabilities to a class. To do this, we needed to have our class implement the `trait` class. This means that pretty printing is a compile time dependency, which means the trait needs to be added to the class in the source code. The big benefit of the trait is the fact that we can neatly package the functionality we want to add into a `trait` class.

This is sort of what we are trying to do with our pretty print AST transformation. AST transformations happen at compile time, so what if we could extend a class with a trait as part of an AST transformation? This will save us a lot of AST node manipulation in the transformation. Fortunately, we can actually do this as the following example illustrates:

```
trait PrettyAwesomeTrait {
    void prettyPrint() {
        this.properties.sort { it.key }.each {
            if (it.key != 'prettyPrint' && it.key != 'class')
                println it.key + ": " + it.value
        }
    }
}


@Target([ElementType.TYPE])
@Retention(RetentionPolicy.SOURCE)
@GroovyASTTransformationClass(["PrettyAwesomeASTTransformation"])
public @interface PrettyAwesome {
}


@GroovyASTTransformation (phase = CompilePhase.SEMANTIC_ANALYSIS)
class PrettyAwesomeASTTransformation implements ASTTransformation,
CompilationUnitAware {

    def compilationUnit

    void visit(ASTNode[] nodes, SourceUnit source) {
        ClassNode classNode = nodes[1]

        def traitNode = ClassHelper.make(PrettyAwesomeTrait)
        if (!classNode.implementsInterface(traitNode)) {
            classNode.addInterface(traitNode)
            TraitComposer.doExtendTraits(
                classNode,source,compilationUnit)
        }
    }

    @Override
    void setCompilationUnit(CompilationUnit unit) {
        compilationUnit = unit
    }
}
```

Here, we create a class node for `PrettyAwesomeTrait` using the `ClassHelper` class. We don't want to add this trait if a class already extends it, so we check if the class already implements `PrettyAwesomeTrait` before continuing. If it does not, then we can programmatically add this interface to the class.

Because traits are not just a simple interface implementation, we also need to use the new `TraitComposer` class from Groovy 2.4.0. `TraitComposer` has the method `doExtendTraits`, which does all the heavy lifting for us to build the trait AST and generate all the delegation code that implements the trait. `TraitComposer` needs access to the `CompilationUnit` object, so we need to implement a new interface on our transformation class `CompilationUnitAware`. This interface provides a hook `setCompilationUnit`, which will be called by the compiler to give access to the compilation unit object in our transform:

```
@PrettyAwesome
class Customer {
    int id
    String firstName
    String surname
    String street
    String city
}

given:
def customer = new Customer(id:1001,firstName:"Fred",
surname:"Flintstone",
    street:"1 Rock Road",city:"Bedrock")

when:
        customer.prettyPrint()
then:
"""city: Bedrock
firstName: Fred
id: 1001
street: 1 Rock Road
surname: Flintstone""" == output()
```

Now, we have a `@PrettyAwesome` annotation that works as expected, except that it implements the `prettyPrint` method via trait. This is a really simple application of a trait in an AST. However, I encourage you to think of traits as a means of implementing AST transformations. Remember that unlike interfaces, traits are also able to contain properties, so they can seriously reduce the effort in implementing an AST transformation.

Global AST transformations

Next, we will look at a global AST transformation. Unlike the local transformations we have just encountered, which are targeted at a specific part of the Groovy code, a global transformation is invoked for all AST nodes in the compiled code. Let's take a look at a fully worked global AST transformation example.

A finite state machine DSL

We will be a bit brave with this transformation. In fact, the transformed AST code for this transformation will look nothing like the original compiled code. The goal of this AST transformation is to provide a mini DSL for defining finite state machines. The syntax we are aiming for takes its queue from Spock and uses labels and string literals to be part of the DSL syntax.

Let's start with a simple state machine example, a light controlled by a toggle switch. If the light is off and the switch is pressed, the light turns on and vice versa. Let's first of all express this in pseudo code:

```
state: "OFF"
state: "ON"

event: "toggle"
    when: "ON"
        next = "OFF"
    when: "OFF"
        next = "ON"
```

The preceding pseudo code adequately expresses the state machine for a toggle switch. There are two states, ON and OFF, and we can respond to one event, toggle. The interesting thing about this pseudo code is that it is also valid Groovy syntax. It's composed of some labels (`state:`, `event:`, `when:`), some literal strings (`"ON"`, `"OFF"`, `"toggle"`), and some assignments to a variable (`next = "ON"`).

As pure Groovy the preceding code is useless. Try pasting the preceding code into `groovyConsole` and see what it does. It will run without error, but the only thing it will report is that the result is `"ON"`, which is the evaluated result of the last line of code (`next = "ON"`).

Let's dissect the code a little further. Labels such as `state:` can be placed before any statement in Groovy. The only real use for a label in regular Groovy is as a means of breaking and continuing nested loops. We won't go into that here, it's a feature that is inherited from the Java language that allows you to build clever, but very difficult-to-debug loops. The useful thing about it, from our point of view, is that as a result of this syntax, we can usually stick a label next to almost any statement and then reinterpret the syntax in an AST transformation.

Similarly, placing a string literal in our code without an assignment is mostly a useless exercise. Pretty much the only use that you can make of this construct is to return an immutable string from a method or closure. However, with an AST transformation, we can query the content of the string and turn it into a syntactical element of a DSL.

The assignment to `next` in the preceding code example would result in a compile error if it were in any other scope because it would be interpreted as an assignment to an undeclared variable. However, within a Groovy script is considered to be an assignment to an undeclared variable in the binding scope, so it is legal.

We have some syntactically legal Groovy pseudo code that expresses how we would like a state machine to work. Compiled as it is, it does nothing useful. However, potentially, there are enough clues in this code for a clever DSL to be able to do the rest and transform this into something useful. Let's try doing this, but first let's look at a real piece of Groovy code that implements the toggle light switch state machine.

The state machine pattern

There are many state machine patterns we could use varying from complex to relatively simple. We will implement the toggle switch state machine in a simple pattern of Groovy classes. Once we have this pattern working, we will use this as a target end point for the state machine DSL once it is generated. The pattern we are using is based on the state pattern from the book: *Design Patterns, Elements of Reusable Object-Oriented Software, Addison Wesley*.

 Design Patterns, Elements of Reusable Object-Oriented Software, Addison Wesley written by Erich Gamma, Richard Helm, Ralph Johnson, and John Vlissides (ISBN: 0-201-63361-2).

What we will be aiming for is an AST transform that can parse the DSL at compile time and generate the classes needed to implement this pattern. I find it useful to build the target code that I expect from a transform first, so I have a full understanding of what the expected transformed outcome should be. In fact, in the example code pack, you will find three state machines implemented both in the straight Groovy pattern and with the DSL.

Let's look at the first state machine in detail as a Groovy pattern implementation. Our state machine has several elements as follows:

- **State context**: The context is a holder for the current state of the machine.

- **Concrete state classes**: We will have one concrete state class per available state in the machine. Each state has an event handler method for each event described in the machine. The state will respond to the event by setting the context to the next state in the machine. Note that in a Java version of this pattern, you would also have a `State` interface class. We don't need this in Groovy.

- **Client machine class**: This is the client object for the state machine. All client actions happen via this class. The client class will maintain one state context object for the current state of the machine, and it will implement an event handler method for each event in the machine.

Let's start by looking at the state context class. We declare one `state` property in the class and set its initial value to the off state:

```
class StateContext {
    def state = new OffState(this)
}
```

We need one state class for each of the states represented in the machine, so we implement `OffState` and `OnState` classes:

```
class OffState {
    def context
    OffState(context) {
        this.context = context
    }
    def toggle() {
        context.state = new OnState(context)
    }
    String toString() {
        "OFF"
    }
}


class OnState {
    def context
    OnState(context) {
        this.context = context
    }
```

```
    def toggle() {
        context.state = new OffState(context)
    }
    String toString() {
        "ON"
    }
}
```

Finally, we need the client class, which implements the finite state machine:

```
class LEDToggle {
    def context = new StateContext()
    def toggle() {
        context.state.toggle()
    }
    String getState() {
        context.state
    }
}
```

With all this in place, we can start to write some Spock unit tests to prove the state machine is working as expected:

```
given:
    def ledToggle = new LEDToggle()

expect:
    ledToggle.state == 'OFF'

when:
    ledToggle.toggle()
then:
    ledToggle.state == 'ON'

when:
    ledToggle.toggle()
then:
    ledToggle.state == 'OFF'
```

We have a basic state machine and some unit tests that prove it works as expected. Now, it's time to try and implement an AST transform that converts our previous state DSL into a working version of this pattern. The final proof that it is working is when we can run these tests against a state machine generated from the DSL.

A state machine AST transformation

Unlike the previous examples, we won't need an annotation class for a global AST transformation. AST transformation would get quite unwieldy if we tried to build all the logic into the AST transformation class, so we separate out the responsibilities into four classes:

- `StateMachineASTTransformation`: This is the `GroovyASTTransfromation` class similar to the ones we already encountered in our annotation-based examples.

- `StateMachineParser`: This class implements the `GroovyClassVisitor` interface. This class uses a visitor pattern to allow us to work on any part of the tree of AST nodes in our compiled source. The main responsibility of this class is to produce a simple data model to store the key elements of the state machine.

- `StateMachineModel`: This class stores the data model of the parsed state machine. It describes the possible states, the initial state, the available events, and the allowed transitions for each event.

- `StateMachineBuilder`: This class builds the new AST nodes we need to implement the state machine pattern.

```groovy
@GroovyASTTransformation (phase = CompilePhase.SEMANTIC_ANALYSIS)
class StateMachineASTTransformation implements ASTTransformation {
    def parser
    def builder

    void visit(ASTNode[] nodes, SourceUnit source) {
        if (!nodes) return
        if (!(nodes[0] instanceof ModuleNode)) return
        if (!source?.name?.endsWith('State.groovy')) {
            return
        }
        def model = new StateMachineModel()

        parser = new StatePatternParser(model)
        builder = new StatePatternBuilder(nodes, model)

        for (ClassNode classNode : nodes[0].classes) {
            classNode.visitContents(parser)
        }

        builder.buildStatePattern()

    }
}
```

Global AST transformations are potentially expensive in terms of CPU resources. The visit method of the global transformation will be called for every single AST node it encounters during compilation. For this reason, we want to limit our processing to just the module that contains our state machine DSL. In the preceding example, we check that the file ends with State.groovy. Another valid approach would be to limit the AST transformation to just sources from a particular source folder. Alternatively, the Groovy compiler does allow us to use custom file extensions.

The StateMachineASTTransformation class next creates an empty data model. The data model object is populated during parsing by a StatePatternParser object. Once the data model is populated, it will contain the list of states available in the state machine along a list of all the available events and what transitions are possible in response to these events:

```
class StateMachineModel {
    def states
    def events

    def StateMachineModel() {
        states = []
        events = [:]
    }
    def getInitialState() {
        states[0]
    }
    def addState( state ) {
        if (!states.contains(state))
            states << state
    }
    def addEvent(event) {
        events[ "$event" ] = [:]
    }
    def addTransition(event, transition, next) {
        events["$event"]["$transition"] = next
    }
    def getEvents() {
       events.keySet()
    }
    def getTransitionForState(event, state) {
        def transition = events["$event"]["_all"]
        if (!transition)
            transition = events["$event"]["$state"]
        transition
    }
}
```

The `StateMachineModel` class is really just a wrapper on some lists and maps that contain a representation of the state machine. It has convenience methods for adding the states, events, and transitions as they are encountered during parsing and for accessing these while building the new AST nodes. Next, we will look at how the parser builds the `StateMachineModel` object.

The `StateMachineParser` class is a concrete implementation of the `GroovyClassVisitor` interface. The `StateMachineASTTransformation.visit` method passes the parser each class node it finds to the `visitContents` method:

```
class StatePatternParser implements GroovyClassVisitor {
    def model
    def source

    StatePatternParser(stateMachineModel, sourceUnit) {
        this.model = stateMachineModel
        this.source = sourceUnit
    }
    @Override
    void visitClass(ClassNode node) {
    }
    @Override
    void visitMethod(MethodNode node) {
    // we only need this one
    }
    @Override
    void visitConstructor(ConstructorNode node) {
    }
    @Override
    void visitField(FieldNode node) {
    }
    @Override
    void visitProperty(PropertyNode node) {
    }
}
```

`StateMachineParser` must override all the visit methods available from `GroovyClassVisitor`, but for our purposes, the only one we need to really implement is `visitMethod`. This visitor will be invoked for each method that is encountered in the class.

In order to understand this code better, let's first remind ourselves of the syntax of our state machine DSL. The DSL can represent several different elements of the state machine as follows:

- **States**: The different states are declared with a label and a constant string. So, we are looking in the AST for statements that are constant expressions and have a label `state:`.

- **Events**: The events are declared with a label and string. So here, once again we are looking for constant expressions that have a label `event:`.

- **Transitions**: For each event, we need to define some transitions. We can have a default transition for an event, in which case the `event:` clause should be followed immediately by an assignment to next. Otherwise, it should be followed by one or more `when:` clauses, which define the individual allowable transitions.

Our `StateMachineParser.visitMethod` method looks like this. The Groovy script class that represents our DSL will have a `run` method, which represents the main body of code in the script itself. We limit our AST parsing to this method since this is where we expect to find the DSL code:

```
@Override
void visitMethod(MethodNode node) {
    if (node.name == "run") {
        def event = null
        def when = null
        collectStates(node)
        collectEvents(node)
        handleBaseErrors(node)
        node.code.statements.each { stmnt ->
            def param = getLabelParam(stmnt)

            switch (stmnt.statementLabel) {
                case 'event':
                    event = param
                    when = null
                    break
                case 'when':
                    handleWhenErrors(param, event, stmnt)
                    when = param
                    break
                default:
                    if (event) {
                        handleWhen(stmnt, event, when)
                        } else {
                            addError "Inappropriate syntax.",
                                stmnt, source
                    }
```

```
                    }
                }
            }
        }
```

The state machine DSL should contain at least two state declarations and at least one event declaration to make sense, so we start by collecting this in the model from the ModuleNode object. We do this by traversing all the statements in the ModuleNode object and find all statements that meet the following criteria. The statement is a constant expression, which has the label event for events or state for states:

```
def collectStates(MethodNode node) {
    collectLabeledConstantStrings(node, 'state').each { stmnt ->
        model.addState stmnt.expression.value.toString()
    }
}
def collectEvents(MethodNode node) {
    collectLabeledConstantStrings(node, 'event').each { stmnt ->
        model.addEvent stmnt.expression.value.toString()
    }
}
def collectLabeledConstantStrings(MethodNode node, label) {
    node.code.statements.findAll { stmnt ->
        stmnt instanceof ExpressionStatement &&
        stmnt.expression instanceof ConstantExpression &&
        stmnt.statementLabel &&
        stmnt.statementLabel == label
    }
}
```

Handling the transitions is a little more complex because statement ordering is important. The visitMethod method iterates all statements in the MethodNode object. If the statement we encounter is a labeled constant string, the getLabelParam method will return the constant string. So, the value returned will be state, event, when, or null, depending on whether we find a valid declaration or not:

```
def getLabelParam(stmnt) {
    if (stmnt instanceof ExpressionStatement &&
        stmnt.expression instanceof ConstantExpression &&
        stmnt.statementLabel
    ) {
        return stmnt.expression.value.toString()
    }
    null
}
```

As we traverse the statements in the module, we also record the occurrence of event: and when: clauses. This allows us to correctly handle the transition statement when we encounter it. A transition is declared by assigning a state to next, for example, next = "ON". The handleWhen method handles both the default transition case where no when: clause is provided and the when: clause itself.

```
def handleWhen(statement, event, transition) {
    if (statement instanceof ExpressionStatement &&
        statement.expression instanceof BinaryExpression) {
      BinaryExpression expr = statement.expression
      def var = expr.leftExpression
      Token oper = expr.operation
      def state = expr.rightExpression

      if ( var instanceof VariableExpression &&
           var.accessedVariable.name == 'next' &&
           oper instanceof Token &&
           oper.rootText == "=" &&
           state instanceof ConstantExpression
      ) {
        def next = state.value.toString()
        if (!model.states.contains(next))
          addError "Reference to non existent state",
                  state, source
        if (event && transition) {
          model.addTransition event, transition, next
        } else {
          model.addTransition event, '_all', next
        }
      } else {
          handleBadWhenExpression var, expr, state
      }
    } else {
        addError "when: or next = 'state' is allowed here",
                statement, source
    }
}
```

Here, we are looking in the AST for a binary expression where the left operand is a variable called `next`, the right operand is a constant and the operator is equals. If we find code in the AST that matches this, then we add the appropriate transitions to the model. In the preceding code you can clearly see how the AST is structured as a tree. If we do find the expression we are looking for—that is, `next = "ON"`, then this is composed in the tree as follows:

```
ExpressionStatement       next = "ON"
|_BinaryExpression         next = "ON"
  |_VariableExpression     next
  |_Token                  =
  |_ConstantExpression     "ON"
```

Handling errors – compile errors

Even though state machine DSL written in Groovy is a mini language in its own right. If we add inappropriate code into the source, it can have undesired effects. It's also possible for many potential syntax errors to occur, which could cause the transformed code to behave incorrectly or to fail to transform at all. As far as possible, we should predict all these potential error conditions and respond accordingly. The appropriate response in this case would be to generate compiler errors with an appropriate message and identify the location in the code, which is incorrect.

To help us with generating compiler errors, we are using a helper method in the `StateMachineParser` class, `addError`. This method is borrowed from the `LogASTTransformation`, which is part of the core Groovy sources. This helper method will produce a compile error in the compiler output that looks just like a regular `groovyc` compiler error:

```
def addError(String msg, ASTNode expr, SourceUnit source) {
    int line = expr.lineNumber
    int col = expr.columnNumber
    SyntaxException se =
        new SyntaxException(msg + '\n', line, col)
    SyntaxErrorMessage sem = new SyntaxErrorMessage(se, source)
    source.errorCollector.addErrorAndContinue(sem)
}
```

In the interest of brevity, this DSL example does not contain all the possible error handling we could do. Here are some of the ones we do handle. I'm sure you can think of more.

We should have two or more states and at least one event declared. You will also notice in the `handleWhen` method we encountered previously, we detect if a nonexistent state is referenced and add an error for that:

```groovy
def handleBaseErrors(node) {
    if (model.states.size() < 2)
        addError "State machine must have at least two states",
            node, source
    if (!model.events)
        addError "State machine must have at least one event",
            node, source
}
```

If we then build a toggle state machine that accidentally omits a state and then references that state, we will cause two compile errors to be generated:

```groovy
state: "ON"

event: "toggle"
    when: "ON"
        next = "OFF"
```

This will provide the following output:

```
ErrorState.groovy: -1: State machine must have at least two states
 @ line -1, column -1.
ErrorState.groovy: 7: Reference to non existent state
 @ line 7, column 16.
            next = "OFF"
                   ^
```

Declaring a `when:` clause without a state, or with a nonexistent state, or failing to use a `String` constant to represent, the state should cause an error:

```groovy
def handleWhenErrors(state, event, statement) {
    if (!state)
        addError "Expected state value after when:",
            statement, source
    if (state && !model.states.contains(state))
        addError "Cannot transition from a non existant state",
            statement.expression, source
    if (!event)
        addError "when: must follow event:", statement, source
}
```

```
    state: "ON"

    when: "ON"

    event: "toggle"
        when:
            next = "ON"
        when: "OFF"
            next = "ON"
```

This will provide the following output:

ErrorState.groovy: 5: when: must follow event:
@ line 5, column 7.
** when: "ON"**
**   ^**

ErrorState.groovy: 9: Expected state value after when:
@ line 9, column 9.
**   next = "ON"**
**   ^**

ErrorState.groovy: 10: Cannot transition from a non existant state
@ line 10, column 11.
**   when: "OFF"**
**   ^**

Providing any expression for a transition other than one in the form
next = 'state' should cause an appropriate error:

```
    def handleBadWhenExpression(next, expr, state) {
        def oper = expr.operation
        if (!next instanceof VariableExpression ||
            next.accessedVariable.name != 'next') {
            addError "assignment to next is only allowed",
                next, source
        } else if (oper instanceof Token || oper.rootText != "=") {
            addError "assignment operator is only allowed",
                expr, source
        } else if (!state instanceof ConstantExpression) {
            addError "assigning a valid state only allowed",
                state, source
        }
```

```
    }

    state: "ON"
    state: "OFF"

    event: "toggle"
        when: "ON"
            prev = "OFF"
        when: "OFF"
            next * "OFF"
```

This will provide the following output:

```
ErrorState.groovy: 9: assignment to next is only allowed
 @ line 9, column 9.
        prev = "OFF"
        ^

ErrorState.groovy: 11: assignment operator is only allowed
 @ line 11, column 9.
        next * "OFF"
        ^
```

Building the new AST nodes

Once the `StateMachineParser` class has done its magic, we should have a valid representation of the state machine in the `StateMachineModel` object. From this model, we need to build a new implementation of the state machine pattern. This will involve adding nodes to the AST for the various elements of the pattern.

We will need to generate a client class to implement the state machine itself. We will need a state context class, and we will need a concrete state class for each of the states. We also need to build methods to implement each of the events across all the state classes and the client class and to handle all the individual state transitions that are declared for each event.

We handle all of this in the `StateMachineBuilder` class. The `StateMachineBuilder` class is initialized with the new `StateMachineModel` object we built during parsing. It has a method `buildStatePattern` that does the work of building the pattern classes, but this is subsequently broken down into smaller steps. We will look at each step in detail:

```
class StatePatternBuilder {
    def model
```

```
    ModuleNode moduleNode
    ClassNode classNode
    String className
    ClassNode contextClass
    String contextClassName

    StatePatternBuilder(ASTNode[] nodes, stateMachineModel) {
        this.model = stateMachineModel
        moduleNode = nodes[0]
        classNode = nodes[0].classes[0]
        className = nodes[0].classes[0].nameWithoutPackage
    }

    void buildStatePattern() {
        buildContextClass()
        updateClientClass()
        buildStateClasses()
    }
    void buildContextClass() {
      ....
    }
    void updateClientClass() {
      ...
    }
    void buildStateClasses() {
      ...
    }
}
```

The StateMachinePattern class is initialized with the newly created model and the ASTNode object passed into the transform. For convenience, we extract some objects from the AST and save them locally. This will save us dereferencing them from the AST later. In the pattern, the one class that is referenced across all three components of the pattern is the StateContext class, so this is the first thing we will build:

```
void buildContextClass() {
    def contextClassNode = new AstBuilder().buildFromString
        CompilePhase.SEMANTIC_ANALYSIS, true, """
class ${className}Context {
}
"""

    contextClass = contextClassNode[1]
    moduleNode.addClass(contextClassNode[1])
```

```
    contextClassName = "${className}Context"

    contextClassNode[1].addProperty(
        new PropertyNode(
            "state",
            Modifier.PUBLIC,
            ClassHelper.DYNAMIC_TYPE,
            ClassHelper.make(contextClassName),
            new ConstructorCallExpression(
                ClassHelper.make(
                    "${model.initialState}${className}"
                ),
                new ArgumentListExpression(
                    new VariableExpression('this')
                )
            ),
            null,
            null
        )
    )
}
```

The first thing you will notice here is we use `ASTBuilder.buildFromString`. This is yet another mechanism in the `ASTBuilder` class that is available to us. Using this method, we can formulate the code we need in text and pass it in. `ASTBuilder` will take care of the parsing of this into whatever AST nodes it contains. In this case, this is a `ClassNode` object for the context class. We then make use of this class node with the regular APIs to add the state property, the `StateContext` class. Note that the actual class name of the context class will be derived from the DSL script class name. So, for instance, the toggle example will produce a class called `LEDToggleStateContext`.

The reason we need to use the base APIs here is down to the code we need to generate for the initialization of the state property. We need to add the expression `def state = new InitialState(this)`. The `InitialState` class will be the class for whatever the initial state should be. In the case of the toggle switch, it will be `OFFState`. The problem is that we don't have that class created anywhere yet. If we tried to build the entire state context class using `ASTBuilder.buildFromCode`, then we will get a class not found exception for `InitialState`.

What we have is a classic chicken and egg situation. There is nowhere in the pattern that we can start where we will not encounter the need to reference another pattern class that is not created yet. The solution that you are seeing in the preceding code is where we use `ClassHelper.make(String)` to make a `ClassNode`, which references the as yet uncompleted class. What we end up with at the end of this builder method is an AST structure as follows for the state context class:

```
ClassNode                        class StateContext
|_PropertyNode                   def state
  |_ConstructorCallExpression    new InitalState
   _ArgumentListExpression       this
```

Our DSL does not have a specific means to declare an initial state, so we just assume the first state encountered in the DSL will be the initial default state. The `StateMachineModel` class implements this via the `getInitialState` method.

This newly created `ClassNode` is added to the AST from the module. Now we need a class to implement the client class for the state machine pattern. We won't create a new class node for this. Instead, we will make use of the class created by the compiler for the module. For instance, if our DSL code is in `LEDToggleState.groovy`, we will already have a class `LEDToggleState` in the AST, which is in fact the class that has the `run` method from which we parsed the state machine code.

The next method we encounter in `StateMachineBuilder` is `updateChildClass`. This method adds the elements necessary to the DSL class to turn it into the client class of the state machine:

```
void updateClientClass() {
    buildClientContextProperty()
    buildClientStateGetter()
    buildClientEventMethods()
}

def buildClientContextProperty() {
    classNode.addProperty(
        new PropertyNode(
            "context",
            Modifier.PUBLIC,
            ClassHelper.make(contextClassName),
            ClassHelper.make(className),
            new ConstructorCallExpression(
```

```
                          ClassHelper.make(contextClassName),
                          ArgumentListExpression.EMPTY_ARGUMENTS
                    ),
                    null,
                    null
              )
        )
}
```

The first thing we need in the client class is a property to represent the context object for the state machine. This property is a state context object, which will always contain the current state of the machine. Next, we add a getter for the current state of the machine:

```
def buildClientStateGetter() {
    def callGetContextState = new ExpressionStatement(
        new MethodCallExpression(
            new MethodCallExpression(
                new VariableExpression("context"),
                new ConstantExpression("getState"),
                ArgumentListExpression.EMPTY_ARGUMENTS
            ),
            "toString",
            ArgumentListExpression.EMPTY_ARGUMENTS
        )
    )

    classNode.addMethod(new MethodNode(
        "getState",
        Modifier.PUBLIC,
        null,
        new Parameter[0],
        null,
        callGetContextState
      )
    )
}
```

The `getState` method returns the state of the context object as a string. The code we are looking to generate for the body of the methods therefore is `context.getState().toString()`. In the AST, the nodes needed for the method needs to be in the following structure:

```
MethodNode                             getState()
|_ExpressionStatement
  |_MethodCallExpression               toString()
    |_MethodCallExpression             getState()
    | |_VariableExpression             context
```

```
|  |_ConstantExpression          getState
|  |_ArgumentListExpression
   |_ArgumentListExpression
```

Note how the `toString()` and `getState()` calls in the method body are nested. The `toString()` method is called on the result of the `getState()` call. You can imagine artificially adding scoping brackets around the code to reflect precedence of method calling. Each of the following expressions is equivalent. The last expression however best reflects how the individual expressions are structured in the AST. The outer expressions will be at the top of the AST, whereas the inner expressions will be nested in the following code:

```
context.state.toString()
(context).getState().toString()
((context).(getState)()).(toString)()
```

The last thing we need to do to the client class is add methods for each of the event handlers. These event handler methods simply delegate calls to the equivalent event handler in the current state so the body of a `toggle()` event handler method will just be `context.state.toggle()`:

```
def buildClientEventMethods() {
    for (event in model.events) {
        def methodStatement = new ExpressionStatement(
            new MethodCallExpression(
                new MethodCallExpression(
                    new VariableExpression('context'),
                    new ConstantExpression('getState'),
                    ArgumentListExpression.EMPTY_ARGUMENTS
                ),
                new ConstantExpression("${event}"),
                ArgumentListExpression.EMPTY_ARGUMENTS
            )
        )
        def eventMethodNode = new MethodNode(
            "${event}",
            Modifier.PUBLIC,
            null,
            new Parameter[0],
            null,
            methodStatement
        )
        classNode.addMethod(eventMethodNode)
    }
}
```

This builder method is very similar to the `buildClientStateGetter` method. It iterates all events in the model, creates the body of the method, then creates a new method node with this body and adds it to the class node.

The final thing the `StateMachineBuilder` class needs to do is to create the state classes themselves. We iterate each state in the model, create a state class, and add event handlers for each event in the model:

```
def buildStateClasses() {
    for (state in model.states) {
        def stateNode = buildStateClass(state)
        for (event in model.events) {
            buildStateClassEventMethod(event, state, stateNode)
        }
        moduleNode.addClass(stateNode[1])
    }
}
```

Building the state class is very similar to building the state context class. We use `ASTBuilder.buildFromString` and provide a completed class definition minus the event methods:

```
def buildStateClass(state) {
    def stateClassNode = new AstBuilder().buildFromString
            CompilePhase.SEMANTIC_ANALYSIS, true, """
class ${state}${className} {
    def context
    ${state}${className}(context) {
        this.context = context
    }
    String toString() {
        "${state}"
    }
}
"""
    stateClassNode
}
```

Next, we add the event methods in the usual way. For the individual event methods in states, we need to cater to the allowed transitions. If a state transition is allowed for this state/event pair, then we need to insert the code for that as the method body:

```
def buildStateClassEventMethod(event, state, stateClassNode) {
    def methodStatement = null
    def nextState = model.getTransitionForState(event, state)
    if (nextState) {
```

```
        methodStatement = new ExpressionStatement(
            new BinaryExpression(
                new PropertyExpression(
                    new VariableExpression("context"),
                    new ConstantExpression("state")
                ),
                new Token(Types.EQUALS, "=", -1, -1),
                new ConstructorCallExpression(
                    ClassHelper.make("$nextState$className"),
                    new ArgumentListExpression(
                        new VariableExpression('context')
                    )
                ),
            )
        )
    }
    def eventMethodNode = new MethodNode(
        "${event}",
        Modifier.PUBLIC,
        null,
        new Parameter[0],
        null,
        methodStatement
    )
    stateClassNode[1].addMethod(eventMethodNode)
}
```

The expression we need to add to an event method for a state transition must set the state property of the context class to the next state. So, for instance, the toggle event of an OFFState needs to be context.state = new ONState(context). We build an AST structure as follows:

```
MethodNode                      toggle()
|_ExpressionStatement           (expr)
  |_BinaryExpression            (expr) = (expr)
    |_PropertyExpression        (context).(state)
    | |_VariableExpression      context
    | |_ConstantExpression      state
    |_Token                     =
    |_ConstructorCallExpression new ONState
      |_ArgumentListExpression  context
```

Testing the state machine DSL

With our state machine complete, we hope now that it will work as well as the hand crafted pattern, which fortunately it does. We can test that by modifying the Spock test used for the original state pattern classes. All we need to do is change the class name to the name of the DSL script:

```
given:
def ledToggle = new LEDToggleState()

expect:
ledToggle.state == 'OFF'

when:
ledToggle.toggle()
then:
ledToggle.state == 'ON'

when:
ledToggle.toggle()
then:
ledToggle.state == 'OFF'
```

However, what's even better is that we now have a reusable DSL for building state machines. What would a regular ON/OFF light switch look like in this DSL?

```
state: "OFF"
state: "ON"

event: "switchOn"
        next = "ON"

event: "switchOff"
        next = "OFF"
```

Note here how we can omit the `when:` clause from the DSL because the next state when we switch on is always on and when we switch off is always off. We can write a test to confirm this also works as we expect it:

```
given:
    def ledSwitch = new LEDSwitchState()

expect:
    ledSwitch.state == 'OFF'

when:
```

```
        ledSwitch.switchOn()
then:
        ledSwitch.state == 'ON'

when:
        ledSwitch.switchOn()
then:
        ledSwitch.state == 'ON'

when:
        ledSwitch.switchOff()
then:
        ledSwitch.state == 'OFF'

when:
        ledSwitch.switchOff()
then:
        ledSwitch.state == 'OFF'
```

Both these state machines use just two states. What if we have a more complex state machine with multiple states, events, and transitions? The following is a state machine that mimics the operation of an old cassette type tape machine:

```
state: "EMPTY"
state: "LOADED"
state: "RUNNING"
state: "PAUSED"

event: "load"
    when: "EMPTY"
        next = "LOADED"

event: "start"
    when: "LOADED"
        next = "RUNNING"
    when: "PAUSED"
        next = "RUNNING"

event: "pause"
    when: "RUNNING"
        next = "PAUSED"

event: "stop"
    when: "RUNNING"
        next = "LOADED"
```

```
        when: "PAUSED"
            next = "LOADED"

    event: "unload"
        when: "LOADED"
            next = "EMPTY"
```

Those old tape decks were quite stateful. You could only press pause if the tape was running. You could only unload a tape if the tape was loaded but not running or paused. There is a full state pattern version of the tape deck example in the example code. Have a look; it has six classes and over a hundred lines of code. Yet this complexity was all captured earlier in less than 25 lines of code. It also behaves exactly as we expect. Here are just some of the allowed transitions in action. The examples have a full test for them all:

```
given:
    def tape = new TapeDeckState()
expect:
    tape.state == 'EMPTY'

when:
    tape.load()
then:
    tape.state == 'LOADED'

when:
    tape.start()
then:
    tape.state == 'RUNNING'

when:
    tape.start()
    tape.pause()
then:
    tape.state == 'PAUSED'

when:
    tape.start()

when:
    tape.pause()
    tape.stop()
then:
    tape.state == 'LOADED'
```

Compiling and packaging an AST transformation

Within the code examples in this chapter, we have two categories of code, the code implementing the AST transformations, for example, `PrettyAwesome`, `PrettyAwesomeASTTransformation`, `PrettyAwesomeTrait`, and the code, which is being transformed by the transform. However, when we try to run these examples, we need to be aware of when in the compilation process each is used, so we can package them appropriately.

The first thing to be aware of is that the AST transformation code is used in the compilation process, and in effect, becomes an extension of the compiler. This means that in order to use the AST transformation the compiler must already have access to a compiled version of that code. So, we cannot simply have the AST transformation code and the target class in the same source package and hope it will work. If we do this, the AST transform will get compiled, but it will be invisible to the compiler at that point and won't get applied to the target class.

If we take a look at the example code package, we can see how this is circumvented. The example code is built using Gradle and has two distinct compilation tasks. The first, `compileGroovy` compiles all sources in the `src/main/groovy` directories. The second, `compileTestGroovy` compiles all sources in the `src/test/groovy` directories.

For the purposes of the book examples, we only care if the AST transformations are available in the test package. This means we can separate the two parts of the code by placing the AST transformations in `src/main` and the target classes in `src/test`. When we run the tests, the AST transformations are first compiled by the `compileGroovy` task and then the target classes are complied by the `compileTestGroovy` task at which point the AST transformations are available for use.

When implementing your own AST transforms, you will want to package them in such a way as they can be consumed as a dependency by your application. The Groovy AST class files can be packaged into a separate JAR file. For a local AST, this is all you need to do. For a global AST transformation, you need to tell the compiler where to find your transformation. The compiler looks for the `org.codehaus.groovy.transform.ASTTransformation` file in the `META-INF/services` directory of your JAR file. This file should contain the fully qualified package and name of the AST transformation class. So, for our state machine transformation, in the examples pack this might be:

```
com.dearle.groovydsl.transforms.StateMachineASTTransformation
```

We mentioned earlier that the Groovy compiler supports custom file extensions. If we add a META-INF/services/org.codehaus.groovy.source.Extensions file to our JAR with a list of file extensions we want to support, then the compiler will also compile any files it finds with these extensions.

Summary

This chapter has been quite a deep dive into the relatively complex subject of AST transformations. We've covered both local and global AST transformations and even used AST transformation to build a mini DSL.

In the next chapter, we will look at some of the publicly available Groovy DSLs. We will describe how to use them, but we will also be taking a critical view of how they might be implemented given the knowledge we now have about the Groovy MOP and Groovy AST transformations.

Existing Groovy DSLs

By now, we have covered a lot of ground in describing the DSL-enabling features of Groovy. In this chapter, we will look at two of the existing Groovy DSLs that are freely available for download. The purpose of this chapter is not to try to give a comprehensive tutorial on either of them. We will explore each in turn in order to understand how they work, but more importantly, we will go through them in order to understand how they are implemented using the Groovy features and techniques that we have covered in the book so far. In this chapter, we will discuss:

- **Grails object relational mapping (GORM),** which is a core component of the Grails web application framework and uses DSL-style techniques to apply persistence to regular Groovy classes. We will be looking at how GORM decorates regular POGO classes to add persistence semantics to them.

- Spock, which is a **behavior-driven development (BDD)** tool. We have already encountered Spock throughout the book. In this chapter, we will look at how the Spock framework implements its DSL-style features.

Grails object relational mapping – GORM

The Grails framework is an open source web application framework built for the Groovy language. Grails not only leverages Hibernate under the covers as its persistence layer, but also implements its own object relational mapping layer for Groovy, known as **GORM**. With GORM, we can take a POGO class and decorate it with DSL-like settings in order to control how it is persisted. GORM can be considered a DSL as it uses many of the cool DSL features that we have discussed in previous chapters, in order to add its own mini dialect to Groovy in order to implement persistence.

Grails programmers use GORM classes as a mini language for describing the persistent objects in their application. In this section, we will do a whistle-stop tour of the features of Grails. This won't be a tutorial on building Grails applications, as the subject is too big to be covered here. Our main focus will be on how GORM implements its object model in the domain classes.

Grails quick start

Before we proceed, we need to install Grails and get a basic app installation up and running. We can use GVMTool to install Grails. Once it has been installed, navigate to a workspace directory and issue the `grails create-app` command:

```
$gvm install grails 3.0.0.RC3$cd ~/workspace

$grails create-app GroovyDSL

cd GroovyDSL

grails run-app
```

This builds a Grails application tree called `GroovyDSL` under your current workspace directory. If we now navigate to this directory, we can launch the Grails app. By default, the app will display a welcome page at `http://localhost:8080`.

[

The example code already has a `GroovyDSL` Grails app created in the `GroovyDSL` subdirectory.
]

The grails-app directory

The `GroovyDSL` application that we built earlier has a `grails-app` subdirectory, which is where the application source files for our application will reside. We only need to concern ourselves with the `grails-app/domain` directory for this discussion, but it's worth understanding a little about some of the other important directories:

- `grails-app/conf`: This is where the Grails configuration files reside.
- `grails-app/controllers`: Grails uses a **Model View Controller** (**MVC**) architecture. The controller directory will contain the Groovy controller code for our UIs.
- `grails-app/domain`: This is where Grails stores the GORM model classes of the application.
- `grails-app/services`: Any classes found here will be assumed to be service beans.
- `grails-app/view`: This is where the **Groovy Server Pages** (**GSPs**), the Grails equivalent to JSPs are stored.

Grails has a number of shortcut commands that allow us to quickly build out the objects for our model.

 In this section, we will take a whistle-stop tour through GORM. You might like to dig deeper into both GORM and Grails yourself. You can find further online documentation for GORM at `https://grails.github.io/grails-doc/latest/guide/GORM.html`.

Building a GORM model

The `grails` command can be used as a shortcut to carve out GORM domain classes. We can create a domain class for `Customer` by issuing the following `grails` command from the `GroovyDSL` application directory:

```
grails create-domain-class Customer
```

This will create a stub `Customer.groovy` file in the `grails-app/domain` directory, as follows:

```
class Customer {

package groovydsl

class Customer {

    static constraints = {
    }
}
```

If we add some fields to this class, we can peek into the database to see how GORM automatically creates a table for this class:

```
class Customer {
    String firstName
    String lastName
    static constraints = {
    }
}
```

Now, if we restart Grails by issuing the `grails run-app` command, we can inspect the resulting table. If we are running grails in development mode as shown in the preceding code, we can access the H2 database console with `http://localhost:8080/dbconsole`.

GORM has automatically created a customer table for us in the devDB database. The table has two fields by default, for the row id and the object version. The two fields we added to Customer have been mapped to the first_name and last_name fields of type varchar(255) columns in the database.

Using domain classes

If the Customer class was a normal POGO class, this will only allow us to construct it and interact with its properties at this point. However, Grails has added some persistence methods to the Customer class. We won't build a full-blown Grails app with controllers and views in this chapter, but we have several options for exercising our GORM objects without that. The first is to use Groovy Console. To do so, we need to launch it indirectly via the grails command:

```
$grails console
```

This will launch the groovyConsole app we've used before with the GORM objects fully ready to use. I recommend this as a great way to explore your GORM objects and see how they work. In keeping with the rest of the book, we will illustrate how the GORM persistence methods work with a Spock test. We will want a Spock integration test that actually uses GORM persistence rather that a unit test that uses mocks. We can create a template integration test for the Customer class from the grails command line:

```
$grails create-integration-test Customer
```

Next, we edit this to add some interactions with the GORM persistence model for Customer:

```
@Integration
@Rollback
class CustomerSpec extends Specification {
  void "Gorm has added methods for persistence"() {
    given: "We save a domain object with save"
    def barney = new Customer(firstName: "Barney",
    lastName: "Rubble")
    barney.save()

    when: "we get it from the database"
    def fred = Customer.get(1)

    then:
    fred.firstName == "Barney"
```

```
    when:
    fred.firstName = "Freddie"
    fred.save()

    def customers = Customer.list()

    then:
    customers[0].firstName == 'Freddie'
  }
}
```

The preceding example saves a new customer `"Barney"` to the database, gets the customer object for `"Fred"`, and updates the `firstName` field. The `list` method returns all customers as a regular list collection.

Let's take a second to look at what Grails has done to our class. The `Customer` class that we declared had no base class to inherit methods from, and it did not define these methods. Grails has somehow used the features Groovy to add these methods. Given what we know already from previous chapters, we can probably guess some of the ways this might have been achieved.

We know that we can add methods to a class at runtime via `metaClass`. So, this might be one approach:

```
Customer.metaClass.static.get = { ... }
Customer.metaClass.static.list = { ... }
Customer.metaClass.save = { ... }
```

Grails is built on top of Spring, so we could hook into the initialization of `ApplicationContext` and enhance the `Customer` `metaClass` directly with the properties and methods we need to implement persistence. An alternative approach, as we have learned, is that we could use an AST transformation to add the individual methods to the `Customer` class at compile time.

A third and better approach would be to declare a trait for persistence, which could have the additional persistence properties we need such as `ID` and `VERSION` and the additional persistence methods such as `save()`, `list()`, and `get()`. This trait could then be added to the `Customer` class via a Global AST transformation.

Grails uses the convention that all classes in the `grails-app/domain` folder are considered to be domain classes that should be persistent. So, if we were to use the build system to compile all classes in the domain folder in one compilation task, and if we were to apply a Global AST transformation during this compilation, then we could enhance all the domain classes as we pleased.

So what does Grails actually do? The answer is all of the tasks mentioned earlier, depending on which version of Grails you look at. The 1.x.x versions of Grails took the `metaClass` approach and added methods at runtime into all the domain classes. By version 2.x.x, some new requirements were being considered for GORM within the Groovy eco system, including the ability to use GORM as a standalone persistence layer outside Grails.

This led to the rewriting of the GORM enhancement methods so that GORM persistence could be added to a class via an `@Entity` annotation. To do this, the injection of the GORM operations such as `count()`, `save()`, `get()`, and so on were refactored into an AST transformation.

In Grails 2.x.x the GORM operations, methods were fully implemented in a standalone API class. At compile time, the AST transformations would take over and clone the fully formed properties and methods from the AST nodes of the API class and inject them into the domain classes. This is a common pattern that is used in the 2.x.x Grails sources to enhance all the Grails artifact classes. It saves building out the AST manually using `ASTBuilder` or the AST APIs directly. In Grails 3.x.x, this is being improved even further by turning these API classes into traits that can be applied to the artifact classes via AST transformations.

Modeling relationships

Storing and retrieving simple objects is all very well, but the real power of GORM is that it allows us to model the relationships between objects, as we will now see. The main types of relationships that we want to model are **associations**, where one object has an associated relationship with another, for example, `Customer` and `Account`; **composition relationships**, where we want to build an object from subcomponents; and **inheritance**, where we want to model similar objects by describing their common properties in a base class.

Associations

Every business system involves some sort of association between the main business objects. Relationships between objects can be one-to-one, one-to-many, or many-to-many. Relationships may also imply ownership, where one object only has relevance in relation to another parent object.

If we model our domain directly in the database, we need to build and manage tables, and make associations between the tables by using foreign keys. For complex relationships, including many-to-many relationships, we may need to build special tables whose sole function is to contain the foreign keys needed to track the relationships between objects. Using GORM, we can model all of the various associations that we need to establish between objects directly within the GORM class definitions. GORM takes care of all of the complex mappings to tables and foreign keys through a Hibernate persistence layer.

One-to-one

The simplest association that we need to model in GORM is a one-to-one association. Suppose our customer can have a single address, we will create a new Address domain class using the `grails create-domain-class` command, as before:

```
class Address {
    String street
    String city
}
```

To create the simplest one-to-one relationship with Customer, we just add an Address field to the Customer class:

```
class CustomerHasAddress {
    String firstName
    String lastName
    Address address
}
```

When we rerun the Grails application, GORM will recreate a new address table. It will also recognize the address field of CustomerHasAddress as an association with the Address class, and create a foreign key relationship between the customer and address tables accordingly.

This is a one-directional relationship. We are saying that a Customer "has an" Address but an Address class does not necessarily "have a" Customer.

We can model bi-directional associations by simply adding a Customer field to the Address class. This will then be reflected in the relational model by GORM adding a customer_id field to the address table:

```
class Address {
    String street
    String city
    CustomerHasAddress customer
}
```

These basic one-to-one associations can be inferred by GORM just by interrogating the fields in each domain class. To denote ownership in a relationship, GORM uses an optional static field applied to a domain class called `belongsTo`. Suppose we add an `Identity` class to retain the login identity of a customer in the application. We would then use:

```
class CustomerHasIdentity {
    String firstName
    String lastName
    Address address
    Identity identity
}

class Address {
    String street
    String city
}

class Identity {
    String email
    String password

    static belongsTo = CustomerHasIdentity
}
```

 Classes are first-class citizens in the Groovy language. When we declare `static belongsTo = Customer`, what we are actually doing is storing a static instance of a `java.lang.Class` object for the `Customer` class in the `belongsTo` field. Grails can interrogate this static field at load time to infer the ownership relation between `Identity` and `Customer`.

Here we have three classes: `CustomerHasIdentity`, `Address`, and `Identity`. `CustomerHasIdentity` has a one-to-one association with both `Address` and `Identity` through the `address` and `identity` fields. However, the `ident` field is "owned" by `CustomerHasIdentity` as indicated in the `belongsTo` setting. What this means is that saves, updates, and deletes will be cascaded to `identity` but not to `address`, as we can see in the following code. The `addr` object needs to be saved and deleted independently of `CustomerHasIdentity`, but `id` is automatically saved and deleted in sync with `Customer`:

```
void "belongsTo causes cascaded delete"() {
    given:
    def addr = new Address(street:"1 Rock Road", city:"Bedrock")
    def id = new Identity(email:"email", password:"password")
    def fred = new CustomerHasIdentity(firstName:"Fred",
        lastName:"Flintstone",
        address:addr,identity:id)

    addr.save(flush:true, failOnError: true)

    expect: "Only an address is saved"
    CustomerHasIdentity.count() == 0
    Address.count() == 1
    Identity.count() == 0

    when:
    fred.save(flush:true, failOnError: true)

    then: "Customer is save and save was cascaded to Identity"
    CustomerHasIdentity.count() == 1
    Address.count() == 1
    Identity.count() == 1

    when:
    fred.delete(flush:true, failOnError: true)

    then: "Customer deleted an delete was cascaded to identity"
    CustomerHasIdentity.count() == 0
    Address.count() == 1
    Identity.count() == 0

    when:
    addr.delete(flush:true, failOnError: true)

    then: "Now everything is deleted"
    CustomerHasIdentity.count() == 0
    Address.count() == 0
    Identity.count() == 0
}
```

Constraints

You will have noticed that every domain class produced by the `grails create-domain-class` command contains an empty static closure, `constraints`. We can use this closure to set the constraints on any field in our model. Here, we apply constraints to the e-mail and password fields of `Identity`. We want an e-mail field to be unique, not blank, and not nullable. The password field should be 6 to 200 characters long, not blank, and not nullable:

```
class Identity {
    String email
    String password

    static constraints = {
        email(unique: true, blank: false, nullable: false)
        password(blank: false, nullable:false, size:6..200)
    }
}
```

From our knowledge of builders and the markup pattern, we can see that GORM could be using a similar strategy here to apply constraints to the domain class. It looks like a pretended method is provided for each field in the class that accepts a map as an argument. The map entries are interpreted as constraints to apply to the model field.

The builder pattern turns out to be a good guess as to how GORM is implementing this. GORM actually implements constraints through a builder class called `ConstrainedPropertyBuilder`. The closure that gets assigned to `constraints` is in fact some markup style closure code for this builder. Before executing the `constraints` closure, GORM sets an instance of `ConstrainedPropertyBuilder` to be the delegate for the closure. We are more accustomed to seeing builder code where the `Builder` instance is visible:

```
def builder = new ConstrainedPropertyBuilder()
builder.constraints {
}
```

Setting the builder as a delegate of any closure allows us to execute the closure as if it was coded in the previous style. The `constraints` closure can be run at any time by Grails, and as it executes `ConstrainedPropertyBuilder`, it will build a `HashMap` of the constraints it encounters for each field.

We can illustrate the same technique by using `MarkupBuilder`. The `Markup` class in the following code snippet just declares a static closure named `markup`. Later on, we can use this closure with whatever builder we want, by setting the delegate of the `markup` to the builder that we would like to use:

```
given:
Markup.markup.setDelegate(new groovy.xml.MarkupBuilder())

when:
Markup.markup() // Outputs xml

then:
"""<customers>
  <customer id='1001'>
    <name firstName='Fred' surname='Flintstone' />
    <address street='1 Rock Road' city='Bedrock' />
  </customer>
  <customer id='1002'>
    <name firstName='Barney' surname='Rubble' />
    <address street='2 Rock Road' city='Bedrock' />
  </customer>
</customers>""" == output()
```

One-to-many

A one-to-many relationship applies when an instance of class such as `CustomerWithInvoice` is associated with many instances of another class. For example, a customer may have many different invoices in the system, and an invoice might have a sale order object for each line on the invoice:

```
class CustomerWithInvoice {
    String firstName
    String lastName
    static hasMany = [invoices:Invoice]
}

class Invoice {
    static hasMany = [orders:SalesOrder]
}

class SalesOrder {
    String sku
    int amount
    Double price
    static belongsTo = Invoice
}
```

To indicate the "has many" associations between `Customer`/`Invoice` and `Invoice`/`SalesOrder`, we insert a static `hasMany` setting. We can also indicate ownership by using the `belongsTo` setting. In the preceding example, a sales order line has no relevance except on an invoice. We apply a `belongsTo` setting to bind it to the invoice. The `belongsTo` setting will cause `deletes` to cascade when the owning object is deleted. If an invoice is deleted, the `delete` will cascade to the sales order lines. `Invoice` does not belong to `Customer`; so for auditing purposes, the invoice object will not be automatically deleted even if the customer is removed.

From the Groovy DSL point of view, `hasMany` is just a static table containing a `map` of IDs and `Class` objects. GORM can analyze this map at load time in order to create the correct table mappings.

GORM will automatically take care of the mapping between the `Customer`, `Invoice`, and `SalesOrder` classes by creating `invoice_sales_order` and `customer_invoice` join tables.

`Customer` objects are linked to `Invoice` objects through the `customer_invoice` join table. `Invoices` are linked to `sales orders` via the `invoice_sales_order` join table, using foreign keys.

The `hasMany` setting is defined as a `Map` containing a key and class for each domain object that is associated. For each `hasMany` key encountered on a domain class, GORM will inject an `addTo(key)` method. This translates to an `addToOrders` method, which is added to `Invoice`, as the key used was `Orders` and an `addToInvoices` method is added to `Customer`. Invoking these methods will automatically save an order or invoice in the database and also update the join tables with the correct keys:

```
given:
def fred = new CustomerWithInvoices(firstName:"Fred",
lastName:"Flintstone")
fred.save(flush:true, failOnError: true)

expect:
CustomerWithInvoices.count() == 1
Invoice.count() == 0
SalesOrder.count() == 0

when:
def invoice = new Invoice()
invoice.addToOrders(new SalesOrder(sku:"productid01",
                                  amount:1, price:1.00))
```

```
invoice.addToOrders(new SalesOrder(sku:"productid02",
                                   amount:3, price:1.50))
invoice.addToOrders(new SalesOrder(sku:"productid03",
                                   amount:2, price:5.00))

then: "Invoice or sales orders are not yet persisted"
CustomerWithInvoices.count() == 1
Invoice.count() == 0
SalesOrder.count() == 0

when:
fred.addToInvoices(invoice)
fred.save(flush:true, failOnError: true)

then: "Saving cascades to invoice and sales orders"
CustomerWithInvoices.count() == 1
Invoice.count() == 1
SalesOrder.count() == 3
```

Many-to-many

Many-to-many associations are rarer than any of the other associations, and can be tricky to model. In GORM, all we need to do is to make the association bi-directional and give ownership to one side by applying a belongsTo setting. GORM will take care of the rest.

A tunes database needs to model the fact that artistes perform on many songs but also that artistes collaborate on songs, so songs can have many artistes. Modeling this in GORM is the essence of simplicity:

```
class Artist {
    String name
    static hasMany = [songs:Song]
}

class Song {
    String title
    static belongsTo = Artist
    static hasMany = [artists: Artist]
}
```

When maintaining a database, it does not matter whether we add songs to artistes or artistes to songs—GORM will maintain both sides of the relationship:

```
given:
def richWoman = new Song(title:"Rich Woman")
def killingTheBlues = new Song(title:"Killing the Blues")

def jimmyPage = new Artist(name:"Jimmy Page")
def alisonKrauss = new Artist(name:"Alison Krauss")

when:
richWoman.addToArtists(jimmyPage)
richWoman.addToArtists(alisonKrauss)
jimmyPage.addToSongs(killingTheBlues)
alisonKrauss.addToSongs(killingTheBlues)

and:
jimmyPage.save()
alisonKrauss.save()

then:
["Rich Woman","Killing the Blues"] ==
        jimmyPage.songs.collect { it.title }
["Rich Woman","Killing the Blues"] ==
        alisonKrauss.songs.collect { it.title }

["Jimmy Page", "Alison Krauss"] ==
        richWoman.artists.collect { it.name }
["Jimmy Page", "Alison Krauss"] ==
        killingTheBlues.artists.collect { it.name }
```

We add both artistes to `richWoman` and then add `killingTheBlues` to both artistes. We only need to save the artiste objects that are the owners of the relationships, and all associations are preserved.

Composition

Composition is used when, instead of having separate tables for each business object, we would like to embed the fields of a child object in the table of its parent. In the previous one-to-one examples, it might be useful for us to have `Address` and `Identity` classes to pass around in our Groovy code, but we may prefer the data for these to be rolled into one database table. To do this, all we need to do is to add an `embedded` setting to the `Customer` domain class, and GORM takes care of the rest:

```
class Customer {
    String firstName
    String lastName
    Address billing
    Address shipping
    Identity ident
    static embedded = ['billing','shipping','ident']
}

class Address {
    String street
    String city
}

class Identity {
    String email
    String password
}
```

We can see a useful application of embedding in the previous code snippet, where we needed two addresses—one for billing and one for shipping. This does not warrant a full one-to-many association between `Customer` and `Address` because we only ever have the two addresses. The fields from `Address` and `Identity` get mapped into columns in the `customer` table.

Inheritance

By default, GORM implements inheritance relationships with a table-per-hierarchy. A class column in the table is used as a discriminator column:

```
class Account {
    double balance
}

class CardAccount extends Account {
    String cardId
}

class CreditAccount extends Account{
    double creditLimit
}
```

All of the properties from the hierarchy are mapped to columns in an account table. Entries in the table will have the class column set to indicate what class the object in the entry belongs to.

Mapping

We can use the mapping setting to apply a table-per-subclass strategy to inheritance mapping. This will overcome the need to allow all properties to be nullable. Mapping also allows us to map GORM domain classes onto a legacy database as it gives us fine control over both table and column names in the relational model that we map to:

```
class Account {
    double balance

    static mapping = {
        table "fin_account"
        balance column:"acc_bal"
    }
}
```

The `mapping` closure is implemented in Grails in a fashion very similar to `constraints`. The mapping closure is executed, having set its delegate to an instance of `HibernateMappingBuilder`. Within the closure code for `mapping`, we can use any of the built-in methods to control how mapping should occur, or we can name the column field itself for more fine-grained control over the mapping of a column. To apply a table-per-subclass strategy and turn on caching, we can add the following:

```
static mapping = {
    tablePerSubclass = true
    cache = true
}
```

Querying

We've already seen in the examples some basic querying with `list()` and `get()`. The list method can be used with a number of named parameters that gives us finer control over the result set returned:

```
// list all customers
Customer.list().each {
    println "${it.firstName} ${it.lastName}"
}
// List the first 10 customers
Customer.list(max:10).each {
    println "${it.firstName} ${it.lastName}"
}
// List the next 10 customers
Customer.list(max:10, offset:10).each {
    println "${it.firstName} ${it.lastName}"
}
// List all customers in descending order sorted by last name
Customer.list(sort:"lastName",order:"desc").each {
    println "${it.firstName} ${it.lastName}"
```

We've seen the `get()` method in action, which uses the database ID to return an object. We can also use the `getAll()` method when we want to return more than one object, as long as we have the IDs that we need:

```
def customers = Customer.getAll(2, 4, 5, 7)
```

Dynamic finders

GORM supports a unique and powerful query function through the use of **dynamic finders**. A dynamic finder is a pretended method applied to a domain class, which can return one or many queried objects. Finders work by allowing us to invent method names, where the syntax of the query is bound into the method name. All finders are prefixed by `findBy` or `findAllBy`:

```
// Find the first customer called Fred
def fred = Customer.findByFirstName("Fred")
// Find all Flintstones
def flintstones = Customer.findAllByLastName("Flintstone")
// Find Fred Flintstone
def fred_flintstoner = Customer.findByFirstNameAndLastName("Fred",
"Flintstone")
```

Finder names can also include comparators, such as `Like`, `LessThan`, and `IsNotNull`:

```
// Find all customers with names beginning with Flint
def  flints = Customer.findAllByLastNameLike("Flint%")
```

We can include associations in queries. Here, we can find all invoices for Fred:

```
def fred = Customer.findByFirstNameAndLastName("Fred",
"Flintstone")
def invoices = Invoice.findAllByCustomer(fred)
```

Dynamic finders open up a huge range of possible finder methods that can be used with a class. The more fields there are, the more possible finder methods there are to match. Rather than trying to second-guess what all of the possible combinations might be and adding them to the `metaclass`, GORM takes a slightly different approach.

From Groovy 1.0, we can add a method called `methodMissing` to the `MetaClass` object. This differs slightly from the `invokeMethod` call that we provided in previous chapters because `methodMissing` is called as the last chance saloon before Groovy throws a `MethodMissingException`, whereas `invokeMethod` will be called for every method invocation.

In earlier version of Grails, it would add its own `methodMissing` implementation, which catches all of the missing method invocations with the prefixes `find` and `findAll` the first time that they occur. At this point, the actual method implementations were registered in the `metaClass`, so subsequent calls to that finder will not suffer the overhead. The later versions of Grails transform finders as they are encountered in the code and turned them into individual Hibernate criteria style queries.

GORM as a DSL

We've only scratched the surface of what can be done with GORM and Grails. For a more comprehensive view of GORM, take the time to look at the Grails reference at http://www.grails.org. What is most interesting about GORM in relation to this book is how it achieves its goals through a suite of mini DSLs implemented in Groovy. Domain classes could be designed and written by a database architect who can also be insulated from the intricacies of the Groovy language.

Spock as a DSL

Test-driven development (TDD) has become an essential capability for software developers over the past decade. TDD can mean different things to different organizations. It can mean the adoption of a full-blown test first style of coding, where unit tests are written before any functional code. It could just mean that you write extensive unit tests for every piece of functional code in the system. It may or may not mean the use of continuous integration builds that run a battery of unit tests after each code check in. Whatever TDD means to your organization, the chances are that flavors of xUnit test frameworks, including JUnit, WEBUnit, and HTTPUnit have been essential tools in your software developer's arsenal for some considerable time now.

The problem with xUnit-style testing is that these are all tools that are designed by programmers, for programmers. Your QA staff might be familiar with running xUnit tests and reporting on problems that they encounter, but they are less likely to be involved in originating the code tests with these frameworks. Unit tests tend to be written to test features at the class and method level rather than testing the intended behavior of the software.

Two alternate models of testing — **acceptance test-driven development (ATDD)** and **behavior-driven development (BDD)** — have been advocated, primarily within the agile community, as a solution to this issue. The key to promoting ATDD and BDD is the creation of tools that allow all of the stakeholders, including developers, business analysts, and QA, to be able to use a common tool with a common language. Testing begins with a specification of the intended behavior for the software, which will be entered into the tool. This implies being able to develop a specification in a language that can be written and understood by of all the stakeholders, and not just the developers.

The common language of ATDD and BDD revolves around defining behavior in user-centric terms. Whether we are writing acceptance tests or defining behavior, we end up using terms such as **given**, **when**, and **then** as follows:

- **Given** a precondition
- **When** certain actors perform certain actions
- **Then** we expect a predetermined result

Of course, this type of terminology is ripe for using a mini-language or DSL to define the tests or behavior. And this is exactly what is happening. There are a plethora of BDD style testing frameworks out there already, the most notable being **RSpec**, a BDD-style framework implemented by using Ruby's dynamic features.

Spock

We have been using Spock BDD style syntax throughout the book to illustrate the code examples. So, you are already well familiar with the given/when/then semantics of BDD. I hope that using this syntax has brought clarity to the code examples. In effect, the Spock DSL has become part of the primary narrative of the book.

In *Chapter 3, Essential Groovy DSLs*, we took a detailed look at how to use Spock. Now, we will take a look at how some of the DSL-like features of Spock are implemented. First, let's recap on some key elements of a Spock specification. For the purpose of this chapter, we will just focus on feature methods and blocks:

- **Fixture methods**: Fixture methods are to set up and teardown test data, that is, `setup()`, `cleanup()`, `setupSpec()`, and `cleanupSpec()`.

- **Feature methods**: A feature method in Spock is used to describe a single test scenario. It can have any valid Groovy method name, but typically by conventions, we use the Groovy; string as method name syntax, so the method name also becomes part of the test documentation. The thing that separates feature methods from other methods in Spock is the fact that they contain blocks.

- **Blocks**: Blocks in Spock are the given, when, and then clauses of the BDD semantics. They are denoted by an equivalent Groovy label, for example, `given:`, `when:`, `then:`, followed by an optional descriptor string and any number of code statements. The block is terminated by the next valid block or at the end of the enclosing feature method.

- **Helper methods**: Any method that is not a fixture method or does not contain any valid blocks is considered to be a helper method.

The following code is a simple Spock specification that tests some of the features of the `java.util.Stack` class:

```
class ChapterNineSpec extends SpockScriptSpecification {
  def "initial size is zero"() {
    given:
    def stack = new Stack()
    expect: stack.size() == 0
  }

  def "pop from empty stack throws exception"() {
    given:
    def stack = new Stack()
    when: stack.pop()
    then: thrown(EmptyStackException)
  }

  def "peek from empty stack throws exception"() {
    given:
    def stack = new Stack()
    when: stack.peek()
    then: thrown(EmptyStackException)
  }

  def "after push size is one and we can peek"() {
    given:
    def stack = new Stack()

    when: stack.push("elem")

    then:
    stack.size() == 1
    stack.peek() == "elem"
  }
}
```

JUnit

The Spock test framework is built on top of the JUnit test framework. If we were to rewrite the preceding feature method in a JUnit test case, it might look a little like this:

```
public class ChapterNineTest extends TestCase {

    public void testStack() {
        Stack stack = new Stack();

        assert stack.size() == 0;
        stack.push("elem");
        assert stack.size() == 1;
        assert stack.peek().equals("elem");
    }
}
```

I've kept this simple as an old style JUnit test without annotations so that we can start to use our knowledge of Groovy to imagine how a Spock-like DSL could be achieved. It should be clear that the only way to achieve this would be by using a Global AST transformation.

One possible way to achieve this using AST transformations would be to transform the `ChapterNineSpec` class by extending it from `TestCase`. The feature method would need to be transformed by creating a new method starting with test. Each of the blocks would have to be cloned and injected into the new method in sequence and each statement line in the `then:` block would need to have an `AssertStatement` `ASTNode` object added to it.

In fact, this is not far removed from what Spock actually does do under the covers. One important difference is that Spock does not actually try to transform the `Specification` class into a test case class. This can be avoided because Spock implements its own JUnit `Runner` class. This runner class understands how to find each feature methods in turn and invokes it using Java reflection.

Spock creates a brand new feature method in the AST. It builds up the body of the feature method from the blocks contained in the original `Specification` class, and when it is done, it deletes the AST nodes for the original feature methods from the AST.

You can explore this a little yourself by launching a Spock test in the debugger of your favorite IDE. Place a breakpoint on a line within the first feature method of your spec. When the debugger hits the breakpoint, you will notice by looking at the call stack that you are not in the feature method you defined in the test, but in a method called `$spock_feature_0_0`. The Spock AST transformation has created this new method for you.

Try stepping through the lines of code in a block. You will notice that the debugger stays in sync. This is because Spock clones the original source location from the original AST objects into the newly created ones. The `ASTNode` class has a method specifically for doing this: `ASTNode.setSourcePosition(ASTNode node)`. This is an important feature to use if you are going to build an AST transformation-based DSL, which you hope to behave well in a debugger.

Spock does a lot more sophisticated stuff than this under the covers. In fact, it is one of the first DSLs produced in Groovy that exploited the AST transformations feature when it was added to Groovy. I encourage you to explore the Spock sources. They can be found on GitHub at `https://github.com/spockframework/spock`.

Summary

In this chapter, we looked at two existing Groovy DSLs that are in current use and are free to download. GORM implements a full persistence layer over Hibernate that layers over standard Groovy classes. GORM allows us to decorate a regular POGO with settings for applying the most common associations and relationships that we can expect in our object models.

Much of what GORM provides in terms of querying via dynamic finders requires a Groovy-knowledgeable developer to appreciate and use them. However, the basic object modeling semantics provided through the `belongsTo`, `hasMany`, and other persistence settings could be used quite readily by a data-modeling architect who has little or no knowledge of the Groovy language. The domain classes can be viewed as an independent model specification language, which has the advantage of being immediately usable by Groovy developers responsible for other parts of the system.

Spock brings BDD style specification-based testing to the Java/Groovy platform. Each provides a means to write specifications by using given/when/then style semantics that are easier to interpret than regular xUnit style testing frameworks. The pseudo-English style syntax of this DSL should mean that the specifications can be understood by business stakeholders even if they still need to be coded by a Groovy-proficient developer.

Most importantly, in this chapter, we have seen how all of these projects exploit different Groovy features in order to implement DSL-style structures and syntax.

In the next chapter we will cover the techniques that you can use to build your own builder. In *Chapter 7, Power Groovy DSL Features*, we took a brief look at how builders worked. In *Chapter 10, Building a Builder*, we will look in detail at how we can use closures and the Groovy MOP to implement the Groovy builder pattern in our own applications.

10
Building a Builder

Builders are a powerful feature of Groovy. The Groovy libraries contain an expanding set of builders for everything from XML and HTML markup to managing systems via JMX. Even so, you will always come across circumstances where the semantics of a builder would be useful in your own application.

We've seen how to build a rudimentary builder using the Groovy MOP and pretended methods, in *Chapter 7, Power Groovy DSL Features*. Thankfully, the Groovy libraries provide us with an easier means of developing our own builders. In this chapter, we will look at some of the ways in which we can use Groovy and the MOP to create our own builder classes:

- To begin with, we will recap the Groovy features that enable the Groovy builder pattern, in order to understand how they work

- We will look at how to build a rudimentary builder with features from the Groovy MOP

- We will implement our own database seed data builder by using two of the builder support classes provided in Groovy: `BuilderSupport` and `FactoryBuilderSupport`

The builder code structure

The real beauty of Groovy's builder paradigm is the way in which it maps the naturally nested block structure of the language to the construction process.

The process of defining parent-child relationships between objects through nested code blocks is well-established through other markup languages, such as XML and HTML.

The transition from writing XML or HTML to the `GroovyMarkup` equivalent is an easy one. To make use of a builder, we don't need to have an intimate understanding of the Groovy MOP or of how the builder is implemented. We just need to know how to write the builder code so that it conforms to the correct language semantics. The code structure of the builder pattern relies on just a few Groovy language features:

- **Closure method calls**: The distinctively nested block structure in the builder pattern is facilitated by Groovy's special handling of closures when they are passed as method parameters. This allows the closure block to be declared inline after the other method call parameters.

- **Closure method resolution**: When a method is invoked within the body of a closure and that method does not exist in the closure instance, Groovy uses a resolve strategy to determine which object (if any) should be tried to locate that method.

- **Pretended methods**: The Groovy MOP allows us to respond to method calls that do not exist in a class — in other words, to "pretend" that these methods exist.

- **Named parameters**: When we pass a `Map` parameter to a method, we can declare the individual map elements alongside the other method parameters, giving the effect of a named parameter list.

- **Closure delegate**: Changing the delegate of a closure allows another class to handle its method calls. When we change the delegate to a `builder` class, this allows the builder to orchestrate how the method calls are handled.

Closure method calls

When we declare a Groovy method that accepts a closure as its last parameter, Groovy allows us to define the body of the inline closure immediately after the method call containing the other parameters. A method call followed by an inline closure block has all the appearance of being a named block of code. It's when we nest these method calls within each other that we get the distinctive builder-style code blocks.

This style of coding is not unique to builders. We can nest other method calls in the same way. In the following example, we have three methods defined within a script: `method1()`, `method2()`, and `method3()`. Nesting calls to these methods gives us some code that is very similar to a builder block, but is not actually a builder block. The cool thing about the builder pattern is that it uses this existing feature from the language and turns it into a whole new coding paradigm.

The success of building our own `builder` class by using the Groovy MOP depends largely on understanding the sequence in which these methods get called. The output gives us an idea of what might be happening and what the true sequence of events is. Let's decorate the code a little to show what is happening. The comments show what scope we are running in:

```groovy
def method1(Map namedParams = [:], Closure closure = {}) {
    println "method1: $namedParams"
    closure.call()
}
def method2(Map namedParams = [:], Closure closure = {}) {
    println "method2: $namedParams"
    closure.call()
}
def method3(Map namedParams = [:], Closure closure = {}) {
    println "method3: $namedParams"
    closure.call()
}

given:
method1(param: "one") { // Closure1 scope
    method2(greet: true) { // Closure2 scope
        method3 greeting: "hello"
    } // End Closure2
    method1( number: 123 ) { // Closure3 scope
        method1 ( nestedcall: "nested" ) { // Closure4 scope
            method3 number: 10
        } // End Closure4
    } // End Closure3
} // End Closure1

expect:
"""method1: [param:one]
method2: [greet:true]
method3: [greeting:hello]
method1: [number:123]
method1: [nestedcall:nested]
method3: [number:10]""" == output()
```

The main block of code runs within the scope of the script. Each inline closure is in fact an anonymous instance of a `Closure` object. For the purpose of this exercise, we will rename these instances from `Closure1` to `Closure4`. The first call to `method1()` occurs in the outer scope of the script, so we will expect this method to be passed to the outer scope. The subsequent method calls all happen within the scope of one or other of the anonymous closure instances, so we expect these methods to be invoked on the individual closure instances.

The resolve strategy – OWNER_FIRST

The one problem with the expected flow in the previous example is that we know that the closure instances don't implement the `method1()` to `method3()` methods. So, we appear to be executing unimplemented methods. When Groovy makes a call to a method on a closure, it does not always expect it to be present.

If a method is not present in the closure itself, Groovy will try to find it by looking in the owner of the closure, or its delegate, or both. The order in which this occurs is called the **resolve strategy** of the closure. The default resolve strategy is `OWNER_FIRST`, which means that the owner of the closure will be queried first for the method, followed by the delegate. If the owner of the closure happens to be another closure, then the resolve strategy will continue its search for a match in the owner of the owner and so on, until a match is found or the outer scope is reached.

> The resolve strategy can be changed for a closure by calling `Closure.setResolveStrategy`. We can change the resolve strategy to any of the following self-explanatory strategies: `OWNER_FIRST`, `OWNER_ONLY`, `DELEGATE_FIRST`, `DELEGATE_ONLY`, and `NONE`.

Although the preceding sequence diagram reflects the first port of call for `each` method invocation, what in fact happens is that the resolve strategy kicks in and the method calls will percolate out through the closure instances. A match will eventually be found in the outer scope, which is the only place where the actual methods exist.

The insight that Groovy designers had when designing the builder pattern was that this natural nesting of closures could be used to map to any construction process that involved a parent-child type of relationship. Even without using a `builder` class, we can nest closures' method calls to create a pseudo builder. In the next example, we declare three methods that we can use to construct a rudimentary tree structure out of map objects.

The `root()` method creates the initial tree map and inserts a root element into it. We can nest as many levels deep as we like with the `node()` method as it will remember its parent node and add sub nodes to it. The `leaf()` method is the only one to take a value and it does not expect to be passed a closure, as it will create the leaf elements in the tree structure:

```
def current
def root (Closure closure) {
    def tree = [:]
    def root = [:]
    tree["root"] = root
    def parent = current
    current = root
    closure.call()
    current = parent
    return tree
}

def node (key, Closure closure) {
    def node = [:]
    current[key] = node
    def parent = current
    current = node
    closure.call()
    current = parent
}

def leaf (key, value ) {
    current[key] = value

}

given:
// pseudo builder code
def tree = root {
    node("sub-tree-1") {
        leaf "leaf-1", "leaf object 1"
    }
    node ("sub-tree-2"){
        node ("node-1"){
            leaf "leaf-2", "leaf object 2"
        }
    }
```

```
    }

expect:
tree == [
root: [
    "sub-tree-1": [
        "leaf-1": "leaf object 1"
        ],
     "sub-tree-2": [
        "node-1": [
            "leaf-2": "leaf object 2"
            ]
        ]
    ]
]
```

Pretended methods

Many Groovy builders rely on the ability to describe arbitrarily named elements. When we make use of markup builders to generate XML, we need to be able to insert whatever tag names are required to conform to the schema that we are using. Given that elements are created in method calls, we also need to be able to make arbitrarily named method calls during the markup process.

With Groovy, we can respond to methods that don't exist as concrete methods of a class. The term we use for these types of methods is **pretended methods**. Groovy provides two means for implementing a pretended method.

invokeMethod

The `PoorMansTagBuilder` class that we covered in *Chapter 5, Groovy Closures*, uses `invokeMethod` as a means of pretending methods. The `PoorMansTagBuilder` class works by handling all method calls to the builder, and invoking the closure argument manually. With `invokeMethod`, we can respond appropriately to any arbitrary method call. In this case, we output the appropriate XML tags:

```
class PoorMansTagBuilder {
    int indent = 0
    Object invokeMethod(String name, Object args) {
        indent.times {print "    "}
        println "<${name}>"
        indent++
        args[0].delegate = this // Change delegate to the builder
        args[0].call()
```

```
            indent--
            indent.times {print "     "}
            println "</${name}>"
        }
    }
```

This is a simple case that we are using just to illustrate the mechanism. Although the technique works for simple cases, extending it to implement a more complete tag builder will rapidly result in complex and hard to maintain code.

methodMissing

Since Groovy 1.5, an alternative to invokeMethod was provided. The methodMissing mechanism differs slightly from invokeMethod, as it is only called when a method call fails to be dispatched to any concrete method. To update the PoorMansTagBuilder class for using methodMissing instead of invokeMethod, all we need to do is replace the method name that we declare:

```
class PoorMansTagBuilder {
    int indent = 0
    def methodMissing(String name, args) {
        indent.times {print "     "}
        println "<${name}>"
        indent++
        args[0].delegate = this // Change delegate to the builder
        args[0].call()
        indent--
        indent.times {print "     "}
        println "</${name}>"
    }
}

given:
def builder = new PoorMansTagBuilder ()

when:
builder.root {
        level1{
         level2 {
         }
     }
}
```

```
then:
        """<root>
    <level1>
        <level2>
        </level2>
    </level1>
</root>""" == output()
```

The closure delegate

Earlier, we looked at how to code a pseudo builder using methods declared within a script. The resolve strategy in that example passed method calls in the nested closure up to the owner of the closure. The builder block in the previous example is also in the scope of a script. Let's decorate it as we did before, to identify the various anonymous closure instances:

```
// method root() called on PoorMansTagBuilder
builder.root { // Closure1
        // method level1 called on Closure1 instance
        level1{ // Closure2
          // method level2 called on Closure2 instance
          level2 { // Closure3
          }
      }
  }
```

The first method call to root() is made against the builder instance, so it will be handled directly by PoorMansTagBuilder.methodMissing(). Nested method calls will first be dispatched to the enclosing closure. The level1() and level2() methods won't be found in the closure instances, so we would normally expect the resolve strategy to dispatch these methods up the chain of owners until a method is found. This normal dispatch chain would end up at the script instance, so these methods would cause MethodMissingException to be thrown.

The secret of how this works is in the handling of the delegate for closure instances. The builder block starts with a direct method call onto the builder instance, builder.root(). The anonymous closure, Closure1, is passed as a parameter. The call to root() will fail and fall through to methodMissing. In this simple example, arg[0] is always the closure because we are not processing parameters on our tags. A more sophisticated version will need to scan the parameters for the closure instance.

At this point, we have access to the closure, so we can set its delegate to the `builder` instance. Now, when the `level1()` and `level2()` calls are encountered, the resolve strategy will try the owner first and then try the delegate as follows:

- The `level1()` call will not be resolved in `Closure1`. It won't be found in the owner of `Closure1`, which is the script, but it will be resolved in the delegate, which is the builder instance. `PoorMansTagBuilder.methodMissing` will field the method and also set the delegate for the anonymous closure, `Closure2`.

- The `level2()` call happens in the scope of `Closure2`, but will not be resolved there. First, its owner, `Closure1`, will be tried, and then its delegate, which once again is the builder instance.

BuilderSupport

Under the hood, all of Groovy's own Builders are implemented using the `invokeMethod` or `methodMissing` methods and delegate techniques that we have described in the previous section. We can choose to start creating our own builder classes by using these features alone. Perhaps the biggest challenge when creating a builder with these features alone is that the MOP concepts of pretended methods and delegate handling don't fit well with the task at hand—namely, the construction of complex objects. It would be nice to have APIs that reflected the task at hand in a better way.

Thankfully, the complexities of managing `invokeMethod` or `methodMissing` calls and figuring out who the delegate should be, are encapsulated into the builder support classes provided in the Groovy packages. The most basic support class is `groovy.util.BuilderSupport`.

BuilderSupport hook methods

`BuilderSupport` provides an interface to the building process that nicely mirrors the node-based construction process on which most builder classes are based. Instead of overriding `invokeMethod` as in the initial example, we will override the node construction methods provided by `BuilderSupport`.

These methods provide the hooks such that, instead of coding at the MOP level with pretended method invocations and delegates, we can code with respect to the node construction process. The important hook methods that we need to know about are listed here. These methods encapsulate the building process out into node creation style events that make far more sense from an object construction point of view. Then, we never need to worry about pretended methods or delegates again:

- `createNode(Object name)`
- `createNode(Object name, Object value)`
- `createNode(Object name, Map attributes)`
- `createNode(Object name, Map attributes, Objects value)`

Called by `BuilderSupport` whenever a pretended method is encountered, the name parameter contains the name of the pretended call. The responsibility of the hook is to return a new object of a type appropriate to the method call. The specific hook to be called depends on what parameters are passed to the method:

- `nodeCompleted(Object parent, Object node)`: This is called after all of the children of a node have been created
- `setParent(Object parent, Object child)`: This is called after `createNode` for each child node, in order to allow any parent-child relationships to be established

> `BuilderSupport` takes care of the nitty-gritty of handling pretended methods for us. Had our `PoorMansTagBuilder` worked only for parameter-less tags, `BuilderSupport` would have detected which type of call was being made and called the appropriate `createNode` for us. The `setParent` method is only called if a parent node exists.

How this all hangs together is best illustrated by way of an example. So, let's start by creating a really dumb `builder` that just logs these methods as they are encountered. This will give us a feel for the sequence in which the methods are called:

```
class LogBuilder extends BuilderSupport {
    def indent = 0
    def createNode(name){
        indent.times {print "  "}
        println "createNode(${name})"
        indent++
        return name
    }
    def createNode(name, value){
```

```
      indent.times {print "   "}
      println "createNode(${name}, ${value})"
      indent++
      return name
    }
    def createNode(name, Map attributes){
      indent.times {print "   "}
      println "createNode(${name}, ${attributes})"
      indent++
      return name
    }
    def createNode(name, Map attributes, value){
      indent.times {print "   "}
      println "createNode(${name}, ${attributes}, ${value})"
      indent++
      return name
    }
    void setParent(parent, child){
      indent.times {print "   "}
      println "setParent(${parent}, ${child})"
    }
    void nodeCompleted(parent, node) {
      indent--
      indent.times {print "   "}
      println "nodeCompleted(${parent}, ${node})"
    }
}
```

To use this builder, all that we need to do is to construct one and start writing some markup with it. Here we have some markup for building customer records, but as this builder does not care what the method tags are, we could write whatever markup we please:

```
given:
def builder = new LogBuilder()

def customers = builder.customers {
    customer{
      id(1001)
        name(firstName:"Fred",surname:"Flintstone")
        address("billing", street:"1 Rock Road",city:"Bedrock")
        address("shipping", street:"1 Rock Road",city:"Bedrock")
    }
}
expect:
```

```
"""createNode(customers)
  createNode(customer)
    setParent(customers, customer)
    createNode(id, 1001)
      setParent(customer, id)
    nodeCompleted(customer, id)
    createNode(name, [firstName:Fred, surname:Flintstone])
      setParent(customer, name)
    nodeCompleted(customer, name)
    createNode(address, [street:1 Rock Road, city:Bedrock],
    billing)
      setParent(customer, address)
    nodeCompleted(customer, address)
    createNode(address, [street:1 Rock Road, city:Bedrock],
    shipping)
      setParent(customer, address)
    nodeCompleted(customer, address)
  nodeCompleted(customers, customer)
nodeCompleted(null, customers)""")""" == output()
```

We can see from the output exactly what the sequence of calling is, and what parameters are being passed. We've used this simple example for illustrating how the BuilderSupport class works, but it is actually a useful debugging tool in general for using with any builder that's not behaving as expected. By replacing any existing builder instance in your code with a LogBuilder class, it will output the construction sequence for you, which may identify the problem.

From this output, we can trace the sequence in which the hooks are called. Nodes are created from the top down. The createNode hook for the parent is called first. The createNode hook for a child is called next, and setParent is called for each individual child after both the parent and the child have been created. The nodeCompleted hook is called only after all of the children have been created and their parent-child relations are set.

The default implementation of BuilderSupport manages the current node cursor by itself. Two additional hooks to consider are:

- setCurrent(Object current)
- Object getCurrent()

Certain builder implementations might want to manage the notion of a "current" node object in order to maintain a cursor on the construction process. If so, both of these hooks will need to be implemented.

Now that we understand the building mechanism, it is a trivial matter to change our `LogBuilder` script to create some actual markup. Here, with a few modifications, we can turn our script into `PoorMansTagBuilder20`:

```
class PoorMansTagBuilder20 extends BuilderSupport {
  def indent = 0

  def createNode(name){
    indent.times {print "  "}
    println "<${name}>"
    indent++
    return name
  }
  def createNode(name, value){
    indent.times {print "  "}
    println "<${name}>" + value
    indent++
    return name
  }
  def createNode(name, Map attributes){
    indent.times {print "  "}
    print "<${name} "
    print attributes.collect {
      "${it.key}='${it.value}'"
    }.join(' ')
    println ">"
    indent++
    return name
  }
  def createNode(name, Map attributes, value){
    indent.times {print "  "}
    print "<${name} "
    print attributes.collect {
      "${it.key}='${it.value}'"
    }.join(' ')
    println ">" + value
    indent++
    return name
  }
  void setParent(parent, child){
    // Don't care since we are just streaming to output
  }
  void nodeCompleted(parent, node) {
    indent--
```

```
        indent.times {print "   "}
        println "</${node}>"
    }

}

given:
def builder = new PoorMansTagBuilder20 ()

when:
builder.root {
        level1{
         level2 {
         }
      }
}

then:
        """"<root>
    <level1>
        <level2>
        </level2>
    </level1>
</root>""" == output()
```

Once again, this is a simple implementation of a tag builder. We are making no interpretation of the method tags that are being passed in, so for each `createNode` call, all we do is output a `<TAG>` tag with parameters and attributes if necessary. The `setParent` call is not relevant to us because we are just streaming output to standard output. We will see in the next example where we need to implement this. Finally, the `nodeCompleted` call just closes the `</TAG>` tag.

Now, we can apply this builder to the same `customers` markup script that we did before, as follows. The only change required is to instantiate `PoorMansTageBuilder20` in place of the original builder class.

As a markup builder, this falls well short of the features in the Groovy `MarkupBuilder` class, but it does show just how easy it is to put together a quick builder to fit the need of the day. Now, let's consider what we've learned, and look at building something a little more useful.

A database builder

Every application that includes a database needs some means of setting up seed, demo, or test data. I have worked on numerous enterprise applications during my career and invariably the management of different datasets becomes as much of an effort over time as the development of the application itself. In my own experience of working with **Independent Software Vendors (ISVs)**, whose applications need to be deployed on multiple customer sites with multiple versions, the problem becomes acute.

ISV companies often have competing needs for datasets. The sales organization needs a predictable dataset for its demos to customers. The test department needs datasets that allow them to test specific features of the application. Project management requires specific seed data to be available, which is tailored to each customer site prior to installation. With all of these competing requirements, the IT department has a limited set of database instances available on which to install and test all of these configurations.

There are various ways of managing datasets. The most common is to maintain SQL scripts that take care of the database insertions. Building a simple database will require multiple insertions into a multitude of tables. The SQL script needs to be written in such a way as to maintain the integrity of foreign key references. It's not an easy thing to do, and requires intimate knowledge of the schema.

Suppose we are working with a Grails application. Take for example the one-to-many relationship we looked at in *Chapter 6, Example DSL – GeeTwitter*:

```
class Customer {
    String firstName
    String lastName
    static hasMany = [invoices:Invoice]
}

class Invoice {
    static hasMany = [orders:SalesOrder]
}

class SalesOrder {
    String sku
    int amount
    Double price
    static belongsTo = Invoice
}
```

Grails has a migration plugin that can be installed. The migration tool will execute a SQL update script to migrate our database between versions. To use the migrate tool to add some simple test data for the preceding classes, we need to know how GORM maps from the Groovy POGO objects to relational tables.

In *Chapter 9, Existing Groovy DSLs*, we also saw how these classes in fact map to five tables in the relational database. There are three main tables that represent the business objects (`customer`, `invoice`, and `sales_order`) and there are two mapping tables used to manage the foreign key mappings (`customer_invoice` and `invoice_sales_order`) that relate customers to invoices and invoices to sales orders.

To set up a simple test case with one customer, one invoice, and three sales orders would require nine insertions across these tables. Apart from being error prone and difficult to maintain, the script will be incomprehensible to anyone who is not intimately acquainted with SQL. What starts out as a simple data input spec for a test case becomes a development task for a domain SQL expert who understands the GORM mapping model.

An alternative to this approach is to use the GORM APIs to build the test data. At least if we do this, then we don't have to concern ourselves with the foreign key relationships between tables. The following script will set up our simple dataset with one customer, one invoice, and three sales orders:

```
def fred = new Customer(firstName:"Fred", lastName:"Flintstone")

fred.save()

def invoice = new Invoice()

invoice.addToOrders(new SalesOrder(sku:"productid01", amount:1,
price:1.00))
invoice.addToOrders(new SalesOrder(sku:"productid02", amount:3,
price:1.50))
invoice.addToOrders(new SalesOrder(sku:"productid03", amount:2,
price:5.00))

fred.addToInvoices(invoice)
```

This is somewhat better than the SQL script approach, but it does impose a procedural construction onto the data, where the test data is typically defined declaratively. While I've used GORM to illustrate my point here, the same issues will crop up with whatever persistence mechanism we use.

Ideally, we want to be able to describe our data in a declarative style. The syntax of the data definition should match the structure of the resulting data as closely as possible. This is an ideal situation in which to use a builder to take care of construction. With a builder, it should be possible to create a declarative markup style script for building datasets. The builder can take care of the complexities of construction.

Let's first of all imagine how a builder for customers may look in use. We probably want to handle multiple customers, so a top-level `customers` method is useful. We could have multiple customer blocks nested in the following code. Nesting is a good way of depicting ownership in a one-to-many relationship, so our `Customers` markup would probably look something like the following:

```
builder.customers {
    customer{
        invoice {
            salesOrder()
            salesOrder()
            salesOrder()
        }
    }
}
```

We need to be able to set the fields for each entity as it is created. We could have a pretended method for each field as follows:

```
builder.customers {
  customer {
    firstName("Fred")
    lastName("Flintstone")
    invoice {
      salesOrder {
      sku("productid01")
      amount(1)
      price(1.00)
      }
      salesOrder {
        sku("productid02")
        amount(2)
        price(1.00)
      }
      salesOrder {
        sku("productid03")
```

```
            amount(3)
            price(1.00)
          }
        }
      }
    }
```

This will work. However, it is not immediately clear to a reader of this script that `lastName` is an object attribute and invoice is a new subsidiary object. A better option is to set object attributes as mapped parameter values. The following script is far clearer in its intent, so this is the one we will try to implement:

```
builder.customers {
    customer(firstName:"Fred",lastName:"Flintstone") {
        invoice {
            salesOrder(sku:"productid01", amount:1, price:1.00)
            salesOrder(sku:"productid02", amount:2, price:1.00)
            salesOrder(sku:"productid03", amount:3, price:1.00)
        }
    }
}
```

As it happens, the `BuilderSupport` hook methods and their calling sequence work perfectly in step with the GORM APIs that we need in order to construct our customer records:

- The `createNode` method will be called in the correct top down sequence, allowing us to create the appropriate `Customer`, `Invoice`, or `SalesOrder` class as required

- The `setParent` hook is called after both parent and child objects have been constructed, allowing us to call `Customer.addToInvoices` or `Invoice.addToOrders` when we need to

- The `nodeCompleted` hook can be used to intercept when an object needs to be saved

The following code snippet contains a rudimentary builder class based on `BuilderSupport` that constructs customer, invoice, and sales order objects through GORM. The same style of builder could work equally well with whatever other persistence method we choose:

```
class CustomersBuilder extends BuilderSupport {
  def createNode(name){
    Object result = null
    switch (name) {
      case "customer":
```

```
          return new Customer(firstName:"", lastName:"")
        case "invoice":
          return new Invoice()
        case "salesOrder":
          return new SalesOrder(sku:"default",amount:1,price:0.0)
    }
  }
  def createNode(name, value){
    Object result = createNode(name)
    if (value instanceof Customer && result instanceof Invoice)
      value.addToInvoices(result)
    if(value instanceof Invoice && result instanceof SalesOrder)
      value.addToOrders(result)
    return result
  }
  def createNode(name, Map attributes){
    Object result = null
    switch (name) {
      case "customer":
        return new Customer(attributes)
      case "invoice":
        return new Invoice(attributes)
      case "salesOrder":
        return new SalesOrder(attributes)
    }
  }
  def createNode(name, Map attributes, value){
    Object result = createNode(name,attributes)
    if (value instanceof Customer && result instanceof Invoice)
        value.addToInvoices(result)
    if(value instanceof Invoice && result instanceof SalesOrder)
        value.addToOrders(result)
    return result
  }
  void setParent(parent, child){
    if (child instanceof Invoice && parent instanceof Customer)
      parent.addToInvoices(child)
    if (child instanceof SalesOrder && parent instanceof Invoice)
      parent.addToOrders(child)
  }
  void nodeCompleted(parent, node) {
    if (node != null)
      node.save()
  }
}
```

Here, we have implemented all four `createNode` methods. The method tag is passed as the `name` parameter to `createNode`. So, we construct a `Customer`, `Invoice`, or `SalesOrder` object based on the tag that we are processing. We will allow a `parent` object to be set in the value parameter to the method. This allows us to construct a `child` object outside the scope of a parent, and set its parent later.

The `setParent` method takes care of adding invoices to customers, and sales orders to invoices. Testing the `instanceof` both parent and child ensures that we don't attempt to add an invoice if it is declared outside of the customer.

All that remains for `nodeCompleted` to do is to save the node object that we have created to the database. When we put all of this together, we can make use of our `CustomerBuilder` to build a simple test database as follows:

```
given:
def builder = new CustomersBuilder()

def customers = builder.customers {
    def fred = customer(firstName:"Fred",lastName:"Flintstone") {
        invoice {
            salesOrder(sku:"productid01", amount:1, price:1.00)
            salesOrder(sku:"productid02", amount:2, price:1.00)
            salesOrder(sku:"productid03", amount:3, price:1.00)
        }
    }
    def invoice2 = invoice(fred)

    salesOrder(invoice2, sku:"productid04", amount:1, price:1.00)
    salesOrder(invoice2, sku:"productid05", amount:1, price:1.00)
    salesOrder(invoice2, sku:"productid06", amount:1, price:1.00)
}

expect:
CustomerWithInvoices.count() == 1
Invoice.count() == 2
SalesOrder.count() == 6
```

By allowing a `parent` object to be passed as the value parameter, we have made the markup script more flexible. As you can see from the preceding code, `invoice` and `salesOrder` tags can be declared directly as children of a `parent` object, or they can be declared independently. This gives us a bit more flexibility in what types of mapping relationships we can support where ownership between parent and child might be optional, or in more complex scenarios where many-to-many relationships might need to be declared.

FactoryBuilderSupport

`BuilderSupport` is the base class for many of the builder classes provided in the Groovy packages. As we can see from the previous examples, it is easy to work with. We have built quite a useful database builder tool in relatively few lines of code.

However, one issue with `BuilderSupport` is that the hook functions are in effect funnels for handling all of the possible tags that we might like to process in our markup. In our `CustomerBuilder`, we are handling just four different tags.

This is not a realistic scenario for most database schemas. We could expect to have dozens more tag types that we need to handle if we wanted to expand this example into something that would work with a typical database schema for even a modestly sized application. Funneling all of these tags into one `createNode` would create an unwieldy mess of code:

```
def createNode(name){
  Object result = null
    switch (name) {
      case "customer":
        return new Customer(firstName:"", lastName:"")
      case "invoice":
        return new Invoice()
      case "sales_order":
        return new SalesOrder(sku:"default",amount:1,price:0.0)
      case "another_object":
        return new Something()
      ........ and more!
  }
}
```

Groovy provides a second builder support class that neatly overcomes this problem. The `groovy.util.FactoryBuilderSupport` class is based on the factory pattern, and delegates the handling of individual tag objects to Factory classes. Originally, this support class was just provided as part of the `SwingBuilder` class. Since it was clear that this was more generally useful, the code was then refactored to be generally usable as a standalone `Builder` class. Since then, it has become the basis for other builders, such as `JmxBuilder`, and is available to us for deriving our own factory-based builders.

`FactoryBuilderSupport` works by orchestrating the construction process in concert with Factory classes. When the `FactoryBuilderSupport` class encounters a method tag, it constructs an appropriate `Factory` object to handle it. The factory provides method hooks that implement the construction of the individual object and the setting up of parent-child relationships between the objects.

To implement a builder with the `FactoryBuilderSupport` class, we must first declare a Factory class for each object type that we wish to process. Factory classes are derived from the `groovy.util.AbstractFactory` class and need to overload some or all of the following methods from the `AbstractFactory` class:

- `newInstance`: This method is called by `FactoryBuilderSupport` whenever it wants an object of a particular type to be constructed. It is similar to the `createNode` methods of `BuilderSupport` except that there is just one `newInstance` method, which accepts all argument types regardless of whether a value or attributes are supplied or not.

- `onHandleNodeAttributes`: This method allows the `Factory` class to take over the management of attributes. It can stop the builder from processing attributes by returning `true`.

- `setParent` and `setChild`: These methods provide hooks for managing the parent-child relationships between objects.

- `isLeaf`: We set this method to return `true` if the method tag being handled should be a leaf node and stops the builder treating any subsequent method calls as object declarations.

- `onNodeCompleted`: This method is called when a node is completed, in order to allow any finalization of the object to be performed. It is similar to `nodeCompleted` in `BuilderSupport`.

To build a replacement for the `CustomerBuilder` class with `FactoryBuilderSupport`, we first need to define Factory classes for each of the tag methods that we need to process. The first of these is the `customers` tag, which is straightforward enough. This tag does not cause any objects to be created, so all we do is return the tag name as the object created:

```
public class CustomersFactory extends AbstractFactory {

  public boolean isLeaf() {
    return false
  }

  public Object newInstance(FactoryBuilderSupport builder,
      Object name, Object value, Map attributes
  ) throws InstantiationException, IllegalAccessException {
    return name
  }

}
```

We then define a factory class for the `customer` object. The methods that we need to implement are `isLeaf` (returns `false`), `newInstance` (to create the `customer` object), and `onNodeCompleted` (to save it):

```
public class CustomerFactory extends AbstractFactory {

  public boolean isLeaf() {
    return false
  }

  public Object newInstance(FactoryBuilderSupport builder,
  Object name, Object value, Map attributes
  ) throws InstantiationException, IllegalAccessException {
      Customer customer = null
      if (attributes != null)
        customer = new Customer(attributes)
      else
        customer = new Customer()
      return customer
  }

  public void onNodeCompleted(FactoryBuilderSupport builder,
  Object parent, Object customer) {
      customer.save()
  }
}
```

The factory for `invoices` is equally straightforward. The only addition is that we need to take care of the parent-child relationship between customer and invoice. We do this by adding a `setParent` method, which will call `addToInvoices` on the `customer` object if required. We also need to check the value parameter passed to `newInstance` to see whether a `parent` is being set at this point:

```
public class InvoiceFactory extends AbstractFactory {

  public boolean isLeaf() {
    return false
  }

  public Object newInstance(FactoryBuilderSupport builder,
    Object name, Object value, Map attributes
    ) throws InstantiationException, IllegalAccessException {
      Invoice invoice = null
      if (attributes != null)
        invoice = new Invoice(attributes)
```

```
      else
        invoice = new Invoice()
      if (value != null && value instanceof Customer)
        value.addToInvoices(invoice)
      return invoice
  }

  public void setParent(FactoryBuilderSupport builder,
    Object parent, Object invoice) {
      if (parent != null && parent instanceof Customer)
        parent.addToInvoices(invoice)
  }

  public void onNodeCompleted(FactoryBuilderSupport builder,
    Object parent, Object invoice) {
      invoice.save()
  }
}
```

The factory for sales orders is identical to invoices except that we now return `true` from `isLeaf` because a `sales order` object will always be a leaf node in our tree:

```
public class SalesOrderFactory extends AbstractFactory {
  public boolean isLeaf() {
    return true
  }

  public Object newInstance(FactoryBuilderSupport builder,
    Object name, Object value, Map attributes
    ) throws InstantiationException, IllegalAccessException {
      SalesOrder sales_order = null
      if (attributes != null)
        sales_order = new SalesOrder(attributes)
      else
        sales_order = new SalesOrder()
      if (value != null && value instanceof Invoice)
        value.addToOrders(sales_order)
      return sales_order
  }

  public void setParent(FactoryBuilderSupport builder,
    Object parent, Object sales_order) {
      if (parent != null && parent instanceof Invoice)
```

```
            parent.addToOrders(sales_order)
    }

    public void onNodeCompleted(FactoryBuilderSupport builder,
      Object parent, Object sales_order) {
        sales_order.save()
    }
}
```

All of the intelligence of how to orchestrate the construction process is encapsulated in the FactoryBuilderSupport class. So, literally all we need to do for the whole builder to work is to register the Factory classes with appropriate tag names:

```
public class CustomersFactoryBuilder extends FactoryBuilderSupport {
    public CustomersFactoryBuilder(boolean init = true) {
        super(init)
    }

    def registerObjectFactories() {
      registerFactory("customers", new CustomersFactory())
        registerFactory("customer", new CustomerFactory())
        registerFactory("invoice", new InvoiceFactory())
        registerFactory("sales_order", new SalesOrderFactory())
    }

}
```

FactoryBuilderSupport uses reflection at runtime to detect what registration methods to run. By scanning the list of methods in the MetaClass instance and looking for methods that begin with register, FactoryBuilderSupport detects whether any additional registration methods are provided in the derived builder class. In the preceding example, the only registration method added is registerObjectFactories, but we could well have written code:

```
def registerCustomers() {
    registerFactory("customers", new CustomersFactory())
}

def registerCustomer() {
    registerFactory("customer", new CustomerFactory())
}

def regiaterInvoice() {
    registerFactory("invoice", new InvoiceFactory())
```

```
    }

    def registerSalesOrder() {
      registerFactory("sales_order", new SalesOrderFactory())
    }
```

`FactoryBuilderSupport` will detect all of these and run them in turn. Which method you use is a matter of choice. The only issue that you need to be aware of is that the registration methods will not be called in any predetermined order. If there are dependencies in your registration code, then it's best to group these into a single registration method.

To finish, we can drop this modified builder right where we previously used `CustomersBuilder`, and it will work in the same way:

```
    given:
    def builder = new CustomersFactoryBuilder()

    def customers = builder.customers {
        fred = customer(firstName:"Fred",lastName:"Flintstone") {
            invoice {
                sales_order(sku:"productid01", amount:1, price:1.00)
                sales_order(sku:"productid02", amount:2, price:1.00)
                sales_order(sku:"productid03", amount:3, price:1.00)
            }
        }
        invoice2 = invoice(fred)

        sales_order(invoice2, sku:"productid04", amount:1, price:1.00)
        sales_order(invoice2, sku:"productid05", amount:1, price:1.00)
        sales_order(invoice2, sku:"productid06", amount:1, price:1.00)
    }

    expect:
    CustomerWithInvoices.count() == 1
    Invoice.count() == 2
    SalesOrder.count() == 6
```

In terms of management and maintenance, this version is far superior. Adding capabilities now for new tables will simply involve writing a new Factory class and registering it.

Summary

In *Chapter 7, Power Groovy DSL Features*, we discussed how builders worked via the Groovy MOP. In this chapter, we have taken a deeper look at how features of the MOP are used to implement the builder pattern. We've looked at the language features used to create a builder, and seen how they involve implementing pretended methods and influence how methods calls are resolved. Implementing a builder directly by using the MOP in this way focuses on the nuts and bolts of the semantics of the builder, rather than the construction process.

In this chapter, we have seen how Groovy provides two useful support classes that make it much simpler to implement our own builders than if we use the MOP. We've seen how to use `BuilderSupport` and `FactoryBuilderSupport` to create our own builder classes.

Using these support classes greatly simplifies the implementation of builders. Hopefully, this will inspire you to see opportunities to develop your own Groovy-based builders for you own applications. You can find the full documentation for all of the classes that we covered here on the Codehaus website. The Groovy document for the classes can be found at `http://groovy.codehaus.org/api/groovy/util/package-summary.html`.

In the next chapter, we will make use of the techniques we learned here and build a DSL that is heavily based on the builder pattern.

11
Implementing a Rules DSL

In this chapter, we will look at how we can use Groovy to build a DSL that is capable of implementing business rules for an application. The example we will use is a system for implementing rewards bonuses of various kinds as part of a promotions system for an online broadband media provider.

Our provider hosts a service that allows users to view videos and play games online. The provider needs to be able to deploy offers to his users rapidly and with the minimum amount of development time. We will come up with a Groovy-based DSL that expresses rewards in such a way that they can be rapidly developed and deployed in a language that can also be understood by business stakeholders.

This DSL relies on a new concept that we have not covered yet, which is the use of Groovy binding. To begin with, we will look at Groovy bindings—how they work and how we can make use of them to improve our DSLs. We will cover a number of useful techniques that make use of binding.

- Using the binding in combination with closures to introduce built-in methods into a DSL

- Adding closures to the binding to implement structured named blocks in a DSL

- How Boolean and other values added to the binding can be used to build contextual data for a DSL

- How to return values and results from a DSL script

We will use all of these techniques in concert, and build a sample DSL step by step.

Groovy bindings

Every Groovy script has an associated binding object. The binding is where instances of variables referenced within the script are stored. The binding is an instance of the class `groovy.lang.Binding`, and we can access it in any script by referencing the built-in variable binding, as the next example will show.

 When we reference a previously undeclared variable in a script, Groovy creates an instance of the variable in the binding. On the other hand, variables that are defined within the script are considered local variables and are not found in the binding. The latter provides a convenient placeholder where Groovy can store these variables. This also presents the DSL with an opportunity. By manifesting variables in the binding, we can manipulate the script with predefined values. By adding a closure to the binding, we can provide built-in methods for the DSL.

In the following example, when we reference a new variable named `count` in a script, we see how that variable is stored in the binding. If we explicitly declare the variable `local` with `def`, we can use both variables interchangeably, but only `count` is stored in the binding.

```
count = 1

assert count == 1
assert binding.getVariable("count") == 1
binding.setVariable("count" , 2)
assert count == 2
assert binding.getVariable("count") == 2

def local = count

assert local == 2
try {
    binding.getVariable("local")
    assert false
} catch (e) {
    assert e in MissingPropertyException
}
```

Most of the examples we have encountered in the book are written to be run as Spock tests. The next few examples in this chapter are best run from the command line. You could also run this in the Groovy console but the Groovy console maintains a single binding object. So, each time you execute a script from the buffer, you are inheriting objects that were probably stored there during the previous runs. The examples in this chapter all assume a clean binding, so running successive examples in groovyConsole will lead to unpredictable results.

The power of bindings with regard to their use in DSLs comes from the fact that we can add a variable to the binding on the fly. If count does not exist as a variable in the script, then it can be added by a call to setVariable, as follows:

```
binding.setVariable("count" , 1)

assert binding.getVariable("count") == 1

binding.setVariable("count" , 2)

assert binding.getVariable("count") == 2
```

The binding class also implements the property access APIs, such as setProperty, getProperty, and getProperties. This means that the binding will allow bean-like access, including the use of the subscript operator.

```
binding.count = 1

assert binding.getProperty("count") == 1

binding.setProperty("count" , 2)

assert binding.count == 2
```

These examples might look like a clumsy way of getting and setting variables in a script, but the binding becomes really useful when we execute a script that we have loaded. Here we set a property message in the binding and then use the GroovyShell class to execute a script snippet that uses it.

```
def Binding binding = new Binding()

binding.message = "Hello, World!"

shell = new GroovyShell(binding)

shell.evaluate("println message")
```

This will output the string `Hello, World!` to the console. In other words, we have managed to introduce a variable into this script called `message` that has the preset value `Hello, World`.

Exploiting bindings in DSLs

There are numerous ways in which we can use bindings in our DSLs. In this section, we will discover how to use closures in the binding to implement several different DSL styles. We will also look at how simply adding properties to the binding can be an effective way to augment a DSL with shorthand.

Closures as built-in methods

We can add any property to the binding. This includes properties of the type `Closure`. If we add a closure to the binding then the binding variable can be addressed as if it were a built-in method. Here we add a `greet` property to the binding which acts as a `greet` method in the evaluated script.

```
def Binding binding = new Binding()

binding.greet = { subject ->
    println "Hello, $subject!"
}

shell = new GroovyShell(binding)
shell.evaluate("greet 'World'")
```

Closures as repeatable blocks

We've seen how using a closure within the binding can give the impression of having built-in functions in our DSL. We can also use closures in the binding to allow a nested block structure to be represented in the DSL. Using this style, we can repeat a block multiple times within a single script. This is useful when we have a DSL that needs to define multiple instances of the same entity or logic within the same script. Take the following script example:

```
block {
  nestedBlock {
  }
}
block {
  nestedBlock {
  }
}
```

We can implement this structure by adding two closures to the binding called `block` and `nestedBlock`. The `block` and `nestedBlock` closures accept a closure as their only parameter. We saw in *Chapter 5, Groovy Closures*, how this is exactly the same mechanism that is used to implement builders. The `block` and `nestedBlock` closures need to manage their delegates in order to ensure that the expected binding scopes are preserved.

```
binding.block = { closure ->
    def cloned = closure.clone()
    cloned.delegate = delegate
    this.enclosing = "block"

    println "block encountered"
    cloned()
}

binding.nestedBlock = { closure ->
    assert closure.delegate.enclosing == "block"
    def cloned = closure.clone()
    cloned.delegate = delegate
    this.enclosing = "nestedBlock"

    println "nested block encountered"
    cloned()
}

block {
  nestedBlock {
    }
}
block {
  nestedBlock {
    }
}
```

 In these examples, we cloned the passed-in closure before changing the delegate. This is considered the best practice with a DSL, in case the original closure is also used externally. This is also advisable if we make any changes to the closure resolve strategy.

By adding an `enclosing` property to the `block` and `nestedBlock` closures, we ensure that `nestedBlock` is only allowed within `block`. Placing `nestedBlock` outside of `block` will trigger the assertion. Running the original script with these closures in the binding will give the following output:

```
block encountered
nested block encountered
```

Using a specification parameter

If we like, we can also use closures that take one or more parameters in addition to the `closure` parameter; a common style, when using a structured block.

DSL, as mentioned earlier, is used to add a specification parameter to identify individual blocks.

The implementation can choose to ignore this parameter, or it can be used as a means of identifying the individual blocks.

```
binding.block = { spec, closure ->
    def cloned = closure.clone()
    cloned.delegate = delegate
    this.enclosing = "block"

    println "${spec} encountered"
    cloned()
}

binding.nestedBlock = { spec, closure ->
    assert closure.delegate.enclosing == "block"
    def cloned = closure.clone()
    cloned.delegate = delegate
    this.enclosing = "nestedBlock"

    println "${spec} encountered"
    cloned()
}

block ("first block") {
  nestedBlock ("first nested"){
    }
}
block "second block", {
    nestedBlock ("second nested"){
    }
}
```

This outputs:

```
first block encountered
first nested encountered
second block encountered
second nested encountered
```

In the previous code snippet, we see two styles of declaring a specification parameter:

```
block ("spec") {
}
block "spec", {
}
```

The first uses the Groovy "function call" style, passing the closure after the method parentheses. The second uses a parameter list, where one of the parameters is the inline closure. Which one you choose is a matter of personal preference and style.

Some developers have a preference for the latter style in their examples. My own personal preference is for the former, for the simple reason that it is easier for non-technical users to grasp the necessity for a `(something) {}` syntax rather than a `something, {}` syntax.

Closures as singleton blocks

The previous DSL style allows us to implement logic in repeatable named blocks. A DSL script of this style could be run just once or many times. For instance, the DSL could describe a set of business rules to be executed every time we encountered a certain event. Sometimes we need a DSL to define logic that is only ever going to be run once, or that needs to be stored and executed at will at some later date. In this case, it may be better to limit the user to a single block instance, by having them define the closure directly.

```
setup = {
    println "Initialized"
}

teardown = {
    println "finished"
}
```

Here we declare two named closures: setup and teardown. We can now provide default implementations of setup and teardown in the runtime that we use to load and evaluate this script:

```
def binding = new Binding()
binding.setup = {
    println "Setup block is missing"
    throw new Exception("Setup block is missing")
}

binding.teardown = {
    println "Teardown block is missing"
    throw new Exception("Teardown block is missing")
}

def shell = new GroovyShell(binding)
shell.evaluate(
"""setup = {
    'setup called'
  }
  teardown = {
    'teardown called'
  }
"""
)

setup = binding.setup
assert setup() == 'setup called'
// ... do something now and save teardown closure for later
teardown = binding.teardown
assert teardown() == 'teardown called'
```

> For brevity, in some of the following examples, we will use GroovyShell to evaluate our DSL scripts from GString. In most real life DSL scenarios, you will want to externalize your DSL code. GroovyShell can also be used to load and evaluate a script from a file.

An exception will be thrown if either setup or teardown has not been provided. This is a useful tactic to use to ensure that one and only one block is executed from the DSL. It also gives us control over the timing of when the blocks are actually executed.

The only word of caution to heed is that while using both this style of block and the previous in a single DSL, users will need to beware of the subtle difference between block {} and block = {}. Groovy allows a user to specify either, and this can give unexpected results that might be confusing to the general user.

Using binding properties to form context

Most DSLs need to have some predetermined knowledge of the domain within which they operate. So, for instance, if we were to write a DSL that described the rewards that a user might get for making purchases, it makes sense that the DSL would have built-in access to the user's account details and his purchasing history, rather than requiring complex lookups to be performed within the DSL.

The binding is the ideal place in which to store these details. Depending on the sophistication of the DSL target audience, we could decide to embed existing domain objects in the binding or, alternatively, we could look up or pre-calculate values that make sense to the DSL, and embed these.

```
class Account {
    double spend = 11.00
    double balance = 100.00
    boolean active = true

    void credit (double value) {
        balance += value
    }
}
def binding = new Binding()
binding.reward = { closure ->
    closure.delegate = delegate
    closure()
}

binding.apply = { closure ->
    closure.delegate = delegate
    closure()
}

// lookup account in binding
def account = new Account()
binding.account = account
binding.monthSpend = account.spend
binding.credit = account.&credit
```

```
assert account.balance == 100.00

def shell = new GroovyShell(binding)
shell.evaluate(
"""     reward {
            apply {
              if (account.active && monthSpend > 10.00)
                  credit 5.00
            }
         }
"""
)

assert account.balance == 105.00
```

Here we embed an `account` object in the binding, along with a calculated value for the user's monthly spend to date. We have also introduced a shortcut for the `account credit` method, by including a closure called `credit`, which is taken from the address of the `Account.credit` method.

Another useful technique is to predetermine states and `boolean` conditions, and store them in appropriately named binding variables. For the rewards DSL, some common tests that we might need to make are whether the account is active, and whether the minimum spending threshold has been reached. Setting these conditions into binding variables will further improve the readability of the DSL.

```
reward {
   apply {
      if (ACTIVE && REWARD_THRESHOLD_EXCEEDED)
         credit 5.00
   }
}
```

Storing and communicating results

Capturing the values of variables set in the DSL can also be done through the binding. The delegate is set by each calling closure, so any variables defined in the scope of the DSL blocks will be available as binding variables to the calling closures.

```
def binding = new Binding()
binding.outerBlock = { closure ->
   closure.delegate = delegate
   closure()
   println "outerBlock: " + binding.message
```

```
    }

    binding.innerBlock = { closure ->
        closure.delegate = delegate
        closure()
        println "innerBlock: " + binding.message
    }

    def shell = new GroovyShell(binding)
    shell.evaluate(
    """    outerBlock {
            innerBlock {
             message = "Hello, World!"
            }
        }
    """
    )
    println "caller: " + binding.message
```

In the preceding example, the `message` variable is set in the innermost block of the DSL, but we can reference it from the outer block closure, and also from the calling script. Variables set like this in the binding are global to the script, so care must be taken to initialize them to default values before referencing them. Otherwise, subsequent blocks within the DSL will reuse the values. In the following code, the `Hello, World!` message value is still set when the second `outerBlock` is evaluated:

```
    outerBlock {
        innerBlock {
            message = "Hello, World!"
        }
    }
    outerBlock {
        println message
    }
```

The output produced by this will not be what we expected. Setting a default value for the message in the closure definition for `binding.outerBlock` will overcome this.

```
inner: Hello, World!
outer: Hello, World!
Hello, World!
outer: Hello, World!
caller: Hello, World!
```

We know that closures and methods in Groovy will return a value even when no `return` statement is used. The value returned is the result of the last statement executed in the method or closure. We can exploit this in our DSLs. The value returned from `innerBlock` in the preceding code is the result of `message = "Hello, World!"` —in other words, the string `"Hello, World!"`. We can define a closure that captures a string value from the DSL, as follows:

```
binding.messageBlock = { closure ->
    closure.delegate = delegate

    binding.message = closure()
    println "messageBlock: ${binding.message}"
}
```

This allows us to define a message string by using the following DSL code:

```
outerBlock {
    messageBlock {
        "Hello, World!... message"
    }
}
```

Using this style, we can define a DSL block that expects a Boolean return value and use it to define a conditional expression. Going back to the reward DSL we used earlier, we could write the following conditional DSL code:

```
reward {
    appliesWhen {
        ACTIVE && REWARD_THRESHOLD_EXCEEDED
    }
}
```

We can document to our DSL users that `appliesWhen` declares a condition that must be met if the reward between the curly braces is to be awarded.

Building a rewards DSL

The old adage that 80 percent of business comes from your existing customers while 20 percent comes from new customers is as true today as it ever was. Every business, at some point in time, considers offering incentives to its customers in order to increase sales. Rewards can take the form of everything from the selective discounting of end-of-line items, through buy-one-get-one-free promotions, to customer loyalty points schemes.

Marketers constantly devise new ways to promote products and services to customers, but often the problem is that these promotions can be difficult to manage when they need to be implemented in the various backend systems. Configuring a reward could involve applying cross-cutting logic across several systems. Developing and deploying a promotion can take weeks or months to complete, while the marketing department wants to be able to respond to the conditions in the market today.

In this next example, we will take an imaginary broadband service provider that provides access to on-demand video and games content. We will devise a simple Groovy-based DSL that expresses reward programs in simple-to-understand terms. Although the DSL code is not going to be developed by a marketer, a marketer should be able to understand what the code does simply by reading it. This DSL also has the added benefit of being something that can be deployed directly. As such, the DSL should be able to serve as both the specification and the implementation of the reward.

Designing the DSL

Before attempting to design our DSL, it makes sense for us to review our business domain and understand our requirements.

BroadbandPlus

Users of BroadbandPlus, our imaginary broadband service, can subscribe to three levels of access: BASIC, PLUS, and PREMIUM. There is a range of content that a subscriber can consume, including games, movies, and music. Each subscriber can consume any mix of content up to the maximum allowed on their plan, after which they need to pay for any additional content that they consume.

To simplify everything, we will track and allow the subscriber to pick and mix their content. Each type of media consumed has an "access point" value, which is debited from the user's account when they consume it. Each subscriber type is allocated a set number of access points each month, based on their plan. The following table shows how the access points structure works:

Subscription plan	Monthly subscription	Access points
Basic	$9.99	120
Plus	$19.99	250
Premium	$39.99	550

Roughly speaking, an access point equates to 10 cents in value, so basic subscribers are benefiting from a 20 percent bonus versus non-subscribers. Moreover, plus subscribers get 25 percent extra while premium subscribers get a whopping 37.5 percent.

Media	Points	Type of access	Out of plan price
Movies			
New Release	40	Daily	$3.99
Other	30	Daily	$2.99
Games			
New Release	30	3 days access	$2.99
Other	20	3 days access	$1.99
Songs	10	Download	99c

Before consumption of any media is allowed, the system does a canConsume test. This test is passed if the user has enough access points, or if access has been granted already to the content and has not yet expired. If the canConsume test is passed, access to the media is granted when the first consume call is made, otherwise the user is prompted to approve the purchase of the media, followed by the consume call for an authorized purchase.

From the point of view of our rewards program, the APIs that we need to be concerned with are defined in the following stub class for BroadbandPlus:

```
class BroadbandPlus {

  boolean canConsume(subscriber, media) {
  }
  void consume(subscriber, media) {
  }
  void purchase(subscriber, media) {
  }
  void upgrade(subscriber, fromPlan, toPlan) {
  }

}
```

Reward types

We are in the business of encouraging the subscriber to continue to consume content out of plan or to upgrade to a higher plan. So our rewards programs will offer incentives that apply at the time of purchase or upgrade. Rewards usually consist of allocating free points, but we also want to be able to offer free content or extended access.

Our partners are the studios, game developers, and record labels that publish our content. We don't mind what content the subscriber consumes so long as our revenue comes in. As our partners get a revenue share based on which titles the subscriber consumes, they will want to be able to sponsor promotions that target specific content and specific publishers. In other words, these particular types of targeted reward programs need to be activated at the point of consumption rather than purchase.

Some examples of the types of rewards that we might like to deploy are:

* Consume any new release this week and get 10 free access points on your account
* Earn 10 percent bonus points for every game purchased
* Watch any Disney movie for 25 percent off
* Upgrade from basic to plus and get 100 free access points on your account

The reward DSL

Taking all of this into account, we can make an attempt at writing a DSL. The requirements that we have for our DSL can be summarized as follows:

* Rewards need to be triggered by different events in the system. These events are **consumption** (when a user consumes a product—that is, watch a movie, play a game, and so on), **upgrades** (when the user upgrades their subscription plan), and **purchases** (any time that the user spends some cash).
* Rewards need to be based on one or more conditions, such as the user's spending history or the type of media being consumed.
* Rewards can result in the granting of different benefits, for example free access to a video, bonus points, and extended access.

Based on these requirements, and with an understanding of how we can structure a DSL using closures and binding variables, we can make an attempt at how our DSL might look.

```
onConsume = { // or on_purchase or on_upgrade
    reward ( "Reward Description" ) {
        condition {
            // Condition(s) that need to apply
        }
        grant {
            // benefits that can accrue
        }
    }
}
```

We can implement the conditional nature of the preceding code snippet by using a binding variable to collect the result of the condition block. The following closure shows this in action. The condition closure collects the result of its own closure, which in turn dictates whether the grant closure is invoked.

```
binding.condition = { closure ->
    closure.delegate = delegate

    binding.result = (closure() && binding.result)
}

binding.grant = { closure ->
    closure.delegate = delegate

    if (binding.result)
        closure()
}
```

If the target audience for this DSL were to be only software developers, then this would be adequate. A single condition block returning a result could fully capture the logic required to allow or disallow a reward. The problem with this is that the only way to express multiple conditions is through Groovy conditional logic. Programmers don't mind reading this, but other audiences for the DSL will quickly get confused by the Groovy syntax involved. Groovy && and || operators, along with the operator precedence rules, are not going to make for easy reading for the general audience.

Ideally, we want to have a single condition in each block, so we need to allow multiple blocks, and provide an easy way to describe inclusive and exclusive sets of conditions. Adding two more closures to the DSL gives us just that.

```
reward ( "anyOf and allOf blocks" ) {
    allOf {
        condition {
            }
        ... more conditions
    }
    condition {
    }
    anyOf {
            condition {
                }
        +... more conditions
    }
    grant {
    }
}
```

Now we can have multiple condition blocks within a reward. All condition blocks must be true for the reward to be granted. The allOf and anyof condition blocks can each themselves contain multiple condition blocks. For an allOf condition block to be true, all child conditions must be true. For an anyOf block to be true, at least one of the child conditions must be true.

To implement this scheme, we need to tell the condition block whether it should AND (&&) or OR (||) its result to the current condition of the expression. We shall store the current status of the condition in a binding variable called result and decide whether to && or || based on the status of the binding Boolean useAnd. To begin with, for each reward we presume that the reward is passed, and set result to true. We set the default operator to && by setting useAnd to true.

```
binding.reward = { spec, closure ->
    closure.delegate = delegate
    binding.result = true
    binding.useAnd = true
    closure()
}

binding.condition = { closure ->
    closure.delegate = delegate
```

```
        if (binding.useAnd)
          binding.result = (closure() && binding.result)
        else
          binding.result = (closure() || binding.result)
  }
```

To implement the `allOf` closure block, we store the current states of `result` and `useAnd`, before calling the child closure. We `&&` or `||` the stored result with the new result from the closure, giving us the new `boolean` state of the expression. The starting presumption of an `allOf` block is that it is `true`. It will be set to `false` if any one of the child conditions returns `false`.

```
    binding.allOf = { closure ->
      closure.delegate = delegate
      def storeResult = binding.result
      def storeAnd = binding.and
      binding.result = true // Starting premise is true
      binding.and = true

      closure()

      if (storeAnd) {
        binding.result = (storeResult && binding.result)
      } else {
        binding.result = (storeResult || binding.result)
      }
      binding.and = storeAnd
    }
```

The `anyOf` closure block is identical to `allOf` except that the starting presumption is false. The operator that we now use is `||`, so if any one of the child conditions returns `true`, the overall result will be `true`.

```
    binding.anyOf = { closure ->
      closure.delegate = delegate
      def storeResult = binding.result
      def storeAnd = binding.and

      binding.result = false // Starting premise is false
      binding.and = false

      closure()
      if (storeAnd) {
        binding.result = (storeResult && binding.result)
      } else {
```

```
    binding.result = (storeResult || binding.result)
  }
  binding.and = storeAnd
}
```

This gives us a very flexible conditional logic that we can include in the DSL, which is still very legible to a general audience. We can test the effectiveness of this with a few assertions. The `result` binding variable is available to the DSL script, so we can use that to assert that the result is as expected. Next we want try out some of the ways to use our conditional DSL, but first let's put our DSL into a script that we can run from the command line.

This script sets up our mini DSL by adding some closure to the binding. It then invokes the reward script passed to it via the command line. We can test out the validity of our conditional logic by passing some of the following conditional scripts:

- A reward defined without any conditions should always be `true`.

```
reward ( "No conditions" ) {
    assert result == true
}
```

- With a single condition, the state of the reward is dictated by that one condition.

```
reward ( "One false condition" ) {
    condition {
        false
    }
    assert result == false
}
```

- By using `allOf` and `anyOf` combined with a condition, we can nest to any depth without losing legibility.

```
reward ( "nested anyOf and allOf conditions" ) {
  anyOf {
    allOf {
            condition {
                true
            }
            condition {
                false
            }
    }
        condition {
           false
```

```
            }
            anyOf {
                    condition {
                        false
                    }
                    condition {
                        true
                    }
            }
        }
      assert result == true
  }
```

Handling events – deferred execution

Running this particular DSL from the command line is not particularly useful. In order to be useful, our rewards DSL will eventually need to be hooked into the runtime of our broadband provider's backend applications. Rewards need to be applied as the result of different events in these systems. Some rewards will be applied at the point of consumption of the individual media. Other rewards will be applied at purchase time, and others when significant account events occur, such as upgrading from one plan to another.

Placing all of the rewards in a single DSL script means that they will all be executed in sequence when we load and evaluate the script. We could decide to separate the rewards into three script files, one for each type of event. On each event being triggered in the application, we would load and execute the appropriate reward script; for a consumption event, we load the onConsume script, and so on. This would work, but considering the amount of loading and parsing required for each event, it could become a drag on performance.

There is an alternative approach that will allow us to keep all of the rewards in a single script and also allow us to load the full script only once. Earlier on in this chapter, we talked about using closures as a singleton. This means, having a single instance of a named closure when the user supplies the implementation. We can partition the rewards script into three possible sections by using this pattern.

```
onConsume = {
    reward {
        ...
    }
    ...
}
onPurchase = {
    reward {
```

```
        ...
    }
    ...
}
onUpgrade = {
    ...
}
```

By using this structure for the DSL, the loading and evaluating of the script simply causes the three closure assignments to be executed. On completion of the evaluation of the script, there will be three closure variables in the binding, which contain the reward logic. This small change to the structure means that we can now load and evaluate the script just once on initialization, and invoke the specific rewards for consume, purchase, and upgrade as required.

Here we see how we can use GroovyShell to defer execution of a closure block:

```
def binding = new Binding()
binding.saved = {
}

binding.deferred = { closure ->
    closure.delegate = delegate
    closure()
}

def shell = new GroovyShell(binding)
shell.evaluate(
"""
saved = {
        println "saved"
          deferred {
           println "deferred"
          }
    }
"""
)
storeSaved = binding.saved
```

In the preceding snippet, the `evaluate` method of the DSL script will set `saved` to be the closure that is provided within the script. We can store this in a closure variable to be reused later. Evaluating the `saved` closure in `GroovyShell` once again gives us the opportunity to set up the binding to support our DSL. Prior to calling `saved()` in the evaluated script, we need to set its delegate. This ensures that the saved closure inherits the binding that we pass into the script.

```
def binding = new Binding()

binding.saved = store_saved
binding.deferred = { closure ->
   closure.delegate = delegate
   closure()
}

def shell = new GroovyShell(binding)
shell.evaluate("saved.delegate = this; saved()")
```

We now have a means of stripping out the closures defined within the main script and executing them at will.

Convenience methods and shorthand

The final piece of our DSL that we need to take care of is to add some convenience methods and shorthand binding variables, in order to make the DSL more legible. First, we add some actions to be taken when a reward is granted. In the case of our rewards DSL, the actions that we want for now are the ability to extend access to a video or game, or to add points to a subscriber's account.

In reality, we would implement many more of these, including granting access to specific videos or games. The features that we can add to the DSL are limited only by our imagination and the features provided in the backend systems that we are working with. Most likely our DSL would evolve over time, with new action verbs and other shorthand features being added.

```
binding.extend = { days ->
   def bbPlus = new BroadbandPlus()
   bbPlus.extend( binding.account, binding.media, days)
}
binding.points = { points ->
   binding.account.points += points
}
```

We implement the `extend` action through a method call on the `BroadbandPlus` service. The `points` action is just a shorthand way of updating the account points value that is always in the binding. In this way, we can extend the vocabulary of the DSL to include any actions that we might like to perform on the system.

We further improve the legibility of our scripts by adding some shorthand to be used in conditionals. Common tests that we encounter when deciding to grant a reward are the type of media being consumed or purchased, and whether it is a new release or not. We add some shorthand to the DSL by including `boolean` binding variables for these common conditions.

```
binding.is_new_release = media.newRelease
binding.is_video = (media.type == "VIDEO")
```

The offers

Putting all of these DSL features together, we now have a mini DSL that will allow us to define how rewards should be granted to subscribers based on their consumption and purchasing behavior. Earlier in the chapter, we listed some reward types that we would like to support. Let's see now how well we can express those rewards by using the DSL that we have just designed. If we've done our job well, the reward DSL should be all we need to read to fully understand the intent and impact of applying the reward.

```
onConsume = {
  reward ( "Watch a Pixar Movie, get 25% extra points." ) {
    allOf {
      condition {
        media.publisher == "Disney"
      }
      condition {
        isVideo
      }
    }

    grant {
      points media.points / 4
    }
  }
  reward ( "Rent a new release, get extra night rental" ) {
    condition {
      isNewRelease
    }
```

```
        grant {
          extend 1
        }
      }
    }

    onPurchase = {
      reward ( "Earn 10% bonus points on all games." ) {
        condition {
          isGame
        }
        grant {
          points media.points / 10
        }
      }
    }

    onUpgrade = {
      reward ("Upgrade to PLUS and get 100 free points") {
        condition {
          toPlan == "PLUS"
        }
        grant {
          points 100
        }
      }
    }
}
```

The RewardService class

We now have a very usable DSL design that can express the rewards as a script.
All that remains is to implement the means to integrate this DSL into our application.
It makes sense to package all of this functionality into a service class that can
be called by our application when needed. To do this, we provide a class called
RewardService.

The RewardService class provides a static method, loadRewardRules, that needs
to be called first, in order to initialize the rewards. This method takes care of the
initial loading of the rewards from the script file. Initial default implementations
of the onConsume, onPurchase, and onUpgrade closures are provided by the
RewardService class. Their only purpose is to provide a stub, which will be
called if any of these closures has not been provided by the DSL. Once loaded, the
RewardService class maintains static copies of the closure, to be called as needed by
the event hook methods.

`RewardService` provides three event hook methods: `applyRewardsOnConsume`, `applyRewardsOnPurchase`, and `applyRewardsOnUpgrade`. These hook methods are to be called in response to consume, purchase, and upgrade events in the system. The hook methods take care of preparing the binding with the necessary closures and binding variables, before performing a deferred invocation of the `onConsume`, `onPurchase`, or `onUpgrade` closures that were stored earlier. The convenience methods `prepareClosures` and `prepareMedia` set up some of the common binding variables, which implement our built-in action methods and other `boolean` shorthands.

```
class RewardService {
    static boolean on_consume_provided = true
    def static onConsume = {
        on_consume_provided = false
    }
    static boolean on_purchase_provided = true
    def static onPurchase = {
        on_purchase_provided = false
    }
    static boolean on_upgrade_provided = true
    def static onUpgrade = {
        on_upgrade_provided = false
    }

    void prepareClosures (Binding binding) {
        binding.onConsume = onConsume
        binding.onPurchase = onPurchase
        binding.onUpgrade = onUpgrade
        binding.reward = { spec, closure ->
                closure.delegate = delegate
                binding.result = true
                binding.and = true
                closure()
        }
        binding.condition = { closure ->
            closure.delegate = delegate

            if (binding.and)
                binding.result = (closure() && binding.result)
            else
                binding.result = (closure() || binding.result)
        }
```

```
binding.allOf = { closure ->
   closure.delegate = delegate
   def storeResult = binding.result
   def storeAnd = binding.and
       binding.result = true // Starting premise is true
       binding.and = true

   closure()

   if (storeAnd) {
      binding.result = (storeResult && binding.result)
   } else {
      binding.result = (storeResult || binding.result)
   }
   binding.and = storeAnd
}

 binding.anyOf = { closure ->
       closure.delegate = delegate
   def storeResult = binding.result
   def storeAnd = binding.and

       binding.result = false // Starting premise is false
       binding.and = false

       closure()
   if (storeAnd) {
      binding.result = (storeResult && binding.result)
   } else {
      binding.result = (storeResult || binding.result)
   }
   binding.and = storeAnd
}

binding.grant = { closure ->
       closure.delegate = delegate

       if (binding.result)
              closure()
}
binding.extend = { days ->
   def bbPlus = new BroadbandPlus()
   bbPlus.extend( binding.account, binding.media, days)
}
```

```
        binding.points = { points ->
            def bbPlus = new BroadbandPlus()
            binding.account.points += points
        }
    }
    void prepareMedia(binding, media) {
        binding.media = media
        binding.is_new_release = media.newRelease
        binding.is_video = (media.type == "VIDEO")
        binding.is_game = (media.type == "GAME")
        binding.is_song = (media.type == "SONG")
    }
    static void loadRewardRules() {
        Binding binding = new Binding()

        binding.onConsume = onConsume
        binding.onPurchase = onPurchase
        binding.onUpgrade = onUpgrade

        GroovyShell shell = new GroovyShell(binding)
        shell.evaluate(new File("rewards/rewards.groovy"))

        onConsume = binding.onConsume
        onPurchase = binding.onPurchase
        onUpgrade = binding.onUpgrade
    }
    void applyRewardsOnConsume(account, media) {
        if (on_consume_provided) {
            Binding binding = new Binding()
            binding.account = account
            prepareClosures(binding)
            prepareMedia(binding, media)

            GroovyShell shell = new GroovyShell(binding)
            shell.evaluate("on_consume.delegate = this;onConsume()")
        }
    }
    void applyRewardsOnPurchase(account, media) {
        if (on_purchase_provided) {
            Binding binding = new Binding()
            binding.account = account
            prepareClosures(binding)
            prepareMedia(binding, media)
```

```
            GroovyShell shell = new GroovyShell(binding)
            shell.evaluate("on_purchase.delegate =
            this;onPurchase()")
        }
    }
    void applyRewardsOnUpgrade(account, plan) {
        if (on_upgrade_provided) {
            Binding binding = new Binding()
            binding.account = account
            binding.to_plan = plan
            binding.from_plan = account.plan
            prepareClosures(binding)

            GroovyShell shell = new GroovyShell(binding)
            shell.evaluate("on_upgrade.delegate = this;onUpgrade()")
        }
    }
}
```

The BroadbandPlus application classes

In order to show this DSL working, we need to flesh out some classes in order to
implement a rudimentary application skeleton for our imaginary BroadbandPlus
service. We won't scrutinize these classes in too much detail, as their main purpose is
to provide the hooks to exercise our DSL, and not to represent a working system.

To begin with, we need to define an Account class. The Account class maintains
the basic subscription details for a subscriber, including the plan he is on and his
remaining points for this period. It also maintains the current list of media that he
has access to. Once the consumption of an item starts, the media is added to this list,
along with an expiry date. The expiry date can be extended at any time by calling the
extendMedia method.

```
class Account {
    String subscriber
    String plan
    int points
    double spend
    Map mediaList = [:]
    void addMedia (media, expiry) {
        mediaList[media] = expiry
    }
    void extendMedia(media, length) {
        mediaList[media] += length
    }
```

```
      Date getMediaExpiry(media) {
         if(mediaList[media] != null) {
            return mediaList[media]
         }
      }
   }
}
```

The `Media` class is used to describe individual items from the media catalog.
Properties of the class define its price and access points value, along with other
properties that help to categorize it, such as the media type (VIDEO, GAME, or SONG),
the publisher, and whether it is a new release or not.

```
class Media {
    String title
    String publisher
    String type
    boolean newRelease
    int points
    double price
    int daysAccess
}
```

The `BroadbandPlus` class implements the backend services that we expect, and
defines the APIs that we need to manage the consumption of media, purchasing,
and account upgrades. These APIs make calls to `RewardService` as required, in
order to apply the various rewards for `onConsume`, `onPurchase`, and `onUpgrade`.

The `consume` API will add the consumed media to the account's media list on the
first consumption. The purchase API adds the points value of the purchased media
to the account's points balance. Upgrade takes the current period balance into
account by simply adding the points difference between the original and
upgrade plans.

```
class BroadbandPlus {
    def rewards = new RewardService()

    def canConsume = { account, media ->
        def now = new Date()
        if (account.mediaList[media]?.after(now))
            return true

        account.points > media.points
    }
    def consume = { account, media ->
        // First consume add media to accounts access list
```

```
        if (account.mediaList[media.title] == null) {
            def now = new Date()
            account.points -= media.points
            account.mediaList[media] = now + media.daysAccess
            // Rewards only applied on first consumption
            rewards.applyRewardsOnConsume(account, media)
        }
    }
    def purchase = { account, media ->
        rewards.applyRewardsOnPurchase(account, media)
        account.points += media.points
        account.spend += media.price
    }
    def upgrade = { account, newPlan ->
        if (account.plan == "BASIC" && newPlan == "PLUS")
            account.points += 130
        if (account.plan == "BASIC" && newPlan == "PREMIUM")
            account.points += 430
        if (account.plan == "PLUS" && newPlan == "PREMIUM")
            account.points += 300

        rewards.applyRewardsOnUpgrade(account, newPlan)
        account.plan = newPlan
    }
    def extend = {account, media, days ->
        if (account.mediaList[media] != null) {
            account.mediaList[media] += days
        }
    }
}
```

Testing with Spock

Finally, we can test to see if our reward scripts are being triggered as expected, by writing a Spock test specification for it. Here, we can verify that each individual reward that we have defined is being triggered. We do this by setting up consumption, purchase, and upgrade scenarios that we expect to trigger the reward.

In the `setup` method, we create an `account` object with a `BASIC` plan. We set up four different media objects, and load the reward rules. We can assert that the outcome was as expected. For instance, in the first test we consume a Disney video and assert that the bonus points have been added. For completeness, we then consume a non-Disney video and see that no bonus points have been added.

```
def account
def up
def terminator
def halo3
def halo1
def bbPlus


def setup() {
    account = new Account(plan:"BASIC", points:120, spend:0.0)
    up = new Media(title:"UP", type:"VIDEO", newRelease:true,
                price:3.99, points:40, daysAccess:1,
                publisher:"Disney")
    terminator = new Media(title:"Terminator", type:"VIDEO",
                newRelease:false, price:2.99, points:30,
                daysAccess:1, publisher:"Fox")
    halo3 = new Media(title:"Halo III", type:"GAME",
                newRelease:true, price:2.99, points:30,
                daysAccess:3, publisher:"Microsoft")
    halo1 = new Media(title:"Halo", type:"GAME",
                newRelease:false, price:1.99, points:20,
                daysAccess:3,publisher:"Microsoft")
    bbPlus = new BroadbandPlus()
    RewardService.loadRewardRules()

}
def "Disney Reward programme is applied"() {
    expect:
    bbPlus.canConsume(account, up)
    account.points == 120

    when:
    def expected = account.points - up.points + up.points / 4
    bbPlus.consume(account, up)
```

```
            then:
            account.points == expected

            when:
            bbPlus.consume(account, terminator)

            then:
            account.points == expected - terminator.points
        }
        def "Rental extension reward"() {
            given:
            bbPlus.consume(account, up)
            bbPlus.consume(account, terminator)
            def now = new Date()
            expect: "Extension applied to Up but not Terminator"
            account.getMediaExpiry(up).after(now + 1)
            account.getMediaExpiry(
                    terminator).after(now + 1) == false
        }
        def "Purchase reward applied to Games"() {
            expect:
            account.points == 120

            when:
            bbPlus.purchase(account,  terminator)
            bbPlus.consume(account,  terminator)
            then:
            account.points == 120
            when:
            bbPlus.purchase(account,  halo1)
            bbPlus.consume(account,  halo1)
            then:
            account.points == 122

        }

        def "Upgrade to plus reward"() {
            expect:
            account.points == 120

            when:
            bbPlus.upgrade(account,  "PLUS")
            then: "Should have 250 for PLUS and 100 bonus"
```

```
            account.points == 350

            when:
            bbPlus.upgrade(account,  "PREMIUM")
            then: "Should have 550 for PREMIUM and 100 bonus"
            account.points == 650
    }

    def "Upgrade to premium reward"() {
            expect:
            account.points == 120

            when:
            bbPlus.upgrade(account,  "PREMIUM")
            then: "Should have 550 for PREMIUM and 100 bonus"
            account.points == 650
    }
```

Running this test case should pass all of the tests. This would verify that all of
the rewards that we have deployed in the DSL are being activated as expected.
However, the final testUpgradeToPremiumReward fails. This reveals a flaw in
our reward logic. The conditions that we have used allow a bonus for upgrading
from BASIC to PLUS. If the subscriber then upgrades to PREMIUM, they keep the
bonus points. However, a subscriber upgrading from BASIC straight to PREMIUM is
disadvantaged by not receiving the bonus, which was not our intention.

```
onUpgrade = {
    reward ("Upgrade to PLUS and get 100 free points") {
        anyOf {
            condition {
                toPlan == "PLUS"
            }
            allOf {
                condition {
                    toPlan == "PREMIUM"
                }
                condition {
                    fromPlan == "BASIC"
                }
            }
        }
        grant {
            points 100
        }
    }
}
```

Changing the onConsume reward script fixes this anomaly. Running our tests again will show them all passing as expected. So now we have a rewards DSL script with a service class that implements it. We've hooked the rewards service into the domain service so that it is triggered on the important events within the backend services. We've tested out the rewards by using some test cases. We should now have a good degree of confidence that, if BroadbandPlus was a real application service, our reward programs would be getting called at the appropriate times.

Summary

We covered a lot of ground in this chapter. We took a look at Groovy bindings to see how they can be used in our DSL scripts. By placing closures strategically in the binding, we can emulate named blocks of code. We can also provide built-in methods and other shorthand by including closures and named Boolean values in the binding. These techniques can be used to great effect to write DSL scripts that can be read and understood by stakeholders outside of the programming audience.

We've worked through a full implementation of a DSL for customer rewards by using these techniques, and we've seen how such a DSL can be integrated into an existing application. The reader should now have the confidence to start generating their own domain-specific DSLs that implement features in a similar way and integrate them into their own applications.

In the next and final chapter we will cover another fully worked DSL. The DSL we will implement in *Chapter 12, Integrating It All*, will make full use of AST transformations and will build on the techniques we covered in *Chapter 8, AST Transformations*.

Integrating It All

In this final chapter, we will build a fully functioning DSL and integrate it into a web application. In doing so, we will cover the issues you will encounter when integrating your own DSLs into existing applications. The DSL we will look at is a proof of concept DSL that implements a simple state machine style game engine with server-side engine logic, which supports a HTML user interface.

- The DSL was written to support teaching Groovy, so we will start by looking at how we can use DSL techniques to help with teaching programming to kids
- We will see how those ideas evolved into the proof of concept game engine DSL we will build in this chapter
- We will look at how we can structure the game engine as a pattern of Groovy classes and then see how we can implement an AST transform to generate that pattern
- We will see how we can integrate the DSL into a spring boot game server with a MongoDB session store
- Finally, we will build a simple mobile UI for the game with HTML5 and jQuery Mobile

Groovy as a teaching language

I've had the wonderful opportunity in the last year to be involved with the CoderDojo Foundation via my local CoderDojo. CoderDojo is a global movement of free volunteer-led, community-based programming clubs for young people at `https://coderdojo.com`. I joined Wexford CoderDojo as a mentor in January 2015.

The club was teaching a Java class to the more senior students who had already graduated from Scratch and HTML. The mentors were struggling with teaching Java to youngsters. The amount of ceremony needed to set up even a simple `HelloWorld.java` class was hard for the kids to grasp. The fact that you need a class and a main method and all those semicolons caused a lot of puzzled faces and most of the classes were occupied with helping the kids correct simple syntax errors.

My immediate reaction was, "Ouch! I don't want to be teaching Java", so I suggested we try Groovy instead. In that way, all we needed to do for a Hello World script was:

```
println "Hello, World!"
```

Which is what we did. It has turned out to be a great decision. By losing all the extraneous Java syntax we have been able to focus on introducing basic programming concepts in a far more natural order. Starting with variables, conditionals and looping, we then introduced methods and classes only when there was a natural need to do so.

As soon as we started using Groovy, we also started seeing opportunities to use the DSL features of the language to improve the experience for the kids. By building our own script launcher we were able to add built-in features to the coding environment that made life easier, for example:

- While Groovy has `println` as an easily accessible shortcut, there is no easy way to accept input on the command line so we added `readln` and variants.

- We noticed that the stack traces and compile errors were confusing to the kids so we captured those and simplified them.

- We added other goodies like a built-in banner method which produces ASCII text using JFiglet:

```
banner "Groovy"
```

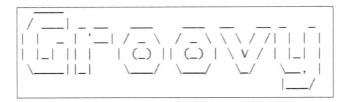

Hiding complexity

Overall, what we found was that, by hiding some of the complexity inside a runtime environment, the kids were able to focus on getting their own pieces of the code to work. This turns out to fit well with what they would have experienced in the other classes. Most would have started programming in the Scratch environment, `https://scratch.mit.edu/`.

Scratch is a visual programming environment for kids where they can plug together logic elements in a drag and drop editor. It's a visual DSL for kids. When they arrive in the Groovy class they are used to having a lot of power at their fingertips. HTML teaches them that syntax is important and that they need to be careful about what they write, but it also gives them an expectation that they can produce a rich user interface.

Entry into the Groovy room is supposed to be a graduation from the Scratch and HTML world and it certainly is. It's the first introduction to *proper* programming so to speak. Groovy, as we know it, is a lot simpler than Java and requires less punctuation but it is still a step beyond either Scratch or HTML. We wanted to avoid the trap whereby the Groovy class was considered too hard or too boring because the kids did not get enough feedback for their efforts.

With this in mind, we began to take the approach that we would provide framework classes as helpers for the kids. The more advanced students would be able to help build the classes while the others were happy to be able to build programs using them.

An ongoing theme during term was a project to build a functioning TicTacToe program. This was a console-based program that started out just taking user input to allow two players to play each other on the same computer. We then started to introduce concepts that allowed the kids to write code to automate the game. By the end, most of the students had understood the concepts and were able to write simple player strategy classes like the following. These are actual classes developed by Nathan and Eoghan, two of the CoderDojo Ninjas.

```groovy
class NathanPlayer extends Bot {
def playRound(grid) {
        if (!Grid.isSolved(grid)) {
            if (Grid.canWin(grid,this.player))
                Grid.playWin grid, this.player
            else if (Grid.canBlock(grid, this.player))
                Grid.playBlock grid, this.player
            else if (Grid.canTakeCenter(grid, this.player))
                Grid.playCenter grid, this.player
            else if (Grid.canTakeCorner(grid, this.player))
```

```
                Grid.playCorner grid, this.player
            else
                Grid.playRandomCell grid, this.player
        }
    }
}
class EoghanPlayer extends Bot {
def playRound(grid) {
        if (!Grid.isSolved()) {
            if (Grid.canWin(grid, this.player))
                Grid.playWin grid, this.player
            else if (Grid.canBlock(grid, this.player))
                Grid.playBlock grid, this.player
            else if (Grid.canTakeCorner(grid, this.player))
                Grid.playCorner grid, this.player
            else if (Grid.canTakeCenter(grid, this.player))
                Grid.playCenter grid, this.player
            else
                Grid.playRandomCell grid, this.player
        }
    }
}
```

Not bad for 10-12 year olds! The preceding code represents two TicTacToe player
bots that implement Nathan and Eoghan's strategies for playing the game. The class
relies heavily on the Grid class, which was a boilerplate we provided. Nathan and
Eoghan would also have helped us flesh out this class. We discovered early on that
coding the methods to detect whether the grid was solved or to play a blocking mode
were beyond the skill level of most students. However most were able to work out
how to implement Grid.canTakeCenter, Grid.playCenter, Grid.canTakeCorner,
and Grid.playCorner.

A game DSL for kids

By the closing weeks of term 2 we had quite a nice console-based TicTacToe game
built. The first of the kids were starting to complete functioning strategy classes and
we could play two strategies against each other in an automated game. It was time
to up the ante. The challenge now was to find a way to allow the kids to get more
return for their efforts. If you asked them what they would like to build, games and
something running on a mobile ranked high on their lists.

So this chapter is a response to that need. It's been coded part-time over a period of a few weeks. What I'll present here is a work in progress and it is presented warts and all. It is, however, a worthy illustration of a real life DSL integrated into lots of the technologies you might end up using yourselves. Let's look at what the goals were when writing this DSL and how they impacted the technology choices I made.

A game DSL – goals

- The first goal for this DSL was to get beyond the console-bound apps that we had been building. Something that could work in conjunction with a web-based UI would be good but ideally something that would allow a mobile app as the UI would be best.

- We needed to build on the existing skills that the kids had acquired.

- There would need to be a very simple interaction between the game logic on the one hand and the user interface on the other. The kids would need to be able, in time, to work on both aspects.

- We used the Cloud9 online web-based IDE `https://c9.io/`. So we needed a solution that would run on a remote workspace. The mentors typically used a premium workspace account but the students worked on free accounts, which limited their VMs to 512 MB RAM and 1 GB disk. Ideally, we wanted to be able to run the environment and compile the DSL code on the student's free accounts.

Architecture and technology choices

We needed a user interface technology that would be familiar to the kids and support both web and mobile. A combination of HTML5 with jQuery mobile is what I picked. jQuery mobile has a good page-oriented model for display purposes which fits well with the page-oriented state model we will implement in the game DSL.

The page content needed to be dynamic based on the current game state, so some sort of page templating engine was needed. Mustache.js is a good fit here. Mustache templates are very close to pure HTML so the kids would be on familiar territory when using them.

The UI works as a **single-page app** (**SPI**) and communicates with the game engine backend via JSON AJAX calls. The game server is a Spring MVC app, which is bootstrapped easily using Spring Boot and responds to all calls in JSONP.

Events are received by the game server and dispatched to the game engine code, which is generated from the DSL. The DSL itself is modeled on the state machine DSL we built in *Chapter 8, AST Transformations*.

The game DSL includes the ability to define state variables. The current value of these state variables is passed back to the UI after each event so that the UI can update its state. Events are sent asynchronously so we need to persist some session states between events. We do this in a MongoDB database which we access via Spring Data mappings for MongoDB.

TicTacToe in a DSL

So let's look at some code. In this section we will look at the DSL representation of a basic TicTacToe game. This DSL works in conjunction with the grid and player classes we mentioned earlier to form the core game logic for the TicTacToe game.

When I build a relatively complex DSL like this one, which uses AST transforms, I like to first get a non-DSL version working as a Java or Groovy implementation. Let's first look at the TicTacToe DSL:

```
import com.dearle.game.engine.Grid

page: "welcome"
page: "players"
page: "roundX"
page: "roundO"
page: "gameover"

state:
    String playerX
    String playerO
    List players
    String winner
    def grid = [
            ' ', ' ', ' ',
            ' ', ' ', ' ',
            ' ', ' ', ' '
    ]


event: "game_start"
    players = getPlayers()
    page = "players"
```

```
event: "select_players"
    playerX = event.playerX
    playerO = event.playerO
    page = "roundX"

event: "play_round"
    def player = getPlayer(event.player)

    player.playRound(grid)

    if (Grid.isSolved(grid)) {
        winner = event.player
        page = "gameover"
    } else {
        if (event.player == 'X') {
            page = "roundO"
        } else {
            page = "roundX"
        }
    }

event: "game_end"
    page = "welcome"
```

The preceding DSL models the basic states and events of the TicTacToe game. We refer to the states as pages since it is easier to explain to the kids how a state corresponds to a page in the game. The state of the game is represented by whatever state variables are declared in the `state:` block of the DSL.

The basic game engine mechanism is simple enough. We declare the pages in the game. A page could be a simple start page or a step in a game. We declare the state variables that the game relies on. Then we declare the events that the engine can respond to. The DSL writer codes the logic of the game in the event blocks. We can optionally assign a new value to the built-in page state variable in the logic. This will cause the game to transition to that page. If no assignment is made, then the game continues on the same page.

This particular game engine also has the concept of automated player bots built in. The code in the event block can be any valid Groovy code. We can call the built-in functions to get a list of players and any assignment to a built-in variable page is assumed to represent a desired page transition in the game. The event block has an implied event parameter, which will contain any parameters passed to it by the UI. Before we look at the AST transformation that implements this DSL, let's first look at a Groovy class pattern that implements the same logic. This pattern of classes is what the AST transform will generate at compile time:

```
class GameEngineClient implements GameEngineTraits {
    def GameEngineClient() {
    }
    def GameEngineClient(session) {
        this.session = session
    }
    Map game_start(Object event = null, Object saved = null) {
        restoreSession('TicTacToeEngine', saved)
        session.page.game_start(event)
        session.asMap()
    }
    Map select_players(Object event = null, Object saved = null) {
        restoreSession('TicTacToeEngine', saved)
        session.page.select_players(event)
        session.asMap()
    }
    Map play_round(Object event = null, Object saved = null) {
        restoreSession('TicTacToeEngine', saved)
        session.page.play_round(event)
        session.asMap()
    }
    Map game_end(Object event = null, Object saved = null) {
        restoreSession('TicTacToeEngine', saved)
        session.page.game_end(event)
        session.asMap()
    }
}
```

This is the class that the game server will interact with. It is quite similar to the state machine client class we encountered in *Chapter 8, AST Transformations*, LEDToggle. The session serves the same role in the pattern as the StateContext class. However, we are going to be persisting the context between events so the term session better fits our understanding of that mechanism.

Each event method takes an optional event parameter and an optional saved session parameter. The type expected for each of these parameters is actually of the type map, however it proved to be difficult to generate a method signature with generics in the AST transform code, so I've used object instead which works fine.

The event method dispatches to the event handler in the current page object. It also ensures that the session is restored first and it returns the session data as a map. Persisting the session will be the responsibility of the game server, as we will see later.

The `GameEngineClient` class will start out life in the DSL as the DSL script class. We need to add some functionality to the class, such as the `getPage` method, a `restoreSession` method and the session property itself. It makes our lives easier in the AST transform if this is all packaged in a trait and we simply inject the trait into the script class. We implement that trait here in the pattern to ensure it will work as expected:

```
trait GameEngineTraits {
  def session

  def restoreSession(engine, sessionData = null) {
    if (!session)
      session = Class.forName("${engine}Session").newInstance()
    if(session && sessionData) {
      session.restoreSession(sessionData)
    }
  }

  String getPage() {
    session.page
  }
}
```

You will see a lot of code in the pattern version of the engine that seems unnecessary. We have used reflection here to create an instance of the `TicTacToeEngineSession` class. That is because this is what we will need to do in the code generated by the AST. The `GameEngineTraits` class needs to be generic if we want to use it for multiple game engines so it needs to generate the session class by name dynamically:

```
class TicTacToeEngineSession extends PersistableSession {
    def playerX
    def playerO
    def players
    def grid = [
    ' ',' ',' ',
```

```
    ' ',' ',' ',
    ' ',' ',' '
]

def TicTacToeEngineSession() {
    super()
    page = new WelcomePage(this)
}
}
```

The `TicTacToeEngineSession` class will be generated based on the state variables declared in the state block of the DSL. The session class extends a `PersistableSession` class, which has methods for marshaling the current session variables to and from a map. It also creates a unique session ID from a UUID:

```
class PersistableSession {
  def sessionId
  def page

  def PersistableSession() {
    sessionId = UUID.randomUUID().toString()
  }
  def restoreSession(Map saved) {
    saved.each { var ->
      if (this.properties.containsKey(var.key)) {
        if (var.key == 'page') {
          page = Class.forName("${saved.page.capitalize()}Page")
                 .getDeclaredConstructor(Object.class)
                 .newInstance(this)
        } else {
          this."${var.key}" = var.value
        }
      }
    }
  }
  Map asMap() {
    Map theMap = this.properties.clone()
    theMap.remove('class')
    theMap['page'] = this.page.toString()
    theMap
  }
}
```

The persisted version of the session saved pages as a string so you can see that the class that represents a page is stored as a string in the saved map. The `restoreSession` method creates a `newInstance` of the page class using reflection. We also need to generate the default starting page in the `TicTacToeEngineSession` constructor. By default, we use the first page as it occurs in the DSL as the start page. Now, let's look at some of the page classes and event handlers:

```
class WelcomePage extends PlayerService {
    def session

    WelcomePage(context) {
        this.session = context
        setClosureDelegates()
    }
    def game_start = { Object event ->
        players = getPlayers()
        page = new PlayersPage(session)
    }
    def select_players = { Object event ->
    }
    def play_round = { Object event ->
    }
    def game_end = { Object event ->
    }
    def setClosureDelegates() {
        if (session) {
            game_start.delegate = session
            select_players.delegate = session
            play_round.delegate = session
            play_round.delegate = session
        }
    }
    String toString() {
        "welcome"
    }
}
```

There is a notable difference between this class and the state classes we implemented in the state machine example in *Chapter 8, AST Transformations*. Here we use closure instances as the event handler methods. We do this so that the event handler can have the session object as its delegate.

Looking back at the DSL code, you will note that the `state:` block where the state variables are declared gets generated in the `TicTacToeEngineSession` class, whereas the event handling code gets generated as part of the page class. We want the event handling code to act like the state variables are in its local scope, which we can achieve by using the delegate mechanism. We resolve this delegate relationship in the `setClosureDelegates` method, which is called when the page is constructed.

Each page class extends `PlayerService`. There is a presumption in this game engine that game rounds are played by automated player classes. The `PlayerService` class provided some helper functions for accessing the available player bots. This is a test version of the class designed to work with the Groovy pattern:

```
class PlayerService {

  def getPlayers() {
    [
      [ playerClass: "NextFreeSpacePlayer"],
      [ playerClass: "RandomPlayer"]
    ]
  }

  def getPlayer = { player ->
    def instance
    if (player == 'X')
      instance = Class.forName("${playerX}").newInstance()
    else
      instance = Class.forName("${playerO}").newInstance()
    instance.player = player
    instance
  }
}
```

Let's look in more detail at an event handler method. Here is an event handler block from the DSL along with the event closure we expect to generate to implement it:

```
event: "play_round"
    def player = getPlayer(event.player)

    player.playRound(grid)

    if (Grid.isSolved(grid)) {
        page = "gameover"
    } else {
        if (event.player == 'X') {
            page = "roundO"
```

```
            } else {
                page = "roundX"
            }
        }

    def play_round = { Object event ->
        def player = getPlayer(event.player)

        player.playRound(grid)

        if (Grid.isSolved(grid)) {
            page = new GameOverPage(session)
        } else {
            if (event.player == 'X') {
                page = new RoundOPage(session)
            } else {
                page = new RoundXPage(session)
            }
        }
    }
}
```

You will notice that, for the most part, the statement block from the DSL is replicated as the statement block in the closure. The one exception is where we assign the page property. This is transformed to a constructor call statement for the corresponding page class. We will see later how to use GroovyCodeVisitor to achieve this.

All these classes together with the Grid class and some player classes make a rudimentary game engine that implements an automated TicTacToe game engine. Let's look at this engine in action with a very dumb player class. The NextFreeSpacePlayer class just looks for the next available space in the grid and selects it. Two of these players against each other will always guarantee a win for X in the fourth round:

```
class NextFreeSpacePlayer extends Bot {
def playRound(grid) {
        if (!Grid.isSolved(grid)) {
            Grid.playNextFreeCell grid, this.player
        }
    }
}
```

We can verify this with a Spock test:

```
given:
    def engine = new GameEngineClient()

expect:
    !engine.session
when:
    def savedSession = engine.game_start()
then:
    engine.session
    engine.page == 'players'
    engine.session.players.size() == 2
    engine.session.players[0].playerClass == 'NextFreeSpacePlayer'
    engine.session.players[1].playerClass == 'RandomPlayer'
when:
    engine = new GameEngineClient()
    savedSession = engine.select_players(
    [
playerX: 'NextFreeSpacePlayer',
playerO: 'NextFreeSpacePlayer'
],
        savedSession)
then:
    engine.page == 'roundX'
when:
    engine = new GameEngineClient()
    savedSession = engine.play_round([player: 'X'], savedSession)
then:
    engine.page == 'roundO'
when:
    engine = new GameEngineClient()
    savedSession = engine.play_round([player: 'O'], savedSession)
    engine = new GameEngineClient()
    savedSession = engine.play_round([player: 'X'], savedSession)
    engine = new GameEngineClient()
    savedSession = engine.play_round([player: 'O'], savedSession)
    engine = new GameEngineClient()
    savedSession = engine.play_round([player: 'X'], savedSession)
    engine = new GameEngineClient()
    savedSession = engine.play_round([player: 'O'], savedSession)
then:
    engine.page == 'roundX'
```

```
        // X O X
        // O X O
        // Expect next X play to win
    when:
        engine = new GameEngineClient()
        engine.play_round([player: 'X'], savedSession)
    then:
        engine.page == 'game_over'
```

We now have a Groovy class-based pattern, which implements our game engine. The DSL will be implemented with an AST transform, which generates classes in that pattern. So we can now focus on building the AST transform. We know we have successfully built the AST transformation when the DSL version works with the preceding test.

Implementing the AST transform

As with all the previous AST transforms, our work begins with writing an `ASTTransformation` class:

```
@GroovyASTTransformation (phase = CompilePhase.SEMANTIC_ANALYSIS)
class GameEngineASTTransformation implements ASTTransformation,
        CompilationUnitAware {
    def parser
    def builder
    def compilationUnit

    void visit(ASTNode[] nodes, SourceUnit source) {
        if (!nodes) return
        if (!(nodes[0] instanceof ModuleNode)) return
        if (!source?.name?.endsWith('Engine.groovy')) {
            return
        }
        def gameEngineModel = new GameEngineModel()
        parser = new EnginePatternParser(gameEngineModel, source)
        builder = new EnginePatternBuilder(nodes,
                gameEngineModel, source, compilationUnit)

        for (ClassNode classNode : nodes[0].classes) {
            classNode.visitContents(parser)
        }
        builder.buildEnginePattern()
    }
    @Override
```

```
        void setCompilationUnit(CompilationUnit unit) {
            compilationUnit = unit
        }
    }
```

You will immediately notice the similarity between this transformation class and
the state machine transformation in *Chapter 8, AST Transformations*. We follow the
same steps as before. We first parse the AST nodes to build an interim model that
represents the game engine. We then use that model to build the game engine
pattern classes:

```
class GameEngineModel {
    def pages
    def events
    def stateDeclarations
    def eventStatements

    def GameEngineModel() {
        pages = []
        events = [:]
        stateDeclarations = []
        eventStatements = [:]
    }
    def getStartPage() {
        pages[0]
    }
    def addPage( page ) {
        if (!pages.contains(page))
            pages << page
    }
    def addEvent(event) {
        events[ "$event" ] = [:]
    }
    def getEvents() {
        events.keySet()
    }
    def addStateDeclaration(declaration) {
        stateDeclarations << declaration
    }
    def addEventStatement(event, stmnt) {
        if (!eventStatements["$event"])
            eventStatements["$event"] = []

        eventStatements["$event"] << stmnt
    }
}
```

There is not much to the game model class, as you can see in the preceding code. While parsing, we build a list of the pages declared in the DSL, and a map of the events declared. We also capture all the statements declared in the state variables block and in each of the event blocks. This aspect of the AST transform is new.

In the state machine DSL, the model was more of a specification language. This DSL contains actual executable code and variable declarations that we need to handle. While parsing, we don't need to do any transformation of this code, we just need to capture it in the correct blocks so we can make use of it later.

The parser class `EnginePatternParser` handles this by scanning the DSL run method for labeled statements. Anything after a `state:` or `event:` is labeled up until the next labeled block is collected and stored in the model:

```
@Override
void visitMethod(MethodNode node) {
    if (node.name == "run") {
        collectPages(node)
        collectEvents(node)
        collectStateVariables(node)
        collectEventMethodBodies(node)
    }
}
def collectStateVariables(node) {
    def collecting = false
    node.code.statements.each { stmnt ->
        if (!collecting && isStateBlock(stmnt))
            collecting = true

        if (collecting && isNonStateBlock(stmnt)) {
            collecting = false
        }

        if (collecting) {
            if (isDeclarationExpression(stmnt)) {
                model.addStateDeclaration stmnt
            } else {
                addError "Declarations only allowed in state block",
                        stmnt, source
            }
        }
    }
}
boolean isStateBlock(Statement stmnt) {
    stmnt instanceof ExpressionStatement &&
```

```
                    stmnt.statementLabel &&
                    stmnt.statementLabel == 'state'
}
boolean isNonStateBlock(Statement stmnt) {
    stmnt instanceof ExpressionStatement &&
            stmnt.expression instanceof ConstantExpression &&
            stmnt.statementLabel &&
            (stmnt.statementLabel == 'page' ||
             stmnt.statementLabel == 'event' ||
             stmnt.statementLabel == 'when')
}
boolean isDeclarationExpression(Statement stmnt) {
    stmnt instanceof ExpressionStatement &&
            stmnt.expression instanceof DeclarationExpression
}
```

Only declaration expressions are allowed in the `state:` block of the DSL. If we encounter anything else, we raise a compile error via the `addError` method. Collecting the `event:` blocks is more straightforward. We just add each statement we encounter to the model:

```
def collectEventMethodBodies(node) {
    def collecting = false
    def event
    node.code.statements.each { stmnt ->
        if (!collecting && isEventBlock(stmnt)) {
            collecting = true
            event = getLabelParam(stmnt)
            return
        }
    if (collecting && isNonEventBlock(stmnt)) {
            collecting = false
        }
    if (collecting && isEventBlock(stmnt)) {
            event = getLabelParam(stmnt)
        }
      if (collecting) {
            model.addEventStatement event, stmnt
        }
    }

}
boolean isEventBlock(Statement stmnt) {
    stmnt instanceof ExpressionStatement &&
            stmnt.expression instanceof ConstantExpression &&
```

```
            stmnt.statementLabel &&
            stmnt.statementLabel == 'event'
}
boolean isNonEventBlock(Statement stmnt) {
    stmnt instanceof ExpressionStatement &&
            stmnt.expression instanceof ConstantExpression &&
            stmnt.statementLabel &&
            (stmnt.statementLabel == 'page' ||
             stmnt.statementLabel == 'when' ||
             stmnt.statementLabel == 'state')
}
```

Building the game engine pattern

Once the parser has completed its work, we should have a full representation of the
game engine in the GameEngineModel class. We next set about generating the classes
of the game engine from this model. The EnginePatternBuilder class takes over at
this point:

```
class EnginePatternBuilder {
    def model
    ModuleNode moduleNode
    ClassNode classNode
    String className
    ClassNode contextClass
    String sessionClassName
    def sourceUnit
    def compilationUnit

    EnginePatternBuilder(ASTNode[] nodes, model, source, comp) {
        this.model = model
        moduleNode = nodes[0]
        classNode = nodes[0].classes[0]
        className = nodes[0].classes[0].nameWithoutPackage
        this.sourceUnit = source
        this.compilationUnit = comp
    }

    void buildEnginePattern() {
        buildSessionClass()
        updateClientClass()
        buildPageClasses()
        removeMethods()
    }

    ...... . .
}
```

Our starting point with this AST transformation will be a single Groovy script class containing the DSL code. We know from earlier chapters that this means we will have an existing class with the same name as the script file. So if we start out with a file named `Engine.groovy`, we will find that the DSL script has a class in it called engine.

That class will already have several methods and constructors in it. By the end of the transformation process, the only part of the original class that we will make use of is its default constructor. By the end of the transformation process, we will have added a constructor and event methods to the original script class. We will have changed the class so it implements a trait and we will have added several other classes to the module.

The first step is to add the session class since this is referenced extensively in the rest of the generated code. At this point in the book, the mechanism for constructing code with the AST APIs should be familiar to you so I won't describe every aspect in detail unless it is a feature we have not encountered already.

In *Chapter 8, AST Transformations*, the simple state pattern we implemented did not have any methods with more than a single line of code. We were therefore able to represent each method body with a single `ExpressionStatement` object. The constructor method in the generated session class has two lines, so we use a `BlockStatement` object to represent the code part of the constructor. A `BlockStatement` object is simply constructed from an array of statements and a scope object:

```
void buildSessionClass() {
    def sessionClassNode = new AstBuilder().buildFromString
        CompilePhase.SEMANTIC_ANALYSIS, true, """
class ${className}Session extends PersistableSession{
}
"""

    contextClass = sessionClassNode[1]
    moduleNode.addClass(sessionClassNode[1])
    sessionClassName = "${className}Session"

    def blockStatement = new BlockStatement([
        new ExpressionStatement(
            new ConstructorCallExpression(
                ClassHelper.make(
                    PersistableSession.class
                ),
                ArgumentListExpression.EMPTY_ARGUMENTS
            )
```

```
        ),
    new ExpressionStatement(
        new BinaryExpression(
            new VariableExpression("page"),
            new Token(Types.EQUALS, "=", -1, -1),
            new ConstructorCallExpression(
                ClassHelper.make(
                    "${model.startPage}Page"
                ),
                new ArgumentListExpression(
                    new VariableExpression('this')
                )
            ),
        )
    )
],
new VariableScope()
)

def constructorNode = new ConstructorNode(
        Modifier.PUBLIC,
        [] as Parameter [],
        [
                ClassHelper.make(Exception, false),
                ClassHelper.make(IOException, false)
        ] as ClassNode [],
        blockStatement
)
sessionClassNode[1].addConstructor(constructorNode)

// Add Properties for each variable declaration in the DSL
model.stateDeclarations.each { stmnt ->
    def statePropertyNode = new PropertyNode (
        stmnt.expression.variableExpression.name,
        Modifier.PUBLIC,
        stmnt.expression.variableExpression.type,
        ClassHelper.make("${className}Session"),
        stmnt.expression.rightExpression,
        null,
        null
    )
    sessionClassNode[1].addProperty(statePropertyNode)
}
}
```

We start off the preceding code by creating a new AST node for the session class. We build the constructor code block and create a `ConstructorNode` for the class. Finally, we use the state variable declarations we found while parsing the `state:` block to add properties to the class to represent each state variable. This newly created class is added to the original `ModuleNode` object for the DSL script.

Next we work on the script class itself. We add a new constructor to it, change it so it implements the trait, `GameEngineTraits` and adds the event handling methods to it:

```
void updateClientClass() {
    addGameEngineTraits()
    buildGameEngineConstructor()
    buildClientEventMethods()
}

def addGameEngineTraits() {
    def traitNode = ClassHelper.make(GameEngineTraits)

    if (!classNode.implementsInterface(traitNode)) {
        classNode.addInterface(traitNode)
    }
}

def buildGameEngineConstructor() {
    def constructorStatement = new ExpressionStatement(
        new BinaryExpression(
            new PropertyExpression(
                new VariableExpression("this"),
                new ConstantExpression("session")
            ),
            new Token(Types.EQUALS, "=", -1, -1),
            new VariableExpression("session")
        )
    )
    def constructorNode = new ConstructorNode(
        Modifier.PUBLIC,
        [
            new Parameter(
                    ClassHelper.make(Object, false), "session")
        ] as Parameter [],
        [
            ClassHelper.make(Exception, false),
            ClassHelper.make(IOException, false)
        ] as ClassNode [],
```

```
                constructorStatement
        )
    classNode.addConstructor(constructorNode)
}
```

Most of the preceding code should be familiar to you. The one aspect we have
not come across before is the construction of the parameter declaration for the
constructor. Earlier in the chapter, I mentioned the difficulties in generating a map as
a parameter to a method. The parameter class constructor requires a `ClassNode` as its
first argument and the recommended method for creating one of these for an existing
object is to use the `ClassHelper.make` method. Unfortunately, this does not seem
to work successfully when you try to create a `ClassNode` for a generic type such
as map.

The same issue occurred when trying to generate the event methods in the following
code. The compromise I settled on was to declare these parameters as an object but to
treat them as map. Here we create block statements for each event method with the
lines of code from the class pattern:

```
def buildClientEventMethods() {
    for (event in model.events) {
        def blockStatement = new BlockStatement( [
            new ExpressionStatement(
                new MethodCallExpression(
                    new VariableExpression("this"),
                    new ConstantExpression("restoreSession"),
                    new ArgumentListExpression(
                        [
                            new ConstantExpression(className),
                            new VariableExpression("sessionData")
                        ]
                    )
                )
            ),
            new ExpressionStatement(
                new MethodCallExpression(
                    new MethodCallExpression(
                        new VariableExpression('session'),
                        new ConstantExpression('getPage'),
                        ArgumentListExpression.EMPTY_ARGUMENTS
                    ),
                    new ConstantExpression("${event}"),
                    new ArgumentListExpression(
                        new VariableExpression('event')
                    )
```

```
                )
            ),
            new ExpressionStatement(
                new MethodCallExpression(
                    new VariableExpression('session'),
                    new ConstantExpression('asMap'),
                    ArgumentListExpression.EMPTY_ARGUMENTS
                )
            )
        ],
        new VariableScope()
    )
    def eventMethodNode = new MethodNode(
        "${event}",
        Modifier.PUBLIC,
        null,
        [
            new Parameter(
                ClassHelper.make(Object, false),
                "event",
                new ConstantExpression(null)
            ),
            new Parameter(
                ClassHelper.make(Object, false),
                "sessionData",
                new ConstantExpression(null)
            )
        ] as Parameter[],
        null,
        blockStatement
    )
    classNode.addMethod(eventMethodNode)
    }
}
```

That concludes the modification we need to make to the engine class. The final part of the pattern we need to generate is the page classes. We create a new page class for each page in the engine DSL:

```
def buildPageClasses() {
    for (page in model.pages) {
        def pageNode = buildPageClass(page)
        for (event in model.events) {
            buildPageClassEventClosure(event, page, pageNode)
        }
```

```
        moduleNode.addClass(pageNode[1])
    }

}
```

Much of the code for building these classes will be familiar already.
One new construct we encounter is the generation of the conditional. The
`setClosureDelegates` method that is added to the class has a conditional block
based on the value of the session property. This is built with an `IfStatement`
object that accepts a `BooleanExpression` object as the condition, and two
`BlockStatements` for the if block and the `else` block. A basic `if` statement is
constructed as an `IfStatement` with an `EmptyStatement` as the `else` block:

```
def buildPageClass(page) {
    def pageClassNode = new AstBuilder().buildFromString
        CompilePhase.SEMANTIC_ANALYSIS, true, """
class ${page}Page extends com.dearle.game.engine.ast.PlayerService{
    def session
    ${page}Page(session) {
        this.session = session
        setClosureDelegates()
    }
    String toString() {
        "${page}"
    }
}
"""
    def closureDelegateStatements = [
        new ExpressionStatement(
            new BinaryExpression(
                new PropertyExpression(
                    new VariableExpression("getPlayer"),
                    new ConstantExpression("delegate")
                ),
                new Token(Types.EQUALS, "=", -1, -1),
                new VariableExpression("session")
            )
        )]
    for (event in model.events) {
        def closureDelegateStatement = new ExpressionStatement(
            new BinaryExpression(
                new PropertyExpression(
                    new VariableExpression("$event"),
                    new ConstantExpression("delegate")
                ),
```

```
                        new Token(Types.EQUALS, "=", -1, -1),
                        new VariableExpression("session")
                )
            )
            closureDelegateStatements << closureDelegateStatement
    }

    def blockStatement = new BlockStatement(
            closureDelegateStatements, new VariableScope() )

    def methodBody = new IfStatement(
        new BooleanExpression (
            new BinaryExpression(
                new VariableExpression("session"),
                new Token(Types.COMPARE_NOT_EQUAL, "!=", -1, -1),
                new ConstantExpression(null)
            )
        ),
        blockStatement,
        EmptyStatement.INSTANCE
    )

    def eventMethodNode = new MethodNode(
        "setClosureDelegates",
        Modifier.PUBLIC,
        null,
        [] as Parameter[],
        null,
        methodBody
    )

    pageClassNode[1].addMethod(eventMethodNode)
    pageClassNode
}
```

Finally, we need to add the event handling closures to the page classes. These are constructed as `PropertyNode` objects where the assignment expression is a `ClosureExpression`. The closure is constructed with a `BlockStatement` object into which we place the original statements parsed from the `event:` block in the original DSL script:

```
def buildPageClassEventClosure(event, page, stateClassNode) {
    def eventStatements = []
    model.eventStatements["$event"].each {
        eventStatements << it
```

```
    }

    def blockStatement = new BlockStatement(
        eventStatements as Statement [],
        new VariableScope()
    )

    PageAssignmentTransformer pageAssignmentTransformer =
            new PageAssignmentTransformer(model, sourceUnit)
    blockStatement.visit(pageAssignmentTransformer)

    def closureExpression = new ClosureExpression(
        [
            new Parameter(
                    ClassHelper.make(Object, false),
                    "event")
        ] as Parameter[],
         blockStatement
    )
    closureExpression.variableScope = new VariableScope()

    def closurePropertyNode = new PropertyNode(
        "${event}",
        Modifier.PUBLIC,
        ClassHelper.DYNAMIC_TYPE,
        ClassHelper.make("${page}Page"),
        closureExpression,
        null,
        null
    )

    stateClassNode[1].addProperty(closurePropertyNode)
}
```

When a page is assigned in the DSL, we need to transform this assignment from a constant string assignment to a constructor call for the corresponding page class:

```
// And assignment like this in the DSL
page = "Welcome"
// Becomes this in the pattern
page = new WelcomePage(session)
```

These assignments can occur anywhere within the `event:` block code. This means they could be nested deep within the AST nodes we have saved. We have a convenient method for finding each of them so we can transform them.

Once we have created a new `BlockStatement` object out of event statements, we can visit all of the AST nodes in the block using the `GroovyCodeVisitor` class. To do so, we need to implement our own visitor class:

```groovy
class PageAssignmentTransformer extends CodeVisitorSupport {
    def model
    def source

    PageAssignmentTransformer(model, source) {
        this.model = model
        this.source = source
    }

    @Override
    void visitBinaryExpression(BinaryExpression expr) {
        def var = expr.leftExpression
        Token oper = expr.operation
        def page = expr.rightExpression

        if ( var instanceof VariableExpression &&
             var.accessedVariable.name == 'page' &&
             oper instanceof Token &&
             oper.rootText == "=" &&
             page instanceof ConstantExpression
        ) {
          def next = page.value.toString()
          if (!model.pages.contains(next)) {
            addError "Reference to non existent state",
                    page, source
          } else {
            expr.rightExpression = new ConstructorCallExpression(
                ClassHelper.make("${next}Page"),
                new ArgumentListExpression(
                    new VariableExpression('session')
                )
            )
          }
        }
    }
}
```

The `PageAssignmentTransformer` class extends `CodeVisitorSupport` and overrides the `visitBinaryExpression` method. `CodeVisitorSupport` has methods for every type of statement and expression you could possibly encounter. As it happens, the only type of expression we care about is `BinaryExpression` where the left expression is the page variable and the right is a constant.

We can therefore target all the places where the statement `page = constant` occurs. We can then make a direct assignment to `rightExpression` and replace the constant with the appropriate `ConstructorCallExpression` for a page class.

Apart from some cleanup to remove the unwanted methods from the engine class, that is the full AST transformation completed.

Testing the DSL

In theory, we should now be able to make use of the game engine DSL. Let's see if the original Spock test will still work if we convert it using the DSL instead of the pattern classes. To do so, we need to load the DSL code from somewhere:

```
given:
    CompilerConfiguration config = new CompilerConfiguration()
    config.addCompilationCustomizers(
            new ASTLogCompilationCustomizer(
                    CompilePhase.SEMANTIC_ANALYSIS,
                    System.out
            ))
    GroovyClassLoader classLoader = new GroovyClassLoader(
            this.class.classLoader, config)
    engineClass = classLoader.parseClass(
            new File("pathto/TicTacToeEngine.groovy"))
    def gameEngine = engineClass.newInstance()

expect:
    !gameEngine.session

when:
    def savedSession = gameEngine.game_start()
then:
    gameEngine.session
    gameEngine.page == 'players'
    gameEngine.session.players.size() == 2
```

In order to create an instance of the game engine class, we use `GloovyClassLoader.parseClass` to parse the class from a local file. If the AST transform is available in the compiler's classpath, that's all we need to do to cause the DSL script to be transformed. For a simple DSL implementation, such as the state machine DSL in *Chapter 8, AST Transformations*, this is all we need to do:

```
GroovyClassLoader classLoader = new GroovyClassLoader()
    stateMachineClass = classLoader.parseClass(
            new File("pathto/SomeState.groovy"))
    def stateMachine = stateMachineClass.newInstance()
```

Class loading issues

All the dependent classes created in this DSL are generated in the original script model for the state machine DSL. So it is entirely self-contained in the parsed module. The game engine DSL makes use of existing classes such as `PersistableSession`, `PlayerService` and the trait `GameEngineTraits`. These classes need to be resolved on the class path when the AST transform is generating code that depends on them.

We can resolve this by creating the `GroovyClassLoader` with a parent `ClassLoader` and any class reference that the compiler cannot resolve in the `GroovyClassLoader` will be delegated to the parent class loader seeking a reference. The three classes we need are already in the class path of the Spock specification via the `ast.jar` file, we will see how this is built in a moment. We can get hold of the default class loader for the specification via the test specification's own class, which is referenced in the test via `this.class.classLoader`.

When we are building our own AST transformations, it is important to understand that the transformation itself becomes part of the compilation process. The transform won't work if you put the AST transformation sources into your main application code because the transform is compiled at the same time as the application.

We managed to avoid this issue in the *Chapter 8, AST Transformations* examples. All the AST examples in the *Chapter 8, AST Transformations* exercise were transforms via Spock tests. The transforms were compiled to classes in the Gradle compile phase and then made use of in the `testCompile` phase.

Gradle subprojects

In order to make use of the game engine AST transform, we will need to compile it into a separate JAR file which is made available in the classpath when we compile the main application code. A handy way to do this is via a Gradle multi-project build.

The example code for this chapter can be found in the TicTacToe directory of the source pack. There are two subdirectories in here, www which contains the HTML5 UI which we will discuss later, and server which contains the game server and DSL sources. The server directory contains a Gradle build script build.gradle.

Underneath server there is another subdirectory ast, this is where the sources for the AST transformation lives. It also contains a build.gradle, which is configured to build a JAR distribution of the game engine AST transformation:

```groovy
apply plugin: 'groovy'

repositories {
    mavenCentral()
}

dependencies {
    compile "org.codehaus.groovy:groovy-all:2.4.3"
    testCompile "org.spockframework:spock-core:0.7-groovy-2.0"
}
```

This will build a JAR file for the AST in server/ast/build/libs/ast.jar. The server build.gradle consumes this JAR as a project dependency with the following entry in its dependencies:

```groovy
dependencies {
    compile project(':ast')
}
```

With this build structure in place, Gradle will ensure that the JAR containing the AST is built first and made available at compile time for the server. The tests for the server and the AST can be run via Gradle on the command line:

```
$gradle clean test
```

Debugging

Debugging an AST transform can be difficult at the best of times. Attaching a debugger via Eclipse or IntelliJ is possible. However, in the early stages of DSL development, I find that the simplest solution is just to put some logging into your AST transform code. You can dump what the DSL is doing at any point in time.

There is one aspect of DSL development that is particularly difficult to debug. That is when your transform has finished and produced an end set of transformed classes, but now these classes don't behave as expected. You don't have the code for these classes to debug them because you generated them dynamically in the transform.

Ideally you want to be able to visualize the code you have just generated. In the above Spock test, you will notice that I've added a `CompilationConfiguration` class with a `CompilationCustomizer` to the `GroovyClassLoader` class. This compilation customizer uses a visitor, `AstNodeToScriptVisitor`, that is part of the `groovyConsole` sources. This visitor traverses the generated `ASTNode` tree and generates a text view of the generated code:

```
class ASTLogCompilationCustomizer extends CompilationCustomizer {
    final PrintStream out

    ASTLogCompilationCustomizer(CompilePhase compilePhase,
                    PrintStream out) {
        super(compilePhase)
        this.out = out
    }
    void call(SourceUnit source, GeneratorContext context,
        ClassNode classNode) throws CompilationFailedException {
          StringWriter writer = new StringWriter()
          new AstNodeToScriptVisitor(writer).visitClass(classNode)
          out.println writer
    }
}
```

Running the tests will produce an HTML report in the `server/build/reports/tests` directory. There is a link in the report to the standard output from the test, which contains the pretty printed version of the generated code. This is tremendously useful when debugging the generated output from an AST transformation.

The game server

Now we will look at building a simple game server that exploits the DSL. The server is built upon Spring MVC using Spring Boot which is a convention over configuration version of the Spring framework that allows you to get up and running quickly—`http://projects.spring.io/spring-boot/`.

The server responds to HTTP requests via AJAX and returns JSONP. Each response will contain the latest version of the game engine state along with a session ID and the name of the next page to go to in the UI. In between requests, the session state is stored in a MongoDB collection. Let's look at the Gradle file that builds this server:

```
buildscript {
  repositories {
   jcenter()
    maven { url "http://repo.spring.io/libs-release" }
  }
```

```
  dependencies {
    classpath (
      "org.springframework.boot:spring-boot-gradle-plugin:1.2.3.RELEASE"
    )
    classpath (
      'com.sourcemuse.gradle.plugin:gradle-mongo-plugin:0.1.0'
    )
  }
}

apply plugin: 'spring-boot'
apply plugin: 'mongo'
apply plugin: 'groovy'

repositories {
  jcenter()
  maven { url 'http://repo.spring.io/release' }
}

dependencies {
  compile project(':ast')
  compile "org.codehaus.groovy:groovy:2.4.3"
  compile "org.springframework.boot:spring-boot-starter-web"
  compile (
    "org.springframework.boot:spring-boot-starter-data-mongodb"
  )
  testCompile 'org.spockframework:spock-core:0.7-groovy-2.0'
  testCompile "org.mongodb:mongo-java-driver:2.12.0"
}
```

As usual, configuring a project with the Gradle DSL is surprisingly easy. All we need to do is apply the plugins for Spring Boot and Mongo and supply the dependencies for the libraries. Running Gradle will cause all the dependent components to be installed. You don't even need to install a MongoDB database since the Mongo plugin will create an embedded MongoDB instance for you. To start the embedded MongoDB, just issue the following Gradle command:

$gradle startMongo

Now we can start the Spring Boot server and try out some responses:

$gradle clean run

This starts the server on localhost port 8080 so we can use `curl` to get a response to the game start event, as follows (alternatively, just enter the URL into a browser):

```
$ curl http://localhost:8080/tictactoe/game_start
{
    "grid": [
        " ",
        " ",
        " ",
        " ",
        " ",
        " ",
        " ",
        " ",
        " "
    ],
    "page": "players",
    "players": [
        {
            "name": "Next Free Space Player",
            "playerClass": "NextFreeSpacePlayer"
        },
        {
            "name": "Random Blocking Player",
            "playerClass": "RandomBlockingPlayer"
        },
        {
            "name": "Random Player",
            "playerClass": "RandomPlayer"
        }
    ],
    "sessionId": "81a6db09-fb78-485f-8cca-3b5e69e5a0df",
}
```

Response is cleaned up and formatted. If you are running on Mac OS X or Linux and have Python installed, try piping output to:

`python -mjson.tool`

Integrating with Spring Boot server

Spring Boot application startup is via the main method of a class. You can put this main method in any class you like. You can build a functioning Spring Boot application with a single controller class that has a main method. A common convention, however, is to create a separate application class that contains the main method, which is what we have done here:

```
@EnableAutoConfiguration
@ComponentScan("com.dearle.game.engine.tictactoe")
class Application {
    static void main(String[] args){
        new SpringApplication(Application).run(args)
    }
}
```

In the main method, we create the `SpringApplication` class and run it. The configuration of components is made easy by using the `@ComponentScan` annotation, which tells Spring Boot to search in the `tictactoe` package for component classes.

 It is important that you only have one main method in the application JAR. If you include any DSL script classes in the JAR they will also have a main method. This is why the DSL AST transform takes care to remove the script main as part of the transformation.

The main work of the server is performed by a single controller class. The component scan will discover that `GameEventController` has the `@RestController` annotation which means that this controller is prepared to handle web requests.

I mentioned earlier that Spring Boot takes convention over configuration. The `@AutoWired` annotation informs Spring to create a bean for `GameSessionRepository` and `GameEngineService` and the instance into the controller. No further configuration is required:

```
@RestController
class GameEventController {
    @Autowired
    GameSessionRepository sessionRepo
    @Autowired
    GameEngineService engineService

    @RequestMapping(value = "/{game}/{event}",
            produces = MediaType.APPLICATION_JSON_VALUE)
    @ResponseBody
```

```
Map event(@PathVariable String game,
        @PathVariable String event,
        @RequestParam Map params ) {
    def session = null
    if (params.sessionId)
      session = sessionRepo.findBySessionId(params.sessionId)

    def client = engineService.getEngineInstance(this, game)
    def state = client."${event}"(params, session?.cache)

    if ( session) {
        session.cache = state
    } else {
        session = new GameSession(
            sessionId: session.sessionId, cache: state)
    }

    sessionRepo.save( session)
    session.cache
    }
}
```

Events can arrive asynchronously to the server and we need to be able to maintain the game state for a player between requests. The event detects if a session already exists and creates one if it does not. It then uses `GameEngineService` to get a game engine client instance to which it delegates the event handling. The latest values for the state are returned by the DSL handler and saved. Finally, the update state is sent back as part of the response body. Let's see how all this works.

Controller annotations

This controller has a single action method `for` event. The `@RequestMapping` annotation tells Spring to map any two-part URL requests to the event controller method. The two `@PathVariable` annotations on the method parameters for game and event ensure that the first part of the URL is passed to the action as the game parameter, and the second as the event. So the URL `http://localhost:8080/ tictactoe/play_round` will be mapped to a call to `GameEngineController` with the statements, `game = 'tictactoe'` and `event = 'play_round'`.

We can control how single parameter values are passed with a `@RequestParam` annotation. Using the `@RequestParam` string `foo` would allow us to map the request parameter `foo` to a named method parameter. When we declare `@RequestParam` as a map, as is the previous case, all the request parameters are marshaled into a single parameter called `params`.

The @ResponseBody annotation will mean the result returned by the event action is automatically placed in the HTTP response body. The @RequestMapping annotation indicates that this action produces MediaType.APPLICATION_JSON_VALUE. Combined, these annotations will ensure that the map that is returned is converted to its corresponding JSON structure.

JSONP

If we were to serve the UI for this server from the same domain then this would be adequate for most purposes. We will be building an embedded mobile client which means that the UI will be served from the phone's own storage whereas the JSON will be served from the Spring Boot app. Some browsers will enforce a same origin policy and will not allow this. We circumvent this problem by using JSONP instead of JSON.

JSONP is an alternative format to JSON whereby the returned value is a JavaScript function call passing the JSON as a parameter. The snippet below shows a simple piece of JSON and the JSONP equivalent:

```
//JSON
{ id: '123' }
//JSONP
callback({ id: '123' })
```

For a more detailed explanation of the JSONP mechanism, see http://json-p.org/. All we need to know is how to generate this format in the response body. AbstractJsonpResponseBodyAdvice is available in Spring 4.1. We extend this class and annotate it with the @ControllerAdvice annotation. ControllerAdvice is a mechanism in Spring for adding additional default functionality such as common exception handlers to all controllers. In this case, we are adding JSONP capabilities to all controllers:

```
@ControllerAdvice
public class JsonpAdvice extends AbstractJsonpResponseBodyAdvice {
    public JsonpAdvice() {
        super("callback");
    }
}
```

Loading the DSL

The transformed DSL classes need to be in the application class path so that the game engine controller can delegate events to them. For this particular DSL, it is a requirement that the DSL can be loaded from a source external to the game server. This is so that the game server, which is not intended to be modified, can be packaged as an application runtime while the game engine DSL can be maintained in a separate source.

The DSL classes need to have access to the application class path when loaded. We also want to minimize the amount of parsing that occurs. This implies creating a GroovyClassLoader that is shared somehow.

Spring components are, by their nature, singletons. We can create a GameEngineService class and annotate it with @Component. The classLoader property in the service is initialized only once. We use getEngineInstance as a factory method which will parse the DSL and return an engine instance:

```
@Component
class GameEngineService {

    GroovyClassLoader classLoader

    def getEngineInstance(obj, engine) {
        if (!classLoader) {
            classLoader = new GroovyClassLoader(
                    obj.class.classLoader)
        }
        def clazz = classLoader.loadedClasses.find {
            it.name == "${engine}"
        }
        if (!clazz) {
            clazz = classLoader.parseClass(
                    new File("engines/${engine}/Engine.groovy"))
        }

        clazz.newInstance()
    }
}
```

Spring Data mapping for MongoDB

In between event requests, we store the latest state of the DSL state variables. These variables can be any fundamental type or a collection of fundamental type objects. Basically, anything that can be marshaled into and out of JSON as is. We therefore need to also have a storage mechanism that allows arbitrary data to be stored.

MongoDB turns out to be a natural fit for this. Mongo is a JSON document store and is schemaless, meaning that we don't have to describe the structure of the data we store. Spring also has a powerful set of libraries that allow it to integrate easily with a Mongo database. This is the entire configuration we need to get working with Mongo using the Spring Data Mongo libraries. First we declare MongoConfig, which configures Spring to use the TicTacToe database:

```
@Configuration
class MongoConfig extends AbstractMongoConfiguration {
    @Override
    String getDatabaseName() {
        "tictactoe"
    }

    @Override
    Mongo mongo() throws Exception {
        new MongoClient()
    }
}
```

A MongoDB database can contain multiple JSON document collections. In our case, we only need one. Here we declare a Spring Data mapping repository for storing the game sessions. Based on the Spring Boot convention over configuration principles, this class declaration will automatically make use of a collection called GameSession. Spring Data also automatically generates the findBySessionId method to query GameSession objects by sessionId:

```
interface GameSessionRepository
        extends MongoRepository<GameSession, BigInteger> {
    GameSession findBySessionId(String sessionId)
}
```

All that remains is for us to declare the GameSession document class, which becomes the data access object for the GameSession collection. GameSession has a database ID, which will be generated by Mongo, a sessionId which we generate on the fly as a stringified UUID, and it has a map in which the game session state will be stored:

```
@Document
class GameSession {
    @Id BigInteger id
    String sessionId
    Map cache
}
```

Surprisingly, that's all the code it takes to build our game server. All that remains is to build a simple UI that can use it.

The Game UI

The nature of the game engine we have built is similar to a state machine. Pages represent the different states so, as we move from state to state, we move from page to page in the UI. We started out with the ambition of building a mobile app to work with this DSL and it turns out that the jQuery mobile framework actually works very well with this notional page model.

With jQuery mobile, we build a single page app, which contains individual "pages". The pages are declared as div element's with a data-role attribute of "page". Here is the play round page of our TicTacToe game. You will notice that the content div element is empty. This will be filled in dynamically from a template as the game is being played:

```html
<div data-role="page" id="roundX" class="engine-page grid-page">
    <div data-role="header" id="header">
        <h1>Play Round</h1>
    </div><!-- /header -->

    <div role="main" class="ui-content" id="content">
    </div><!-- /content -->
    <div data-role="footer" id="footer" data-position="fixed">
        <div data-role="navbar">
          <ul>
            <li>
                <a href="#" onclick="playRound('X');">Play X</a>
            </li>
          </ul>
        </div><!-- /navbar -->
    </div><!-- /footer -->
</div><!-- /page -->
```

The footer of the page contains a link, which calls a JavaScript function. This function matches the `play_round` event in the DSL and causes an AJAX call to be made to the game server. When we get a response from the server, we read the page transition it returns in the response and we display that page:

```
function playRound(player) {
    var params = {
        sessionId: session.sessionId,
        player: player
    }
    event('play_round', params);
}
function event(event, params) {
    var url = "http://localhost:8080/tictactoe/" +
            event +
            "?callback=?";
    if (session.sessionId != null) {
        params.sessionId = session.sessionId;
    }
    $.getJSON(url, params, function(response) {
        session = response;
        if (response.page != "players") {
            $("#" + response.page + " .ui-content").html(
                Mustache.render(
                    MustacheTemplates[response.page], response));
            $("#" + response.page).trigger("pagecreate");
        } else {
            session.sessionId = ""
        }
        $.mobile.changePage("#" + response.page,
            { transition: "slide" });
    });
}
```

The content section of each page is generated dynamically using `MustacheTemplate` like the following one. The state variables transmitted from the server in JSON are passed to the template so that we can reference any of the variables that were defined in the DSL by name. For example, `grid.0` references the `grid[0]` value from the DSL:

```
MustacheTemplates.roundX = [
    "<div class='grid'>",
        "<h1 class='cell'>{{grid.0}}</h1>",
        "<div class='vert-separator'></div>",
        "<h1 class='cell'>{{grid.1}}</h1>",
        "<div class='vert-separator'></div>",
        "<h1 class='cell'>{{grid.2}}</h1>",
        "<div class='horz-separator'></div>",
        "<h1 class='cell'>{{grid.3}}</h1>",
```

```
        "<div class='vert-separator'></div>",
        "<h1 class='cell'>{{grid.4}}</h1>",
        "<div class='vert-separator'></div>",
        "<h1 class='cell'>{{grid.5}}</h1>",
        "<div class='horz-separator'></div>",
        "<h1 class='cell'>{{grid.6}}</h1>",
        "<div class='vert-separator'></div>",
        "<h1 class='cell'>{{grid.7}}</h1>",
        "<div class='vert-separator'></div>",
        "<h1 class='cell'>{{grid.8}}</h1>",
    "</div>"
].join("\n");
```

Put this all together and we have a playable TicTacToe game for mobile devices. I wrote this DSL as a proof of concept to see if a usable DSL could be written for kids to program with.

In terms of hitting our original goals for the DSL, we have achieved a lot of them. At the close of the term we had the kids' own player bots playing each other in the mobile app shown in the following image:

The DSL abstracts out a lot of the complexity for the kids. A normal application with a mobile frontend and a JSON backend would have a lot of framework code to be written for it to work, particularly in the area of data binding.

With this DSL, the kids can just declare their state variables in the DSL and the values of these variables surface with the same names in the UI as part of `MustacheTemplates`. The data binding is all handled by the code generated in the DSL. I'm hoping that in the coming terms it will be possible for them to use the skills that they have acquired to build their own game engines with the DSL. I'm looking forward to evolving this DSL in the future.

Summary

The game engine DSL we built in this chapter was clearly designed with teaching Groovy in mind. However, I also have to admit to a certain amount of contrivance in how it was built. I had also been looking for a good example DSL to use as the final example in this book and I hope this one hit the mark on both counts. The integration problems we needed to solve to get this simple DSL up and running will, I think, be similar to the ones you will face in your own projects.

We have made use of and built on a lot of the concepts in the book. I hope you have had some fun along the way and learned a lot of new things. The journey is not over, however. The next steps are up to you. Happy DSL building!

Index

null safe dereference operator 83
operator overloading 84
spread 82
spread-dot 82, 83

P

plugins, Gradle tasks
  about 40
  Eclipse plugin 41
  Gradle Groovy plugin 40
  IDEA plugin 40
POGO (Plain Old Groovy Object) 59
PoorMansTagBuilder class 252
pretended methods
  about 252
  invokeMethod 252
  methodMissing 253
programming languages
  fourth-generation language (4GL) 5
  evolution 3
  general-purpose languages 4
  third-generation language (3GL) 5

Q

querying, GORM
  about 239
  dynamic finders 240
  GORM, as DSL 241

R

range of values
  defining 77
refactoring 126-128
regex find operator 64
regex match operator 64
regex pattern operator 64
relationships
  about 228
  associations 228
  composition 228, 237
  inheritance 228, 238
resolve strategy 250

rewards DSL
  building 286
  DSL, designing 287
RVM (Ruby Version Manager) 21

S

Scratch
  URL 311
search
  improving 130
shebang scripts 27
shorthand features, Groovy language
  about 53
  default visibility 54
  dynamic types 57
  GroovyBeans 59, 60
  implicit imports 54
  optional dot in method chains 56, 57
  optional parentheses 55, 56
  optional return keyword 57, 58
  optional semicolon 54, 55
  properties 59
single page app (SPI) 313
Spock
  about 42, 223, 242, 243
  as DSL 241, 242
  blocks 242
  feature methods 242
  fixture methods 242
  helper methods 242
  JUnit 244, 245
  URL 50
  used, for testing Gradle 49
Spock specification structure
  about 43
  blocks 43-45
  feature methods 43
  fields 43, 46
  fixture methods 43-47
  helper methods 43, 47
Spock tests
  about 42
  fixture blocks 49

given 42
then 42
when 42
where blocks 48
spread-dot operator 82, 83
spread operator 82
Spring STS
about 32
URL 32
state machine DSL
events 204
states 204
transitions 204
strategies, builders
DELEGATE_FIRST 177
DELEGATE_ONLY 177
OWNER_FIRST 177
OWNER_ONLY 177
TO_SELF 177
SwingBuilder 139, 158-160

T

test-driven development (TDD) 241
TextMate 32
third-generation language (3GL) 5
Twitter
about 113, 114
URL 115
Twitter4J
URL 117
Twitter4J Java APIs
direct message 119
following 121, 122
searching 120, 121
tweeting 118
using 117
Twitter APIs
URL 115
working with 114-117

U

UltraEdit 32

V

virtual machine (VM) 11

W

where blocks 48
Windows Installer
URL 24

Thank you for buying
Groovy for Domain-specific Languages
Second Edition

About Packt Publishing

Packt, pronounced 'packed', published its first book, *Mastering phpMyAdmin for Effective MySQL Management*, in April 2004, and subsequently continued to specialize in publishing highly focused books on specific technologies and solutions.

Our books and publications share the experiences of your fellow IT professionals in adapting and customizing today's systems, applications, and frameworks. Our solution-based books give you the knowledge and power to customize the software and technologies you're using to get the job done. Packt books are more specific and less general than the IT books you have seen in the past. Our unique business model allows us to bring you more focused information, giving you more of what you need to know, and less of what you don't.

Packt is a modern yet unique publishing company that focuses on producing quality, cutting-edge books for communities of developers, administrators, and newbies alike. For more information, please visit our website at www.packtpub.com.

Writing for Packt

We welcome all inquiries from people who are interested in authoring. Book proposals should be sent to author@packtpub.com. If your book idea is still at an early stage and you would like to discuss it first before writing a formal book proposal, then please contact us; one of our commissioning editors will get in touch with you.

We're not just looking for published authors; if you have strong technical skills but no writing experience, our experienced editors can help you develop a writing career, or simply get some additional reward for your expertise.

Mastering Object-oriented Python

ISBN: 978-1-78328-097-1   Paperback: 634 pages

Grasp the intricacies of object-oriented programming in Python in order to efficiently build powerful real-world applications

1. Create applications with flexible logging, powerful configuration and command-line options, automated unit tests, and good documentation.

2. Use the Python special methods to integrate seamlessly with built-in features and the standard library.

3. Design classes to support object persistence in JSON, YAML, Pickle, CSV, XML, Shelve, and SQL.

Mastering JavaScript Design Patterns

ISBN: 978-1-78398-798-6   Paperback: 290 pages

Discover how to use JavaScript design patterns to create powerful applications with reliable and maintainable code

1. Learn how to use tried and true software design methodologies to enhance your JavaScript code.

2. Discover robust JavaScript implementations of classic as well as advanced design patterns.

3. Packed with easy-to-follow examples that can be used to create reusable code and extensible designs.

Please check **www.PacktPub.com** for information on our titles

Swift Essentials

ISBN: 978-1-78439-670-1   Paperback: 228 pages

Get up and running lightning fast with this practical guide to building applications with Swift

1. Rapidly learn how to program Apple's newest programming language, Swift, from the basics through to working applications.

2. Create graphical iOS applications using Xcode and storyboard.

3. Build a network client for GitHub repositories, with full source code on GitHub.

Git Version Control Cookbook

ISBN: 978-1-78216-845-4   Paperback: 340 pages

90 hands-on recipes that will increase your productivity when using Git as a version control system

1. Filled with practical recipes that will teach you how to use the most advanced features of the Git system.

2. Improve your productivity by learning to work faster, more efficiently, and with more confidence.

3. Discover tips and tricks that will show you when and how to use the advanced features of Git.

Please check **www.PacktPub.com** for information on our titles